THE MEANING OF SIN

The Fernley-Hartley Lecture 1956

THE MEANING OF SIN

BY

FREDERIC GREEVES

*Principal, and Randles Tutor in Systematic Theology
and the Philosophy of Religion, Didsbury College, Bristol*

WIPF & STOCK · Eugene, Oregon

Wipf and Stock Publishers
199 W 8th Ave, Suite 3
Eugene, OR 97401

The Meaning of Sin
By Greeves, Frederic
Copyright©1956 Methodist Publishing - Epworth Press
ISBN 13: 978-1-5326-3074-3
Publication date 4/6/2017
Previously published by Epworth Press, 1956

Every effort has been made to trace the current copyright
owner of this publication but without success. If you have
any information or interest in the copyright, please contact the publishers.

CONTENTS

	Page
PREFACE	ix
NOTE ON ABBREVIATIONS	x

PART I
THE PROBLEM OF IGNORANCE

1. A PRELIMINARY SURVEY	3
2. THE PROBLEM OF IGNORANCE	12
3. MODERN QUESTIONS IN OLD FORMS	30

PART II
ATTEMPTS TO SOLVE THE PROBLEM OF IGNORANCE

4. 'SIN *IS* IGNORANCE'	43
5. 'SIN *OR* IGNORANCE'	52
6. 'SIN OR MORAL DISEASE'	66

PART III
THE FACT OF IGNORANCE

7. THE OLD TESTAMENT AND THE FACT OF IGNORANCE	81
8. THE NEW TESTAMENT AND THE FACT OF IGNORANCE	100
9. SIN AND MORALITY	125
10. SIN AND GUILT	142
11. ACCEPTANCE OF THE FACT OF IGNORANCE	161
12. SOME FURTHER CONCLUSIONS AND QUESTIONS	179
INDEX OF SCRIPTURE PASSAGES	195
INDEX OF PROPER NAMES	196
INDEX OF SUBJECTS	198

PREFACE

IS an argument about words ever merely an argument about words? In a time when that question is a matter of keen debate it may appear fool-hardy to claim that a discussion of the meaning of the word *sin* involves more than verbal analysis. Yet such is the conviction which has impelled me to write this book.

It is because I believe that the term *sin* is used in ways which conceal from us the nature of our sinfulness that I have embarked upon this discussion, but I hope that I have made plain that study of the term itself is insufficient to bring us to the meaning of sin. So great, however, is the power that words, both written and spoken, possess that it is unwise to minimize the significance of any word; so frequently does the word *sin* occur in the Christian vocabulary that confusion about its meaning may, and I believe does, hinder acknowledgement of our own sinning and acceptance of our salvation.

No attempt is made in this book to offer a new account of the nature of sin. Many problems that are familiar to theologians are left on one side—in particular, problems about the 'origin' of sin. If I have misconceived the *Christian* doctrine of sin, then my conclusions are certainly false; whether my interpretation of that doctrine in relation to the questions that I raise is valid, the reader must judge.

The most powerful opposition to the use of the term *sin* which I advocate was made by F. R. Tennant, and it is to his books on this subject that I have devoted the most critical attention. So great was the impression made upon me, as upon all his students, by Tennant that it has taken me a quarter of a century to gain courage openly to differ from him. I dare not hope that what I have written would pass his searching scrutiny; I am glad to believe that my purpose in writing would be understood by his wise charity.

My debt to many writers, living and dead, is only partially acknowledged by my references to their works, but it will be obvious to any scholars who may see these pages. One name, however, must be specially mentioned. I discovered, when the theme and argument of this book had been determined, a summary of the Christian doctrine of sin which appears to me to be outstandingly comprehensive and clear. It has been with difficulty that I have refrained, in later chapters, from excessive quotation from Bishop Gustaf Aulén's *The Faith of the Christian Church*. If any reader should be left wondering what I am trying to talk about when I speak of *sin* I would refer him to that volume.

My colleagues at Didsbury College, to whom I have ventured to dedicate this book, have not only read and criticized various chapters, both in typescript and in proof, but have endured, with Stoical endurance and Christian love, my repetitive conversation about it. If I do not say more concerning my debt to them it is only because I fear to associate them with my errors. This work would not have been completed without their encouragement and help. Finally, I wish to express gratitude for the favour conferred upon me by the Trustees of the Fernley-Hartley Lecture.

FREDERIC GREEVES

DIDSBURY COLLEGE
January 1956

NOTE ON ABBREVIATIONS

Kittel: *Bible Key Words from Gerhard Kittel's Theologisches Wörterbuch zum Neuen Testament*, Trans. by J. R. Coates; Volume *SIN*, by G. Quell, etc. (1951).

TWB: *A Theological Word Book of the Bible*, edited by Alan Richardson (1950).

The following works by F. R. Tennant are referred to by the word italicized.

The *Origin* and Propagation of Sin (1902).
Sources of the Doctrine of the *Fall* and Original Sin (1903).
The *Concept* of Sin (1912).

Reference is also made to the same author's article on 'Original Sin' in Vol. IX of *The Encyclopædia of Religion and Ethics* (*ERE*).

Unless otherwise stated, biblical quotations are from the *Revised Standard Version*.

PART ONE

THE PROBLEM OF IGNORANCE

CHAPTER ONE

A PRELIMINARY SURVEY

ANY Christian preacher who is in the habit of inviting his hearers to ask questions receives requests to explain the meaning of religious and theological terms. Words such as 'grace', 'atonement', 'propitiation', and 'spiritual', are examples of words that perplex many who now listen to sermons. It is most unusual to be asked, by a professing Christian, to explain the meaning of 'sin'. The sermons that are heard, the hymns that are sung, and the prayers that are offered make such frequent use of 'sin' and 'sins' that few of those who regularly worship in Church, have asked themselves what these words mean. Indeed, much contemporary preaching suggests that everybody knows what sin is, and that the only necessity is to 'acquire a *sense* of sin'.

It is doubtful whether most Christians fully recognize that sin is a word that belongs to the religious vocabulary and has ceased to be a meaningful and active concept in the minds of those who do not read the Bible or attend Church services. Many non-believers falsely assume that they know what *sin* means to Christians, although what they 'know' appears bewilderingly confused or even unintelligible. There are, of course, others who have a more accurate notion of the Christian belief about sin, and who reject that belief along with the whole Christian faith. Very often, however, unbelief of this kind is partly the result of misunderstanding.

This book does not attempt to 'prove' the Christian doctrine of sin, nor even to expound it in full so that those who are unfamiliar with Christian teaching could be introduced to that doctrine. We are to pursue a limited path, although diversions to a number of side-tracks will be inevitable. Our concern is with the *meaning* of sin, and we start by questioning the assumption that 'everybody knows what sin is'. We begin with the problem of ignorance in its most obvious form—the problem posed by those who confess difficulty in knowing what Christians are talking about. It will soon become clear that 'the problem of ignorance' is greater than such critics recognize. But, first, a brief survey of contemporary perlexities is necessary.

This survey may be made most quickly by noting, with a few examples, the points of view of (1) the intellectual non-Christian, (2) the 'common man', and (3) the Christian evangelist who is sensitively aware of the perplexities of his hearers.

I

'The sense of sin has been one of the dominant psychological facts in history, and is still at the present day of great importance in the mental life of a large proportion of mankind.'[1] Bertrand Russell begins a discussion of sin with this statement of what is presumed to be a fact subject to psychological and historical verification. His next sentence, however, may somewhat shake our confidence in the firmness of this 'fact', for he writes: 'But although the *sense* of sin is easy to recognize and define, the *concept* of "sin" is obscure, especially if we attempt to interpret it in non-theological terms.'

Just how a *sense* of what is itself obscure can be easily recognized and defined Russell does not tell us. It would seem to be at least arguable that if *sin* is obscure, our attempt to examine the *sense of sin*, whether psychologically or historically or in any other way, must require a preliminary endeavour to clear up some of the obscurity in the concept itself. Otherwise it might be feared that our examination would be mistaking some other fact for 'the sense of sin'. And, of course, Russell proceeds to give certain definite, and highly controversial, meanings to the term 'sin', because one can hardly make a serious examination of a *sense* of what is completely indescribable. The inquiry that is to be made in this book will involve asking, both whether the *concept* of sin is as obscure as Russell assumes, and whether the *sense of sin* is as clear as he likewise takes for granted.

There is a further assumption which precedes Lord Russell's quick plunge into his task of examination. His third introductory sentence reads: 'I wish to consider the sense of sin psychologically and historically, and then to examine whether there is any non-theological concept in terms of which this emotion can be rationalized.' The assumption is that a non-theological examination of a *sense* of what is recognized to be a theologically-conceived fact

[1] Bertrand Russell, *Human Society in Ethics and Politics* (1954), p. 89.

can yield knowledge about that fact. Once again it appears to be at least possible that Russell's method needs to be reversed, and that our examination should proceed from an attempt to comprehend the theological meaning of the term *sin* to a consideration of its relation to psychology. It may not be as easy to pass from theological to psychological language as Russell's opening paragraph suggests.

Probably Russell would agree with that doubt, for, as a result of his examination, he writes: 'I conclude that "sin", except in the sense of conduct towards which the agent, or the community, feels an emotion of disapproval, is a mistaken concept, calculated to promote needless cruelty and vindictiveness when it is others that are thought to sin, and a morbid self-abasement when it is ourselves whom we condemn.'[2]

Whatever else may be debatable in that conclusion, it is quite certain that the only meaning of *sin* which Russell allows is not the meaning that has in fact been given to it by the vast number of human beings who have used the term, nor has it been that which most people thought that they were describing when they described a *sense of sin*. That fact does not, of course, prove that Russell is wrong in dismissing all other concepts of sin as mistaken; such matters cannot be decided by majority vote. But, before we accept Russell's conclusion, we shall want to consider carefully the data that he has examined.

For example, he writes: '... many men who do not believe in God nevertheless have a sense of sin.'[3] But this is a very questionable statement. A very great many writers have described sin in terms which make any such statement meaningless. To take but one example (many others will be given later in this book), Aulén writes: 'Sin is a concept which cannot be used except in a religious sense.' This remark is amplified as follows: 'To say that the concept of sin belongs entirely in the religious sphere is the same as saying that all sin is sin against God.'[4] If that be true, then what meaning can be given to the statement that many who do not believe in God have a sense of sin?

So there is at least a prima facie case for starting from the hypothesis that *sin* belongs exclusively to the language of religion and theology. It is, in fact, the assumption that it does so belong

---

[2] ibid., p. 98.   [3] ibid., p. 91.
[4] *The Faith of the Christian Church* (1948), pp. 259, 261.

which makes it an objectionable term in the ears of many of our contemporaries. We have long passed the brief period of human history when many seriously-minded people could ignore or even deny the need for mankind to make use of such terms as 'good', 'bad', 'right', 'wrong'. But by many today, and for many diverse reasons, former explanations of these ethical terms are believed to be (to use Russell's word) 'mistaken'. In particular there are many who are convinced that the only true, and therefore useful, meaning that can be found for ethical terms involves the ruthless separation of them from religion and from religious language. This is Russell's own view, as is clearly shown in the book from which I have quoted. He dismisses the normal use of the term *sin* as a theological and therefore worthless use, but he is too honest a thinker to deny the place of a *sense of sin* in human history. He therefore seeks to find room for a sense of sin, and, more doubtfully, for sin in the language of ethics. He is but one of many who hope that morality can be saved by cutting it adrift from religion, that ethical language can be made respectable by decontaminating it from theological infection.

Other writers are more thorough-going in this purgative task. Miss Kathleen Nott, for example, has thus summarized what she describes as 'the semantic view', but what might be more accurately described as *a* semantic view:

> ... many statements, according to the semantic view, will not be part of this world, this web of human and historic corroboration. They are 'noise', something like the radio operator's 'static', they come out of the ether and return to it, they affect our nerves but not the network of our communication. This is the semantic classification of most of the terms which scholasticism (and idealist philosophy) use; for example, God, Being, Eternity, Sin and Mind (as opposed to Body).[5]

The fact that this list of words has been in common use by theologians having little sympathy with the Scholastics, and by philosophers who are not normally described as Idealists, is important, but is not the immediate point, which is that this author is right when she recognizes that *sin* belongs to the list that contains *God*.

The pages that follow are not a discussion of logical empiricism; they make the more modest attempt to inquire what Christians

[5] *The Emperor's Clothes* (1953), p. 205.

mean—or, if we are not allowed to say so much, what they think that they mean, when they speak about sin. If there are those who believe that we are merely making noises, it is at least worthwhile asking what kind of noise we think that we are making. We may fail in our attempt, both because of our own inability to make ourselves clear and because our critics have already decided what we mean. Miss Nott, in her entertaining and hard-hitting attack upon distinguished lay-theologians such as Mr T. S. Eliot, Miss Dorothy Sayers and Mr C. S. Lewis, finds in 'the dogma of original sin' an object for ridicule and anger. She alleges that this dogma is 'certainly the psychological foundation of Christian orthodoxy', and asserts that it means 'not that we are unwilling to use our reasoning powers upon our own natures but that we are incapable of doing so'. This strange account of an ancient Christian concept is followed by the somewhat condescending remark that whilst Mr T. S. Eliot and her other self-chosen antagonists 'live by or on the use of imagination', 'they ought not to foster mystification'.[6] Without accepting Miss Nott's apportionment of the blame, we must recognize that 'mystification' is very widely felt today. The 'intellectual' but gives expression to the bewilderment that is shared by the common man.

II

This brief and superficial encounter with contemporary philosophy has merely served to suggest that there is much confusion concerning terms such as *sin* and *sense of sin*, which belong to the basic vocabulary of Christians of this, as of preceding, generations. It is important to recognize that similar confusion exists in the minds of those who are not, in any technical sense, philosophers or theologians.

Let us imagine that useful, if mythical, person, the common man, as he hears or reads these words, *sin* and *sense of sin*. They do not belong to the daily speech of most of his associates, nor to the vocabulary of most of the papers and books he reads. But he hears them on his occasional visits to Church or as he listens to radio services; he reads them on Wayside Pulpit posters or in religious articles in his daily paper. It is implied, even if not implicitly stated, that he himself is a sinner; and, because this

[6] ibid., p. 6.

apparently means that he is something that he ought not to be, and because he is a reasonably humble man, he is ready to agree. But *what* does it mean? He is told that all men are sinners, and that seems both to be unfair to a few very good people whom he knows, and also to undermine the significance of his own status as a sinner. He can hardly be blamed for being what every human being is! As he listens a little more carefully he learns that he is supposed to have sinned against God, that, in fact, this is what is really meant by those who call him a sinner. To which his perplexed mind replies: 'I'm not sure that I even believe in God, and anyhow I cannot see what harm I've done to Him. Certainly I never meant to do anything to Him, and whilst I'm sorry if I did, I can hardly be blamed for something I knew nothing about.'

Further shocks await our common man when he is told that we are all involved in the sin of other people. Phrases such as 'the solidarity of the race' and 'corporate sin' puzzle him; and when he is asked in Church to confess 'our sins', or reminded by the preacher of 'our share in the sins of the world', he begins to wonder whether he is being held responsible for the faults of everybody else, including those of the Government which would never have got into power if more people had voted as he did.

If we may stretch our imagination to breaking-point and picture the common man waiting in the local parson's study, and passing the time by dipping into a few of the books, we shall not be surprised if he comes to the conclusion that the 'Experts' are as much confused about sin as he is. For he reads: 'Sin is the Christian name for what ethics calls "moral evil" ';[7] then, opening the next book on the shelf, he learns that 'it is perfectly possible to combine being a sinner with being "good" in the ethical sense; indeed, in the last resort the fact of being or not being a sinner has nothing to do with the difference between the morally "good" and the morally "evil". . . .'[8] He is told on one page that he is 'totally depraved', and on another page that his 'good works' cannot 'save' him. How, if he is totally depraved, can he perform any good works? He is blamed for knowing that he is a sinner and not repenting, and he is rebuked for not recognizing that he is a sinner.

It is hardly necessary for us to pursue this summary of confusions farther, by attempting to analyse the thoughts of those whose

[7] F. R. Tennant, *Concept* (1912), p. 67.   [8] E. Brunner, *Man in Revolt* (1939), p. 154.

learning comes chiefly from newspapers and films. We must not forget, however, that to very many, sin appears to be a nebulous something that the Church is against. It is recognized to be a word that is used about wrong things, so that there is both a muddled sense of guilt and a feeling that we all suffer unjustly through other people's sins, yet there is an undercurrent of suspicion that actions are termed sinful merely because they are pleasant.

III

A few words must be added, however, concerning the significance of the term 'sin' for many who listen to the preaching of the Gospel. The Christian evangelist needs to remember that not all who respond to his message have necessarily responded to what he intended them to hear. If that is due to the fact that God has addressed some other word to them, then all is well. But sometimes the preacher's message is interpreted by the hearer's own very different understanding of the words he has heard. This inevitable difficulty of communication is especially great in reference to the words *sin* and *guilt*.

Most physicians and psychiatrists spend much time with men and women whose illness is, at least in part, traceable to morbid feelings of guilt. The evangelist who is also a pastor (and a pastor who listens) will himself be very familiar with that kind of human suffering, so that he will sympathize with the view, widely held by his medical colleagues, that one of the greatest human needs is the need to escape from the sense of sin and guilt. Such understanding exists in the minds of many more Christian ministers than most members of the medical profession suspect. Yet it needs to be more widely recognized that not all responses to evangelical 'appeals' lead to the health of mind which is part of the true meaning of Christian salvation. The reason for this, in many instances, is that by *sin* the hearer means something quite different from the preacher, and by *guilt* he understands only a morbid self-pity or a condition of neurotic anxiety.

Yet when all has been said about the wide-spread 'mystification' concerning sin, the fact remains that, during many generations, great numbers of people, of every imaginable type, have both recognized that they were sinners and become sure that their sins were forgiven. Hosts of men and women have been certain that their lives were quite different as a result of this experience, and they have been confident that they could recognize a similar difference in other people. If that is what Bertrand Russell means by saying that 'the sense of sin has been one of the dominant psychological facts in history', then we must add that, in Christendom, the 'sense' of forgiveness and cleansing from sin has been much more significantly dominant. It is not only the sense of sin which, as Russell admits, needs to be explained; it is the certitude expressed in such terms as 'set free from the power of sin' which calls for explanation by those who would banish the concept of sin from human minds.

The ordinary Christian believer 'exulting in his Saviour' and sure that the Saviour saves from the guilt and power of sin, is a 'psychological and historical fact'. Of course many have attempted to account for him on the assumption that what he claims cannot be true, and the chapters that follow will attempt neither to describe nor to refute those attempts. My inquiry is, rather, about whether both the experience of salvation and the nature of sin are so profoundly misunderstood by many of those who deny the validity of both, that they must be asked to re-frame their criticism before we can attempt to refute it. All too often, in this as in other respects, the Christian and the non-Christian are engaged in a heated debate about different propositions. It is well for the Christian to accept the larger share of blame if his opponent does not know what the Christian is talking about.

With regard to *sin*, this is (as I have roughly indicated and hope more fully to show) a situation most likely to arise. That is not only because so many ambiguous and false meanings have gathered round the word, but also because the very nature of sin is such that it is most difficult for us to know that we are sinners. In the most literal sense we are ignorant of sin; and that is because at the centre, or root, of sin itself is ignorance of more than one kind.

Such is the theme of this book; and, though we may expect the announcement of it to perplex those who, puzzled by much Christian doctrine, assume that at least everybody knows what the Christian means by sin, we may hope that it will not surprise those who believe the Gospel and hold that it is good *news*.

Our inquiry will take us far from the common man, believer or non-believer, into technicalities and problems with which he would probably have little patience. It is well, therefore, to remember at the outset that what gives point to our inquiry is *his* need. For either the Christian doctrine of sin and its remedy is of the utmost importance to him, or, as very many of our contemporaries most firmly and sincerely believe, it is a great hindrance to his well-being. And not the least important aspect of the Christian doctrine of sin is that each one of us is a 'common man'. Words that Forsyth wrote about Christology are equally true of the doctrine that is to be examined here. It

> exists in the interests of the evangelical faith of the layman who has in Jesus Christ the pardon of his sins and everlasting life. We are all laymen here. It is quite misplaced patronage to condescend to lay experience with the superiority of the academic theologian or the idealist philosopher, and to treat such lay experience of the Gospel as if it were good enough for most, and the only one they are yet fit for. . . . It is the evangelical experience of every saved soul that is the real foundation of Christological belief anywhere.[9]

In like manner, author and reader of this book must seek to remember that, whilst we appear to be arguing about words, we are in fact thinking about the desperate plight and the promised release of Everyman.

Bertrand Russell represents many in this generation who seek to maintain the difference between right and wrong actions whilst rejecting the Christian account of sin. ' "Right" actions are those that it is useful to praise, "wrong" actions are those that it is useful to blame'.[10] If the Christian is to resist this attempt, he must seek to show how those who disbelieve in 'sin' may come to know what it means. That task is not as easy as is sometimes imagined.

---

[9] *The Person and Place of Jesus Christ* (1946), p. 9. [10] op. cit., p. 98.

CHAPTER TWO

THE PROBLEM OF IGNORANCE

I. A TWO-FOLD IGNORANCE

OUR preliminary survey has done little more than draw attention to the somewhat obvious fact that the concept of sin mystifies very many people of varied types. There are several reasons for this.

Firstly, many are now seeking to find a meaning for *sin* which does not necessitate belief in God. Like Russell, though rarely as consciously and openly as he, they are seeking a non-theological interpretation of the concept of sin. It is understandable that they should desire such an interpretation; most of us want our physician to describe our sickness in non-medical language, and our solicitor to explain the law in non-legal terms. But we do not, or should not, expect the doctor to diagnose our sickness as though there were no such fact as disease; nor do we ask our lawyer to give his explanation on the assumption that there is no law. To explain sin without reference to God, that is to say as though there were no God, is an impossibility, and not the least of the purposes of this book is to emphasize that the Christian will never help others by concealing this fact.

A second cause for the wide-spread perplexity about the nature of sin is the simple fact that theological language is a technical language. Like all technical vocabularies it needs to be learnt; but, unlike many others, its terms wear a false appearance of familiarity. This is not peculiarly true of the word 'sin'; it is equally true of love (*agape*), fellowship (*koinonia*), grace, justification, and other terms. Indeed, sin should be much more easily recognizable as a technical term than most of the words I have quoted, or than other words associated with sin, especially the word guilt. It is, however, very commonly forgotten that we need to learn the Christian meaning of apparently familiar words.

The third reason why sin, in common with many other words, appears obscure, is that it is impossible to give an adequate, concise *definition*. Of course many works of Christian theology, especially small handbooks of the popular kind, offer a definition; and it must be admitted that it is extremely difficult to imagine a Catechism which does not define. The Bible, however, nowhere offers *a* definition of sin, any more than it does of God, of grace, of *agape* and so on. There are several reasons for this omission: one is that it is not the method of the writers of either Testament; another, that the books of the Bible came from many hands in many periods, and only an individual or a committee (trusting to a majority vote) could provide a definition of the kind that is sought; and a third, that sin, like all the other major terms used in the Bible, has so many characteristics that, even if a definition were attempted, it would need to be of inordinate length.

But there is a much more significant reason than any so far mentioned why a brief definition of sin must be unsatisfactory. A definition is useful in order to pin-point something, to mark it out from other things of the same class and from other classes of things. It would be comparatively easy to define sin if one could say what 'it' is. But sin is not an 'it'; it is not a *thing* in any meaningful sense of that word. 'It is not *something* that is wrong between God and myself. Evil is not a *something* between God and man; it is myself in the wrong position.'[1] We can only find out what sin means by discovering that we are sinners; that is as important a fact about sin as is the fact that we cannot believe in the reality of sin if we deny the reality of God.

It now becomes plain that we have to face a problem of ignorance that is posed by a more significant fact than that many people find the *word* obscure. We have to face the fact that sin can only be known, recognized, and acknowledged as reality by those who have knowledge both of God and of themselves as sinners.

If such knowledge is necessary, it may well be asked, how can the Christian possibly think himself entitled to say that men who have no such knowledge of themselves or of God are sinners? Yet it is a basic tenet of Christian belief that all men are sinners. Again, how can anybody ever come to a knowledge of sin? Has it not often been said by Christian preachers that a man must 'have a sense of sin' before he can be 'saved'? There are even more searching questions that must be asked, for Christians most

[1] E. Brunner, *The Theology of Crisis* (1929), p. 55.

certainly speak of the *guilt* of sin, and of sinners as being guilty. Can a man be blamed for not knowing God? Can a man be condemned for not knowing himself; indeed do any of us fully know ourselves, our complex nature, our motives and desires, our unconscious as well as our conscious mind?

I can now underline a statement that I have previously made: 'In the most literal sense we are ignorant of sin; and that is because at the centre, or root, of sin itself is ignorance of more than one kind.' We now see that this ignorance is two-fold in character; it is ignorance of self and ignorance of God. How great is that ignorance, and how relevant it is to our understanding of both the nature of sin and the manner of the Divine Remedy for sin, the remainder of this book seeks to examine. Because the words 'ignorance of self' and 'ignorance of God' will occur so frequently in succeeding chapters, something must be said about them by way of introduction.

I shall use the term *ignorance of self* to cover several facts (or what I hope to show to be facts)—the fact that no man fully knows himself, his motives and intentions, his character and personality; the fact that the natural man (man as he is prior to the working of Divine grace) does not, and cannot, comprehend that he is a sinner. This term will also be used to cover our ignorance of other selves, although, at a later stage, it will be necessary to distinguish ignorance of myself from my ignorance of other people. The term *ignorance of God* will be used both in reference to the ignorance of all finite beings and to the particular problems presented by agnosticism and atheism. Finally, by way of explanation of a convenient but intentionally ambiguous terminology, *knowledge of* will be employed for both aquaintance with and knowledge about.

For the purposes of discussion the two kinds of ignorance will frequently need to be separated, but, in actual experience, they are bound up with each other. Moreover, because of the complexity of the issues involved and the differences of opinion that exists about them, the greater amount of space in the following chapters will be devoted to ignorance of *self*. It is, however, most important to note at the outset that it is our human ignorance of God, until He makes Himself known to us, which is of much greater significance both for our understanding of our sinfulness and our acceptance of salvation. We men and women are prone to be most interested in the less important questions, and we are specially apt to be more interested in ourselves than in God.

Probably no Christian theologian ever set before us what I have termed 'the problem of ignorance' more clearly than did F. R. Tennant. He offered a number of definitions of sin of which the following is typical: 'Sin is an activity of the will, expressed in thought, word or deed, contrary to the individual's conscience, to *his* notion of what is good and right, *his* knowledge of the moral law and the will of God.'[2] This definition implies that a man can only be said to sin if he fully understands what he is doing, knows that he ought not to do it, and knows that, in so doing, he offends God's will. If there is any lack of knowledge either of what he himself is doing, or of what God commands him to do, he cannot be described as a sinner, nor need he accuse himself of sinfulness. (In Dr Tennant's terminology, wrong actions done with any such ignorance would be described as due to 'moral imperfection', not to 'sin'.)

Tennant's position will be discussed later, but the considerations that led him, and have led many others, to that position are not difficult to appreciate. If we begin by asking questions about moral responsibility, about guilt, and about punishment for wrong-doing, it appears to be obvious that a man can only be blamed for an entirely voluntary act. Further, it seems that an act can only be described as voluntary if the performer is both free from any kind of coercion and fully aware of the significance of his action. If we have doubts about the existence of any of those conditions, then moral responsibility must be denied, or at least judged to be non-proven.

What, then, are we to say about the two-fold ignorance to which reference has been made? Can a man be a sinner if any such ignorance, however partial, exists? That is the question with which we are here concerned. It is not a new question; few of our questions are new. In Part II several authors of various past centuries will be quoted, and the number of such quotations could be indefinitely extended. But in each generation we must deal with problems as they appear to us, not as they appeared to our ancestors, nor as they may appear to our grandchildren. We are

[2] I quote from notes of lectures by Dr Tennant at Cambridge (1931-2). References to his published works are given in Chapter 5.

often helped by seeing how our predecessors answered their own questions, although we must be very careful not to assume that they saw those questions as we see ours. It is well, therefore, to begin by asking how this two-fold ignorance of God and self appears to us, and we start with ignorance of God.

II. IGNORANCE OF GOD

Whatever else the Christian may mean when he speaks of sin, he most certainly refers to the relationship between man and God. He may use different adjectives, nouns and verbs in describing sin, partly from personal choice and partly because there are many aspects of sin; but the reference to God will always be implicit if not explicit. He may speak of disobedience or transgression, of rebellion and consequent alienation, of self-dependence or self-centredness; he may describe the 'root', or the 'essence' of sin in many diverse ways; he cannot complete any statement about the nature of sin without reference to God.

Here we meet, for the first time, a particular cause of confusion concerning the Christian meaning of sin. It is often said that we must distinguish between 'sin' and 'sins'. The distinction, in that form, is not a scriptural one, although there is a tendency in St Paul's terminology toward a distinction between sin (*hamartia*) and trespass (*paraptoma*) and transgression (*parabasis*). It would make for clarity if some fixed distinction could thus be made between the basic, underlying sin and the many acts which are called sinful. Any attempt, however, to keep rigidly to such a distinction between sin and offences (sins) is fraught with difficulties. What must never be lost sight of, however, is the fact that when the Christian speaks about 'many sins', he is using that term in a secondary, not in a primary sense. There are many offences: they include thoughts and words, as well as deeds; they embrace offences against ourselves, as well as against other people; they may be distinguished as sins of commission and sins of omission. But the Christian affirms, with the Hebrew Psalmist: 'Against thee, thee only, have I sinned' (Psalm 51[4]).

Many of our contemporaries, both learned and unlearned, fail to recognize this God-ward reference in the Christian concept of sin, and assume that a particular type of 'sin' (offence) must be *the* Christian definition of sin. The nature of that particular

THE PROBLEM OF IGNORANCE

offence is variously understood. By some it is taken to be selfishness; by others it is thought to be curiosity, the attempt to use our reasoning faculties;[3] by most, perhaps, it is assumed to be sensuality. It must frankly be admitted that much careless teaching by professing Christians, and perhaps some heretical views that have infiltrated Christianity, have given some justification for this misunderstanding. It is so serious, especially in regard to the assumption that the root of all sin is *sensuality*, that a somewhat lengthy digression is necessary.

The most superficial reading of the Gospels shows that Christ did not isolate sensual sins from other offences, much less 'explain' human need in terms of fleshly desires and misdeeds. Whence comes this wide-spread assumption that all sinfulness is the result of sensuality?

Perhaps there are three reasons for this disastrous error. It is due to the particular feeling of guilt that is often associated with physical desires and activities. It is due to the fact that Christian morality does indeed condemn such 'sins' as fornication and gluttony; professing Christians have often confused sensual desire and enjoyment with such sins. It is also due to the somewhat unfortunate fact that the word 'flesh' has a different meaning in the writings of St Paul from the meaning it commonly bears today. There would seem to be urgent need for Christian propaganda concerning the Pauline (and Johannine) use of the term *sarx*.[4] It must suffice here to state categorically that the explanation of sin in terms of a dualism between 'soul' and 'body', or between 'flesh' and 'spirit', is contrary to Scripture, although it is typical of the Manichæan heresy which has always been the most destructive of all the false beliefs which have infected Christian thought.

It is sometimes implied, both by Christian and non-Christian writers, that the account of sin in terms of man's relationship to God is a mere whim of contemporary theology. That is a total misapprehension. The profound myth of Adam and Eve establishes the meaning of sin as disobedience, the desire to be 'as God'.

---

[3] cf. K. Nott, *The Emperor's Clothes*, pp. 6, 22, 25, 71, 229, etc. Miss Nott understands 'the dogma of original sin' to mean that man should not and cannot use his 'reasoning powers' upon his own nature. Alongside this reiterated charge against Christian teaching she also asserts that the 'literary theologians' (whom she mainly discusses) leave us 'with the half-hearted understanding that the sin by which Adam fell, and in which we are born, is either sexuality or curiosity' (p. 300).

[4] cp. *TWB*, 'Flesh', 'fleshly', etc.

There we first meet the description of man's denial of his creatureliness, his attempt to claim 'a divine sovereignty in his own affairs'.

Whilst there have been many differences of emphasis, and not a few points of controversy, concerning sin among the great teachers of the Church, in this God-ward emphasis they have not differed. A few examples must suffice.

So emphatic was Aquinas on this matter that he found it necessary to discuss how it was possible for sins to be 'fittingly divided into sin against God, against oneself, and against one's neighbour' in view of the fact that 'to sin against God is common to all sins'.[5] Whether Augustine was ever completely liberated from the Manichæan influences of his youth may be a matter of debate, and certainly his account of the significance of the sexual act in reference to the 'transmission' of sin was erroneous, but it was certainly not his intention to lay the cause of our sinfulness in our physical constitution.

If any man say that the flesh is the cause of the viciousness of the soul he is ignorant of man's nature, for the corruptible body does not burden the soul. . . .

The flesh is good, but to leave the Creator and live according to this created good is the mischief.[6]

It was Augustine who, commentating on Psalm 19, described *pride* as the beginning of all evil. This, said Calvin, 'was not far from the mark', and, he added, concerning Adam's fall: 'The common idea of sensual intemperance is childish. . . . We must, therefore, look deeper. . . . Infidelity was at the root of all evil. From infidelity, again, sprang ambition and pride, together with ingratitude. . . .'[7] To add but one other illustration, E. Gordon Rupp has reminded us that Luther, in the more mature teaching about sin in his lectures on Romans, offers 'a more radical diagnosis of the sin of man [than in the lectures on the Psalms], the seat of which, under all disguises and idolatries, is his egoism, lifting itself in rebellion against God'. Rupp adds: 'Concupiscence is no longer for Luther the desire of the flesh, and inbred sin is

---

[5] *Summa*, II, Q. 72, A. 4.
[6] *De Civitate Dei*, XIV. 3 and 5.
[7] *Institutes*, II.i.4. For the way in which Augustine came to single out pride (*superbia*) from other perversions (*curiositas* and *lascivia*) as the root of all sin, see J. Burnaby, *Amor Dei*, pp. 185, 189.

more than a mere material, a tinder (*fomes peccati*); it is a restless egotism which is active and working even in our dreams.'[8]

It is this understanding of sin in terms of rebellion against God which makes the attempt to comprehend it as a non-theological concept not only difficult, as Russell and others have seen, but impossible. And it is this basic fact about sin which most acutely raises in our minds the problem of ignorance of God.

If sin is thought of purely in terms of specific moral misdemeanours, whether they are regarded as offences against a particular moral code or are judged in relation to some moral standard or ideal, the problem of ignorance is a straightforward one; we then have only to decide whether, and to what degree, ignorance of the law, standard or ideal is a *moral* excuse. Even so, if sin be viewed as transgression against the will of *God*, further questions arise. One of the values of Bertrand Russell's book, to which reference has previously been made, is that it forces such questions on our notice. He makes merry with a list of prohibitions which various religions hold to possess divine sanction.[9] His jests may irritate those who, for example, consider it 'sinful' to fornicate but right for a widow to avoid suttee, but the irritation is not to be avoided. Christians have been no more free than members of other religions from readiness to identify changing ethical beliefs with the will of God.

When, however, sin is conceived as a false personal relationship with God, questions concerning man's belief in God and varied ideas about Him come to the fore. They are not new questions; the opening chapters of Romans make some reference to them, if not, perhaps, in the way that is often assumed. In this generation, however, the problem of unbelief is more manifest than in any other. Plato wrote about atheists in the tenth book of *The Laws*, but now a large part of the world's population lives in countries where atheism is both officially upheld and zealously propagated. Agnosticism, whether the denial of the possibility of knowledge of God or doubt concerning His existence, is, at least in Great Britain, more common than atheism. The size of an intellectual

---

[8] *Luther's Progress to the Diet of Worms, 1521* (1951), p. 40. Dr Rupp adds that Luther discarded the Aristotelian doctrine of a *habitus* within the soul, and the Platonic and Neo-platonic division between soul and body, and returned to 'the biblical division between "flesh" and "spirit", the conception of man as a sinner confronted in all his personal existence by the person of the living God'.

[9] *Human Society in Ethics and Politics*, p. 138.

problem is not to be measured by a counting of heads, but the extent to which the problem of unbelief calls for attention is affected by the growth of agnosticism and atheism.

If it be said that only deliberate disobedience to the known will of God is sin, how can the unbeliever be called a sinner? Tennant, whose definition of sin, as will be noted later, has been followed by very many Christians, was exceptional in avowing the consequences of his own definition. He wrote that, if sin were to be defined in the only way which he believed to be legitimate,

> then it will follow that persons, if any there be, possessing no religion —who would confess, that is to say, to entertaining no ideas of deity or of the supernatural, and to feeling no religious sentiment of any sort— cannot be accounted sinners at all, in the sense in which we agree to use that term, however morally evil, even from their own point of view, may be their lives.[10]

Russell quotes these words of Tennant's and confesses himself puzzled by them. He remarks that much may depend upon what Tennant meant by 'religious sentiments', but he adds: 'I have no "ideas of deity or of the supernatural"', and he wonders, whether, 'in Dr Tennant's view, I am or am not capable of "sin"'.[11] The question is both reasonable and one that demands an answer. Can we, or can we not, describe those who are self-confessed atheists or agnostics as sinners?

If the answer is 'No', then the Christian must abandon his message of more than a thousand years that all men are sinners and that salvation is offered to all. But if we say 'Yes', then we must expect that those who do not believe in God will be puzzled by our assertion that they are sinning against God. It may be necessary that they should be puzzled, but we must be careful that we do not perplex them needlessly and that we help them so far as we can.

III. IGNORANCE OF SELF

If ignorance of God suggests problems which are both ancient and pressingly modern, ignorance of self is a problem of no less antiquity and contemporary significance. Words such as 'free-will', 'determinism', 'responsibility', arouse warning memories of endless disputations. Milton's devils 'on a hill retired' reasoning about these things, finding 'no end, in wandering mazes lost',

---

[10] F. R. Tennant, *Concept*, p. 216.   [11] op. cit., p. 94.

endeavour to frighten us away from our inquiry. But there are facts about our ignorance of self, of our own thoughts, motives and actions, which cannot be denied and must not be ignored. Those facts are particularly brought to our notice by the findings of depth-psychology and the exploration of the unconscious.

Fifty years ago, William James wrote of the 'discovery, first made in 1886, that there is not only the consciousness of the ordinary field . . . but an addition thereto in the shape of a set of memories, thoughts and feelings which are extra-marginal and outside of the primary consciousness altogether, but yet must be classed as conscious facts of some sort, able to reveal their presence by unmistakable signs'. This 'discovery' he characterized as 'the most important step forward' made by Psychology.[12] Writing in 1946, G. N. M. Tyrrell said: 'Few as yet realize the full implications of the discovery that the conscious mind does not exhaust personality.'[13] James was right in emphasizing the importance of this matter, as Tyrrell is correct in drawing attention to the widespread neglect of it; but James was wrong in dating the 'discovery' of the unconscious.

It is of considerable importance that we should recognize that awareness of unconscious motivation, and of mental processes of which the subject is not aware, or of which he is only partially and confusedly aware, did not begin with Freud. Nor is it sufficient to take note of Freud's immediate predecessors, such as Breuer. 'The conception of the unconscious mind had been in the air for nearly a century . . . ; what Freud did was to make it more definite, and above all, to exploit it in a practical technique.'[14] Mr L. L. Whyte, whose statement I have just quoted, reminds us that the word 'conscious' entered the English language in 1601, and that for Descartes and Locke, thought was co-extensive with consciousness. Unfortunately the Cartesian emphasis became, in this as in other ways, dominant, in spite of the fact that Leibniz had perceived the significance of what was first called the 'unconscious' in 1712. Mr Whyte traces the emergence of the dormant appreciation of the unconscious under the influence of the romantic movement and 'the first translations of Eastern thought'.

It is too often stated that Freud alone was responsible for the

---

[12] *Varieties of Religious Experience* (1907), p. 233.
[13] *The Personality of Man* (1946), p. 25.
[14] Broadcast Lecture, *The Unconscious Mind* (*The Listener*, 15th July 1954). I am indebted to Mr Whyte in this paragraph.

conflict between a Rationalistic conception of mental life and an awareness of the unconscious. But the basic notion of unconscious mental processes has a much longer history than that of the term itself. Mr Whyte comments that Pascal's, 'the heart has its reasons which reason does not know', is not far from Freud; yet we must go farther back than that. It is fascinating to imagine Plato studying Freudian theories as a comment upon his own words about the 'unjust man', as 'the old approved beliefs about right and wrong which he had as a child [are] overpowered by thoughts, once held in subjection, but now emancipated . . .'.

When he was still under the control of his father and of the laws, they broke loose only in sleep; but now that his passion has set up an absolute dominion, he has become for all his waking life the man he used to be from time to time in dreams. . . .'[15]

It is, however, to Augustine that we must look for the most significant anticipation. Little imagination is needed to speculate concerning the use that great thinker might have made of his own insight, had he been able to work with a later psychology. At least, he might have been spared some of his tortuous explorations of the problem of 'free-will'. As Edwyn Bevan pointed out, Augustine found Hebrew psychology inadequate and 'was thrown on the resources of his own vivid genius'.

And how enormously the Christian's perception of the psychological problem went beyond the wisdom of the ancient schools! How much that had once seemed so easy to read off, so distinct and simple and classifiable, was found to be dim and complicated and infinitely mysterious! 'The abysmal depths of personality'; it was Augustine who first gave men an inkling of what that meant. The very phrase is his—'*abyssus humanae conscientiae*'.[16]

Bevan, adding a further quotation from Augustine—'A man comprises something which not even the spirit of the man, which is in him, knows'—rightly suggests that this is a truth which modern psychology has developed, so that Augustine may be called 'the father' of descriptive psychology. We shall not, therefore, be surprised that his account of human nature, with all its limitations, is nearer to the truth about man than is much superficial description by rationalistic philosophers.

[15] *The Republic* (Cornford's Trans.), IX.574.
[16] Edwyn Bevan, *Hellenism and Christianity* (1930), pp. 139f.

In spite of this centuries-long awareness of what has come to be called the unconscious, remarkably few *theologians* have devoted attention to it. A similar neglect has been shown by ethical writers. An important exception among the latter is Erich Fromm, whose humanistic, non-religious, writings offer one of the most forceful attempts to found an ethic upon a psychological basis. He himself notes how surprising is this neglect in view of the fact that 'psychoanalytic theory has made contributions which are particularly relevant to the theory of ethics'.[17] I would add that the ethical writers who have paid most attention to contemporary psychology have been (whether or not Freudian) unsympathetic to Christian beliefs. When we add to this fact the indifference to psychological inquiry shown by theologians and moralists, do we not see a further example of the way in which a branch of scientific study tends to become secularized if neglected, or merely opposed by Christian thought?

Why has this lack of interest in unconscious mental processes been so common among Christian thinkers? There are reasons which, although they do not justify this neglect, spring from commendable motives. A few attempts that were made to explain sin in terms of the unconscious failed as they were bound to fail. Again, psychology is a difficult discipline, in which a very small measure of agreement has yet been attained, and it is always unwise for theologians to make hasty use of scientific hypotheses. Moreover, whatever may be the truth about unconscious motivation, a very large part of our daily behaviour is consciously motivated. True as it is that we often do not know 'what we are doing', yet we often do know quite well. The theologian, like the moralist, must be careful not to exaggerate the significance of the unconscious. Neither, however, must he minimize its significance.

The 'unconscious' (it must always be remembered) is but a hypothesis; Freud himself, and, to a greater extent, his disciples, passed from experiment and classification to metaphysical theories. Few students of theology have the qualifications and the time to be professional psychologists, and in an age of specialization there are few who can escape the necessity of keeping to their own trade. The theologian resents the theologizing-psychologist, and the psychologist is justly annoyed by psychological pronouncements made by those not trained in his discipline. But we need to take notice

---

[17] *Man for Himself* (1949), p. 31.

of each other's work, and most of all in matters so closely related to human welfare. There are questions raised by contemporary psychological research, although not first nor exclusively thus raised, which no theologian or Christian student can lightly dismiss.

Much psychological, and even psychiatric, work can and does proceed without paying attention to the hypothesis of the unconscious. All existing theories based upon that hypothesis may conceivably be proved to be false or inadequate. It is almost certainly true that the tendency to think of the unconscious as though it were in fact a separate 'part' or quasi-spatial 'level' of personality (suggested by other terms such as 'subliminal' and 'subconscious') has obscured rather than clarified understanding of human nature. It remains true, however, that 'the present-day psychologist is compelled to postulate an unconscious psychic life whether he likes it or not. Apart from the reality of the unconscious, any explanation of the regular processes of conscious phenomena is simply impossible.'[18]

Victor White has reminded us that, whilst experimental study of such phenomena, and the use of 'unconscious' as a collective noun to describe them, are modern developments, the phenomena themselves have been 'familiar from time immemorial'. 'Dreams, automatisms of various sorts, the influence of "forgotten" experience or unacknowledged desires upon conduct, alternating personalities, the phenomena of trance, abnormal and paranormal psychological phenomena of many kinds; none of these was new in human experience.'[19]

That the Christian *pastor* needs to be aware of these phenomena, and of the attempts that are made to interpret their significance, has for long been recognized; that the *theologian* can safely ignore them has, too often, been assumed. Can we, however, discuss the Christian meaning of sin with no reference to the facts of human motivation?

Who can dispute that all of us are continually acting under the influence of 'motives' whose existence, or at least whose nature, is unrecognized by ourselves? This is not merely a matter of taking

[18] N. Ach, quoted by Victor White, O.P., *God and the Unconscious*, p. 35. White adds: 'There is fairly general agreement that this postulate is demanded by (1) the phenomena of involuntary mentation . . . and (2) the seeming purposiveness of nonconscious biological functioning.'

[19] ibid., pp. 23f.

note of instinctive drives or urges, of appetites which most moralists would judge as non-moral, but which play a part in actions that are morally judged. Even more significant is the fact that, from earliest childhood, unrecognized and unexamined processes are taking place 'in our minds'. Environmental influences, and individual responses to those influences in a period of life during which nobody judges us to be morally responsible, have helped to shape our personality and character. What we *do*, we do because of what we *are;* what we *are* has been greatly affected by what we have *done*. There is no escape from that apparently circular statement.

Especially relevant to the point at issue is the process of *repression*. Dr Ryder Smith, during an examination of the biblical attitude to 'sins of ignorance', remarks: 'No doubt there were people then as now, who, driving the sense of guilt into the subconscious, persuaded themselves that some sins were not sins, but this is not innocent ignorance.'[20]

There are, and always have been, such people, but that is not what the psychiatrist means by repression. Repression is itself an unconscious process, clearly distinguished from the deliberate act of suppression. Or, to use a different terminology, we must distinguish between the deliberate suppression of an act or of an impulse, and unwitting suppression of the *awareness* of an impulse. Any pastor's study provides sufficient evidence of this last kind of suppression (which Freud taught us to call repression). There can hardly be need, today, for illustrations of the way in which men and women can be completely unaware of deep and strong impulses which they have unconsciously repressed, but which have motivated their actions with all the greater strength. This is only one of the many ways in which we often know not *why* we do what we do.

Whilst I am anxious not to imply that the problem of ignorance of self is a problem that only emerges for those who accept the hypothesis of the unconscious and allow for the facts which it seeks to interpret, one further word about contemporary psychology needs to be said. At this point we must move with much caution, for we are in a very partially explored territory.

Evidence for some kind of *telepathic* communication is rapidly increasing. Were the amount of research devoted to this subject,

---

[20] *The Bible Doctrine of Sin* (1953), p. 147. See pp. 153ff, *infra*.

and to other branches of parapsychology, which is devoted to many other phenomena, the next generation would perhaps have a far greater understanding of human nature than we can yet claim. Whatever may be the outcome of the study of 'telepathy', there is sufficient evidence already to strengthen the commonsense view that 'we all influence each other'. That simple fact, so deeply rooted in the biblical conception of the solidarity of the race, is another example of the way in which learned men are often slow to recognize the insights of common sense. But medical science seems to be increasingly recognizing this interdependence of us all. One only needs to think of the care with which any modern physician studies the family and social setting of his patient. Nor does he concern himself only with hereditary influences. A large part of modern healing has regard to the living, personal influences that affect total health (which is increasingly understood in psychosomatic terms), and these influences are especially significant for 'mental' health.[21] Who would think of *blaming* the neurotic for the influences of heredity and environment? May not the Christian find himself doing exactly that, if he attaches moral responsibility, in the commonly accepted sense, to all that he calls sin?[22]

It is, then, through these and many other forms of psychological inquiry (including, very significantly, many physiological methods of psychiatric research) that the problem of ignorance of self forces itself upon our notice today. The common man, to return to him for a moment, often with highly confused and exaggerated notions of the achievements of 'psychology', asks his questions. Films and popular writings offer him a pseudo-Freudian interpretation of human behaviour, or introduce him to 'facts' about brain surgery, glandular processes and the like. He asks: 'If I don't understand myself, if I am not wholly responsible for the way I think and behave, how can I be blamed for being what I am?' It appears obvious to him that if he cannot be blamed, he cannot be a sinner. What he hears about original sin and total depravity only adds to his confusion. Yet he is in need, and he knows that he is in need. Is it any wonder, then, that he turns eagerly to those who offer a way of goodness that is not 'complicated' by reference to the will of God, or who offer to deal with the 'self' of which (in his best and worst moments) he is so consciously and painfully ignorant?

[21] See p. 72, *infra*.   [22] See Additional Note, p. 28, *infra*.

Nor does he need to look far to discover those who offer help in both these directions at once.

I am confident that this is not the least of the reasons, for the fact (emphasized by many doctors and others) that very many are turning elsewhere for what the Christian gospel professes to offer. Does this mean that the pastor must turn psychiatrist, the theologian become a psychologist, and the Christian gospel take its turn in the queue of conflicting psychiatric theories? Or can it be that the message of sin and salvation has a direct and unique significance concerning the ignorance of self?

For, it must be noted by way of conclusion, the hypothesis of the unconscious is not relevant merely to mental disease and to what is commonly judged to be morally evil. Unhappily more attention has been paid to what may be described as the murkier aspects of unconscious mental processes. Freud himself said that not only 'what is lowest' but also 'what is highest in the Ego can be unconscious'.[23]

Such study as has been made of the role of the unconscious in genius and in artistic 'inspiration' suggests much further scope for examination. Similarly, all too little has been thought about the ways in which the healing and cleansing power of God works unknown to the consciousness of the recipient. At very least it may be suspected that a concept of sin that limits reference to conscious, deliberate wrong-doing is one that has little reference to the deeper reaches of human personality.

Dr R. Newton Flew is one of the few theologians who have clearly recognized the fact of 'unconscious' sin. He leaves us, however, with the tantalizing comment that 'the acknowledgement that our worst sins may be unconscious opens up a new problem'.[24]

Our preliminary survey of contemporary questions concerning the Christian meaning of *sin* is now completed. It has already become apparent that there are several distinguishable, but related, problems. Problems concerning ignorance of *self*, of the varied types that have been briefly indicated, are bound up with those that relate to ignorance of *God;* but, as will be shown later

---

[23] *The Ego and the Id* (1935), p. 133, quoted E. Fromm, op. cit., p. 33.
[24] *The Idea of Perfection in Christian Theology* (1934), p. 412 note; cf. pp. 332ff, 411ff. See pp. 167ff, *infra*, where reference is made to Dr W. E. Sangster's discussion of the same theme.

in this book, psychological perplexities need to be sharply differentiated from theological discussions. There are, however, two other ways in which any study of sin needs to make distinctions that are sometimes obscured.

Firstly, the problem of human *ignorance* is not the same problem as that of human *impotence*; our ignorance of what is 'right' is the concern that weighs most heavily on our present-day thought, whereas it was man's inability to do the will of God which most deeply concerned the New Testament writers and most of the great teachers of the Church.

Secondly, questions about the nature of *sin* need to be distinguished from those about the nature of *guilt*. As our discussion proceeds, the need to make this distinction will become clearer, but so, also, will the difficulty in making it. It is precisely the desire to make our doctrine of sin harmonious with an ethical conception of individual moral responsibility that has tended to dominate discussion about sin, at least since Augustine wrote *De Libero Arbitrio* with that purpose in mind. We shall see how, in recent years, it has become increasingly customary to explain sin *in terms of guilt*; the consequences and validity of that custom call for examination.

Our main concern in these pages will be with the 'problem of ignorance', but the related problems that have just been noted will inevitably attract our attention. One of our chief purposes will be to see how seriously such problems affect that *knowledge* of sin which the Christian believes to be a necessary element in man's salvation. Therefore, before we turn to some of the attempts to deal with the specific problem of ignorance, it is necessary to look —however briefly—at the way in which our questions appeared to our Christian ancestors.

ADDITIONAL NOTE

I do not wish to overload the argument of this book with discussion of diverse psychological theories which I have not the competence to evaluate, and which are not essential to my main thesis. It is, for example, not necessary for us to await confirmation of telepathic communication before we take note of the power of *suggestion*, operating in many ways to shape our ideas and mould our behaviour. Similarly, so long as the fact of unconscious motivation is recognized, it is not necessary for our present purpose to discuss the varied explanations of the mental processes involved. It should, however, be noticed that there are strong arguments in favour of distinguishing between the secondary unconscious, largely formed by repression, and the primary unconscious 'where the dynamic elements of our basic nature are striving for expression and for a balanced integration'.[25]

Jung's hypothesis of the *collective unconscious* has probably met with less popular interest than has been aroused by Freud's main theories, but it calls for much sympathetic study by Christian students.[26] Few interpreters of Jung, known to me, would see in Jung's theory the suggestion of a racially *shared* 'unconscious'; it appears that by 'collective' Jung means *'common* to all', or 'similar in all cases'. H. H. Price suggests that there is obscurity at this point in Jung's teaching, but he himself, accepting telepathic communication as proven, suggests that 'it becomes at least conceivable that at the unconscious level there are no clear-cut boundaries between this and that. . . . In the study of telepathy we are exploring the fuzziness of boundaries between one mind and another.' He adds the surmise that there may be a 'common unconsciousness, common to all minds'.[27]

It is tempting to postulate something of this kind, and it would provide a fascinating comment upon the Pauline concept of 'in Adam', and upon the orthodox Christian view of the solidarity of the race. But truth is not found by leaping at attractive hypotheses that lack sufficient evidence. Unless and until greater confidence can be placed in this theory of a *shared* 'unconscious' we must be content to take note of the more obvious ways in which, at every 'level' of personality, we influence our fellows and are influenced by them.

[25] L. W. Grensted, *The Psychology of Religion*, p. 85.
[26] cf. V. White, *God and the Unconscious*.
[27] *Some Aspects of Conflict between Science and Religion*, pp. 41ff.

CHAPTER THREE

MODERN QUESTIONS IN OLD FORMS

WHEN we turn from the contemporary world to Christian thought of past generations we move into a universe of thought so different from our own that the greatest care must be taken to avoid reading our questions into the minds of those who did not ask those questions. This danger is most seriously present, as will be noted in later chapters, when we study the Bible.

In great formative periods of the Christian doctrine of sin, such as the Augustine-Pelagius controversy, the work of Aquinas and the birth of Reformation theology, many of the questions that have been raised in the preceding chapters were discussed; but the background of thought, in each of the periods mentioned, differed so greatly from our own ways of thinking that only laborious and patient historical sympathy makes any detailed comparison between their problems and ours possible. Psychological concepts differed greatly from ours, so that it is never easy to be certain that we are not attributing to ancient thinkers notions that are quite foreign to their understanding of human nature. Similarly, just as we must not read Augustine or Aquinas as though they wrote after Descartes, Kant and Freud, so we must not seek from Luther or Calvin *direct* answers to the type of unbelief in God which is current today. Just as each generation of Christians must declare the Gospel in a way that speaks to living minds, so, in each generation, Christians must address themselves to problems that belong to their own and not to some other age.

I shall not, therefore, attempt in this Chapter to bring all the questions that have been summed up under the heading 'the problem of ignorance' to past expressions of Christian orthodoxy. Augustine, however, so stands out in the history of Christian discussion about sin that it is impossible not to devote some attention to him. Through his influence upon Aquinas, on the one hand, and upon Luther, on the other, he has more profoundly influenced both Catholic and Protestant thought than has any Christian apart from the writers of the New Testament.

I wish to suggest, firstly, that one particular attempt made by Augustine to deal with problems concerning ignorance and moral responsibility failed, and, secondly, that his insistence upon two facts which underly those problems remains a necessary insistence. In other words, it will be argued that Augustine was right when he stated facts and problems, rather than when he attempted explanations.

1. THE DISTINCTION BETWEEN 'ORIGINAL' AND 'ACTUAL' SIN

Perhaps the most ill-chosen and unfortunate term in the whole Christian vocabulary is *peccatum orginale*. It focuses our attention precisely where the Scriptures do not focus it, namely upon the historical 'origin' of sin. As there is a striking contrast between the lack of reference to Adam within the books of the Old Testament, in comparison with *extra*-canonical Hebrew writings, so throughout Christian history there has been a tendency to suggest that the responsibility for our sins can be laid on Adam, a tendency which is quite out of harmony with the New Testament. It requires little imagination to conceive the horror with which St Paul would view this outcome of his comparatively incidental references to Genesis. Moreover the term *original sin* has increased the danger of treating sin as a *thing* about which more will be said in later chapters.

We cannot, however, wish away words that are inconvenient; if we could discard the term 'original sin' we should still find ourselves confronted by three facts about human sinfulness, three facts which are inter-related so that we need one word to describe them together. These facts may be briefly summarized as: (1) the totality of sin—it is the whole man, not part of him, that is a sinner; (2) the solidarity of sin—'sinfulness does not belong simply to separate individuals, it is a characteristic of the whole human race';[1] and (3) the 'inevitability' of sin—every man is by 'fallen' nature a sinner.

It should be said at once that I write with the conviction that the three statements just made represent both the teaching of Scripture and a true description of the human predicament.

---
[1] G. Aulén, *The Faith of the Christian Church*, p. 273. Aulén describes original sin under my first two headings; what he has to say about (3) appears under my (2).

Every book must have its presuppositions and these are some of my presuppositions. If they were not true, a large part, but not all, of what I have termed 'the problem of ignorance' would disappear. We shall not be surprised, therefore, to find that many proffered answers to our questions involve the denial of one or more of these facts. For Augustine they were unquestionably true, and all of them were included in his understanding of *peccatum originale*.

Yet Augustine also believed that man chooses, *wills* to sin. This was more than a legacy of his thought prior to the Pelagian controversy.[2] For Augustine the essential truth was a *double-truth;* man *is* a sinner; man *chooses* to sin. As Brunner has written about Augustine:

Inspired by the sense of a divine commission and the truth of the Scriptures [he defended] against the liberalism of his day ... the unity of inescapable necessity and responsibility which cannot be shaken off, sin as a totality which determines the person, and at the same time sin as a personal act.[3]

It was, of course, this double-truth that Augustine sought to affirm against Pelagius. The whole of his often highly involved, and at times almost unintelligible, discussion of this matter is misunderstood if we forget that he was as anxious to affirm personal responsibility as to assert the 'inevitability' of sin. There are sentences in Augustine's writings which might have been written by Kant. 'Sin is so much voluntary evil that it is not sin at all unless it is voluntary.'[4] 'Nothing can possibly be conceived in the world, or even out of it, which can be called good without qualification except a good will.'[5] To that extent Augustine and Kant are, somewhat surprisingly, comrades in arms. But, of course, Augustine also held that 'a man's free choice avails only to lead him to sin, if the way of truth be hidden from him',[6] and, further, that the way of truth is hidden from natural man. Thus, for Augustine, the fact of ignorance is bound up with the fact of impotence; man is neither able to do that which God requires, nor does he know what he needs to know.[7]

[2] F. R. Tennant's article on Original Sin (*ERE*) IX. 561.
[3] *Man in Revolt*, p. 121. [4] *De Vera Religione*, xiv. 27.
[5] Kant, *Grundelegung zur Metaphysick der Sitten*. [6] *De Spiritu et Littera*, 5.
[7] In *Enchiridion*, 'Ignorance and infirmity' are the twin 'causes' of sin, the negative aspects of *curiositas* and *lascivia*, which, with *superbia* are 'the soul's threefold defection from the love of God'. Cf. J. Burnaby, *Amor Dei*, p. 189; and p. 133, *infra*.

It is not necessary to examine in detail the ways by which Augustine sought to reconcile this ignorance and this impotence with the fact of *guilt*. The central point in his explanation is his understanding of original sin as the punishment for *Adam's* sin (*poena peccati*), a punishment involving guilt. The difficulties into which he was led by his attempt to hold to this guilt, whilst conceiving all sin as 'voluntary' (an act of will), is exemplified by his discussion of original sin in infants. This is the punishment of Adam's sin, yet it, too, can be thought of as voluntary, because 'we apply the word "sin" not only to what is properly called sin, that is what is committed knowingly and with free will, but also to all that follows as the necessary punishment of the first sin'.[8]

In that sentence Augustine came, not for the only time, very near to anticipating later attempts to combine a Pelagian view of sin with an Augustinian understanding of divine grace. When in *Retractions* he looked back on that passage in *De Libero Arbitrio* he reiterated this insistence upon the voluntary character of *Adam's* sin (so that original sin in an infant could be called 'voluntary'), but he also added a further analysis of what we mean by 'voluntary' to which I shall refer later. F. R. Tennant has said that Augustine was a 'psychological indeterminist' and a 'theological necessitarian';[9] it seems to me, rather, that, in spite of occasional lapses into a Pelagian view of 'will', Augustine gave the death-blow to that indeterminism which has needlessly complicated discussion about moral responsibility. The inconsistency in his teaching, if such there be, arose, as it must inevitably arise, through the attempt to treat original and actual sin as two quite separate entities, to each of which guilt must be ascribed.

In seeking to explain how we may justly be termed guilty for *Adam's* sin Augustine's thought hovered between the seminal notion, i.e. the belief that the whole race was 'in' Adam, and emphasis upon our sin as inherited from Adam. It was the latter explanation which grew increasingly emphatic in Augustine's own teaching, and which became dominant in subsequent thought. The important point, for our present discussion, is that Augustine thus paved the way for a clear-cut distinction between original and actual sin. The deeper insight of Augustine (and of the New Testament), that *all* sin is both original and actual (if we are to

---

[8] *De Libero Arbitrio*, 3.xix (Tr. *Library of Christian Classics*, 1953).
[9] *ERE*, 'Original Sin.'

retain those words at all), was lost sight of, and was not wholly regained until Luther.

Aquinas gave this same account of the two kinds of sin. He echoed Augustine's words: 'The disorder which is in this man born of Adam is voluntary, not by his will, but by the will of his parent.'[10] As in Augustine, we find in Aquinas the two-fold explanation of this original sin in terms of the human race as a single organism,[11] and in terms of hereditary defect. In giving the second explanation Aquinas taught that guilt for this sin belonged to individuals not as 'private persons', 'but when men are taken as members born of one descent-group; when they appear as one man, then sinfulness is incurred because a voluntary factor is at work, namely the actual sin of our first parents'.[12]

This effort to justify *blame* for 'original' sin has occupied much of the thought of later Christians. Here, too, we notice that separation of original from actual sin which remains characteristic of Roman Catholic Moral Theology. Thus, a present-day Roman Catholic writer finds himself able to combine a definition of sin as 'essentially voluntary' with belief in original sin:

> Sin being essentially voluntary, is also essentially conscious. . . . Sacramental confession . . . is concerned solely with actual sins committed after baptism: it is not concerned with inherited sin, whose remedy lies within the province of Baptism itself.[13]

The author was concerned, in that passage, with the relation between the work of the psychiatrist and that of the priest, a matter to which we shall return. I quote his words now in order to stress that this isolating of original sin, as a 'congenital defect', (to use Aquinas's words),[14] to which guilt is attached, but which is wholly 'removed' by Baptism, leaves the way open for a treatment of actual sin as purely deliberate, voluntary, conscious wrong-doing. 'Ignorance' and 'infirmity' no longer need to be taken into account.

This method has manifest advantages: it enables us to treat actual sin as a matter of wrong thought and acts (vices as contrasted with virtues), without all the complications brought about

[10] *Retractions*, I.xiii.
[11] *Summa Theol.*, lxxxi.1 (Tr. T. Gilby, *St Thomas Aquinas, Theological Texts*, p. 122).
[12] *Disputations*, iv, de Malo, 1 (Tr. ibid., pp. 121-2).
[13] V. White, *God and the Unconscious*, p. 166.
[14] *Disputations*, ibid.

by the three-fold character of original sin as it has been summarized earlier in this chapter. We can now forget all about the totality, the solidarity, the 'inevitability' of sin. Original sin becomes primarily inherited guilt, whereas in fact the all-important truths concealed within that unhappy term are truths about *sin*, not about guilt, and, in particular, they are truths about man's self-estrangement from God. That it is impossible thus to separate 'original' and 'actual' sin will, I hope, be more positively demonstrated in later chapters.

Before concluding this section, however, a few words must be said about 'Catholic' moral theology. Perhaps its strength lies in its emphasis upon, and analysis of, particular 'sins'. If the 'Protestant' tends to be very impatient with this kind of ethical inquiry (as he does), he often appears to the 'Catholic' to be thinking of a 'salvation' which has little moral content. Whereas the 'Protestant' sees the 'Catholic' so minimizing justification by grace through faith that he loses the essential meaning of sin, from the 'Catholic' view-point the 'Protestant' appears to ignore the laborious task of morality because of his trust in justification. It is sometimes useful to see ourselves through each other's eyes, especially if we then proceed to examine *ourselves*. In later pages I shall suggest dangers against which Protestants must be on guard; I shall only venture a brief indication of the limitations that at least some Protestants find in Catholic moral theology.

It is typical of Aquinas's treatment of sin that his main discussion of 'the cause of sin on the part of man' comes in his *Treatise on Habits*. A recent Anglican presentation of Thomist moral teaching[15] makes an exhaustive study of motive and intention, of habit and choice, of different types of sin and degrees of moral responsibility, and thus provides, with contemporary illustrations, a modern commentary upon Aquinas's great work. One is struck by how little comparable study is made by Protestant Christians. Yet it is impossible not to notice also two other facts. First, the whole area of human personality studied by depth psychology is left out of purview. Dr Mortimer gives a very thorough study of 'unawareness',[16] distinguishing between 'vincible' and 'invincible' unawareness, and showing how, for example, blame may be attached to actions performed under alcoholic influence if the

[15] R. C. Mortimer, *The Elements of Moral Theology* (1947), Chaps. 3 and 4.
[16] ibid., pp. 45ff.

consequences of such influences 'were to any extent foreseen'. The far more troublesome facts about unconscious motivation are all left to the psychotherapist.

More significantly, the essential nature of sin as man's self-estrangement from God, the biblical insight that we are all *alike* in our sin, seems to give place to a measuring of degrees of responsibility, based upon the extent of our knowledge of right and wrong; a classification of types of sin seems to eclipse an emphasis upon the basic character of sin itself. I have often wondered what Aquinas can have made of Augustine's remark: 'The weighing-up of which are light and which are grave sins is a matter not for human but for divine judgement.'[17]

To return to our main point, Augustine's attempts to explain the guilt of original sin only serve to distract attention from the meaning of original sin. Augustine, from whose side in the conflict with Pelagius the Christian Church has never found itself able to wander for very long, was a safer guide when he was stressing 'ignorance' and 'infirmity' than when he was yielding ground to Pelagius. It is more important to recognize the facts about our sinfulness than to deny them in the interests of a 'respectable' account of individual responsibility.

II. 'SIN OF IGNORANCE'

Augustine did not hesitate to use the term 'sin of ignorance'. The causes of our sinning are two-fold, either that we do not perceive what we ought to do or that we fail to do what we are already aware ought to be done. 'The former of these is the sin of ignorance, the latter of frailty.'[18] These words come from his last principal discussion of sin. Let us, so far as possible, for the moment leave on one side his attempt to explain the *guilt* of such sins; the important fact is his recognition of the 'sin of ignorance'. Before our task is done we shall have to note many instances of other writers who insist upon the exclusion of all that is done in ignorance from the concept of sin.

Augustine, however, went farther than this acknowledgement that ignorance of what is right is involved in our sinning; he drew attention to the 'ignorance of God'. To those who would say, 'A man cannot sin unless he knows that he is disobeying God',

---

[17] *Enchiridion*, xxi (Tr. Ernest Evans, 1953). [18] ibid., xxii.

Augustine would reply, not only that the sinner does not understand how he is behaving toward God, but that he does not know the one thing he needs to know about his sin, how he may *cease* from sin. A passage in which Augustine taught this is of interest in several ways. It shows, once again, the perplexities in the idea of *guilt;* it shows Augustine, once again, wavering toward Pelagianism and retreating; it sheds some light upon his doctrine of grace, and indicates how he might have avoided the belief in irresistible grace which other aspects of his teaching lead him to hold. (It must, however, be noted that these quotations come from his earlier writings.)

You are not held guilty because you are ignorant in spite of yourself, but because you neglect to seek the knowledge you do not possess. You are not held guilty because you do not use your wounded members but because you despise him who is willing to heal them. These are your personal sins.'

So far, Augustine is conceding to Pelagius. But he continues:

To no man is it given to know how to seek to his advantage what to his disadvantage he does not know. He must humbly confess his weakness, so that as he seeks and makes his confession *He* may come to his aid who, in aiding knows neither error nor difficulty.[19]

Thus Augustine saw the problem of ignorance lying at the very root of sin; he saw this most clearly, as we may, when he thought not about ignorance but about the knowledge that comes from God.

III. 'THE SIN OF FRAILTY'

It was not when Augustine was writing about 'what is properly called sin, that is what is committed knowingly and with free will', but, rather, when he was describing the frailty, the infirmity of the will, that he was most true to his understanding of man's need. We are not surprised, therefore, to find that one who knew so much about the 'abysmal depths' of human personality should have gone far to anticipate that rejection of a false 'faculty' psychology which has taken place in modern times. The illusory belief in a 'will' which is a distinguishable 'part' of us has not yet disappeared from popular notions, nor, indeed, from some theological and ethical writings. The matter is so important that

---
[19] *De Libera Arbitrio,* 3.xix.

somewhat lengthy quotation from Augustine seems desirable. The first reference also sheds light on another error that confuses discussion of moral responsibility, the search for some specific 'cause' of acts of will.

> Since will is the cause of sin, you now ask what is the cause of will. If I could find one, are you not going to ask for the cause of the cause I have found? What limit will there be to your quest, what end to inquiry and explanation? ...
> What cause of willing can there be which is prior to willing? Either it is a will, in which case we have not got beyond the root of evil will, or it is not a will, and in that case there is no sin in it.[20]

In a later passage to which reference has already been made[21] Augustine lays the foundation for a concept of self-determinism as contrasted with indeterminism, and in so doing he unmasks the vain attempt to limit the meaning of *voluntary* to 'will directed by reason', or to actions uninfluenced by passion, unconscious motivation and the like.

> Sins which are not unjustifiably said to be non-voluntary because they are committed in ignorance or under compulsion cannot be said to be committed entirely involuntarily. He who sins in ignorance uses his will to some extent, for he thinks he should do what in fact ought to be done. He who does not do the things that he would because the flesh lusteth against the spirit, may be unwilling, but he lusts all the same, and thereby does not the things he would. If he is overcome, he voluntarily consents to lust, and thereby does what he wishes, being free from righteousness and the servant of sin.[22]

We must not read modern psychological interpretations into that statement, but we may be sure that Augustine would not be surprised by anything he might learn in a psychiatrist's consulting-room, nor would he be compelled by that experience to reformulate his doctrine of sin.

As H. Wheeler Robinson commented,[23] the Pelagian concept of a 'fundamental indeterminism of the human will is psychologically false'. Augustine's conception of will as itself possessing character, and of true liberty as found only when that character

---

[20] ibid., 3.xv. Augustine's argument includes the assertion that a man's *nature* does not 'compel him' to sin. But he is, I think, distinguishing *natura* from what *we* should call 'total personality'.

[21] See p. 34, *supra*.   [22] *Retractions*, I.xiii.

[23] *The Christian Doctrine of Man*, pp. 187f.

is good are truths to which we must hold firmly. In Book 8 of *The Confessions*, Augustine examined what, in later days, has been termed divided (or dual) personality,[24] and, although his language is archaic and his argument unconvincing, his important conclusion is that (however it may appear to the contrary) man has only *one* 'will'. Whatever I think or do, when I am not propelled by some external force, is the outcome of my whole personality.

This emphasis upon total personality, although the term is not his, is also characteristic of *Luther's* teaching. He exposed the folly of trying to separate what the will *does* from what the will *is;*[25] he rejected the notion of a will that is something other than the personality, the self. It is thus that his famous words, 'Freewill lies prostrate'[26] must be understood. 'I wish that the word "free will" had never been invented. It is not in the Scriptures, and it were better to call it "self will" which profiteth not.'[27]

Reinhold Niebuhr claims that Luther heightened Augustine's doctrine to the point of denying moral responsibility.[28] Luther did not, however deny free will ('if we do not like to leave out this term altogether') in the ordinary sense of ability to exercise knowledge and choice in the daily business of living ('the right of using, acting and omitting according to his "free will" '). But in regard to 'the things which pertain unto salvation or damnation, [man] has no "free will", but is a captive, slave, servant, either to the will of God or to the will of Satan'.[29]

Thus, as Aulén has pointed out, Luther, so far from treating original sin merely as a matter of inherited guilt, could describe original sin as *personal* sin. 'Original sin, natural sin, or *personal* sin is the principal sin. If it did not exist, neither would there be any actual sin.'[30] In this, Luther was, I believe, far more in harmony with the teaching of Paul than was Aquinas. That belief, however, can only be demonstrated when we turn to consider the New Testament teaching. For the moment we must

---

[24] Book 8, 21-4; cf. C. S. S. Williams, *The Confessions of St Augustine, Book 8* (1953), p. 53.
[25] *De Servo Arbitrio* (Tr. Henry Cole), p. 125.   [26] ibid., p. 298.
[27] Quoted (from *An Argument in Defense of All the Articles of Dr Martin Luther.* . . .) by H. T. Kerr, *A Compend of Luther's Theology* (1943), p. 91.
[28] R. Niebuhr, *The Nature and Destiny of Man*, I.259.
[29] *De Servo Arbitrio* (T. Henry Cole), p. 79.
[30] (*W.A.*, 10,I,1), quoted by G. Aulén, op. cit., p. 273.

D

be content to notice that for Luther as for Augustine the 'sin' from which man needs to be saved is that which involves the whole man. Man cannot trust to his 'reason' nor to his 'will', as though one or both were uncorrupted parts of his nature by which he might save himself. It is neither by looking in at his own *knowledge*, nor by using his 'reason' to direct his 'will' against the inclinations of 'the flesh', that man can be rescued from that self-estrangement from God, or (to quote Augustine yet once more) from that 'perversity of the will, which turns aside from Thee, O God'.

This brief glance at long-distant teaching has at least served to show that the problems of 'ignorance', as they appear to many in our generation, are almost minor problems compared with the predicament of mankind as our Christian forefathers saw it. Before we turn to notice the all-important truth that they thus realized the gravity of man's condition because they were *assured of the remedy for it*, we must consider some of the ways in which, in our own day, attempts have been made to deal with the questions posed at the outset of this book.

PART TWO

ATTEMPTS TO SOLVE THE PROBLEM OF IGNORANCE

CHAPTER FOUR

'SIN *IS* IGNORANCE'

IT is characteristic of modern man that the problem of ignorance should loom larger in his mind than the problem of impotence; it is lack of knowledge concerning good and evil, rather than the enslavement of will, which appears to our generation as the main obstacle to virtue. Therefore it is with ignorance that most of those who reject the traditional Christian account of sin concern themselves. Whilst our attention in these pages will be mainly given to those who hold the Christian faith but seek to modify the orthodox doctrine of sin, something must first be said about the attempt to explain all moral evil and sin in terms of ignorance.

I. EVIL IS IGNORANCE

Wherever the classical tradition is strong, the element in that tradition which identified vice with ignorance, and virtue with knowledge, is to be found. Amongst our contemporaries are very many to whom this identification offers many obvious attractions. Christians are all too apt to ignore the moral earnestness of non-Christians, and too quick to assume that rationalists are indifferent to ethical problems.

One of the significant aspects of present-day thought is the conviction, shared by many, that the desperate moral dangers by which the human race is faced can only be solved by the substitution of an understanding of moral evil as the result of ignorance for the Christian concept of sin. Such a substitution promises to give an explanation of evil which will be in harmony with scientific explanation; it offers hope that evil will be removed from the realm of the mysterious, in which 'sin' exists. A number of attempts are therefore being made to abandon the vocabulary of religion and of traditional moral philosophy. Difficulty is found in translating terms such as 'sin', 'evil', 'good', 'bad', into other terms; but the attempt is being made. Perhaps the greatest difficulty is to find any meaning for the word 'good' which is not a hedonistic one. This difficulty is strikingly illustrated in the book by Bertrand Russell to which reference has previously been made.[1]

It is important that the Christian should not press too far his criticism of these attempts to explain moral evil in terms of ignorance. We are all familiar with the foolish type of pulpit cliché which denounces the search for knowledge. 'Man is not saved by science.' 'There are those who trust to education . . . to psychology or biology. . . .' These explosive, and often incomplete, utterances are full of ambiguities. They imply that there is one activity termed 'science', and the suggestion is at least implicit that 'science', or the particular science in question, has nothing to contribute to human well-being.

This attitude to man's unfettered search for knowledge has brought Christian belief into contempt, has hindered the moral as well as the physical betterment of human life, and has impoverished the life of the Church itself. Ignorance has very much more relation to moral evil than is often admitted by professing Christians. The painstaking study of all kinds of data concerning human behaviour, the careful analysis of the moral results of varied human activities, the weighing-up of the merits of alternative courses of actions—all these and many other ways of obtaining knowledge are indeed part of the good life. As we shall have cause to note in a later chapter, the Christian faith in God's justifying and sanctifying grace is all too easily misrepresented as a substitute for ethical inquiry and for moral decision.

As more will be said later concerning ethical ignorance—ignorance of right and wrong—no more need be said at this stage than that recognition of such ignorance does not involve identifying *sin* with ignorance. Not only must we include, in the concept of sin, deliberate refusal to do that which is believed to be right, we must also decline to accept any interpretation of sin that excludes reference to God.

It is, then, because *sin* is not to be identified with any concept of moral evil that ignores man's relationship with God that it cannot be identified with human ignorance of right and wrong.

---

[1] *Human Society in Ethics and Politics*, especially Chaps. 3 and pp. 88 and 117. Effects which lead to approval are defined as 'good', and the 'effects' thus described cause pleasure of a type that includes 'intelligence and aesthetic sensibility'. The 'good life' has more in common with a philosopher's paradise than with most people's idea of pleasure.

Only when we begin to understand the sin of the morally upright man do we begin to comprehend the meaning of sin. Then we discover that there is, indeed, ignorance in all sinning, but then, too, we find that goodness is the result of rightness with God and not the way to it. The study of those truths must be postponed to later chapters. There is, however, another legacy of the classical tradition that calls for brief notice.

II. KNOWLEDGE IS VIRTUE

When reference is made today to the 'classical tradition' it is all too often forgotten that the ancient world recognized the need for more than normal knowledge. However profoundly true it is that the Cross was foolishness to the Greeks, it must be remembered that Greeks sought for an enlightenment not to be gained by ordinary intellectual disciplines. There is a world of difference between the quest by worshippers of the Mystery religions for supernatural *gnosis* and Plato's philosophical search, but 'the finer spirits yearned, as Plato yearned, for [a more trusty chariot], a [divine word] in which to make the voyage of life, in place of the poor raft of merely "human" knowledge'.[2]

We are now a long way from Athens, and in our day this yearning for *gnosis*, for a supernatural knowledge that will dispel our ignorance and cure our sins, reveals itself in many different ways. With some it is, still, a desire for and belief in some kind of divine information by which truth is, as it were, injected into passive human minds. The belief that Revelation consists in propositions, theological and ethical statements coercively implanted in the minds of some men and women, is by no means dead; those who share that belief make strange and uncongenial bed-fellows. But similar hunger for miracle-working knowledge is felt by many who have abandoned hope in God.

Many a scientist of our time has expressed his dismay concerning the popular attitude to 'science'. 'The scientists' have become the conscripted high priests of multitudes, and both genuine and pseudo-scientific writings have become the infallible bible of many who have learnt to read but not to think. The humility and reverent agnosticism of the true scientist is almost submerged by the confident cries of the worshippers of this new mystery-religion.

[2] A. W. Mair, 'Sin (Greek)', *ERE*, XI.556a.

If behind this blind faith in the omniscience and omnipotence of scientific inquiry lay reverence for truth and a patient readiness to accept it, there would be no cause for alarm. The painstaking search of the scientific student is not a hindrance to the Gospel; it is the superstitious craving for ready-made knowledge that is a symptom of fear and mental sloth. The 'more trusty chariot', for which the Greeks sought, has become an illusory 'scientific' escalator to happiness and security; the 'word of God' has become the latest item of real or pseudo-scientific writing.

One of the temptations that assail all Christian propagandists today is that of surrendering to the irrationalism of our time. It is fatally easy to present the Christian message as an offer either of individual infallible moral insight or of collective (Church) ethical infallibility. When sin is identified with ignorance goodness tends to be identified with ethical omniscience, and then the rationalist (the ethical humanist, as he is often termed by a prostitution of the word *humanism*) rightly claims that he gives more thought to morality than does the professing Christian. It is, I believe, urgently necessary for Christians to appreciate the fact that they often appear, to those outside the Christian faith, to be lacking in ethical concern. However exaggerated, and sometimes false, such criticism may be, we shall not have removed all grounds for it until we recognize, not only that the morally upright may yet be sinful, but that the 'saved' man may be ethically ignorant.

III. THE DARK SHADOW

There is yet another legacy from the thought of the ancient world which influences contemporary thought about sin and evil, and it has appeared in different guises in many religions and moral philosophies.

Ever in the background, and often in the foreground of ancient thought was the shadow of *Fate*. If in its more popular aspect this was a belief in the gods for whom men were playthings, in more sophisticated minds it appeared as a deep dualism which saw man's potentially perfect mind imprisoned in a corrupt body, and a cyclical view of history which saw all life as a tale without meaning and without end. Most notably of all (as Reinhold Niebuhr pointed out in a summary of the classical tradition as it has influenced our own thinking),³ this dark shadow of despair sees man's doom within himself. Perhaps, I venture to suggest, the Greeks never came nearer to the Gospel than when they considered *hubris*, the vaunting pride that brings man's greatest achievements to ruin and turns his glorious victories into defeat.

Niebuhr contrasts the element of optimism in the 'classical view' of human nature, which, he asserts, existed through its failure to find any defect in the centre of human personality, with contemporary ideas of man. But it seems to me that the recognition of *hubris* brought the Greeks within closer sight of the Christian meaning of sin than are most men today. Moreover, when Niebuhr adds that, 'while it [i.e. the classical view (or, as might better be said, the socratic view)] has perfect confidence in the virtue of the rational man, it does not share the confidence of the moderns in the ability of all men to be either virtuous or happy',⁴ I cannot fail to recall that he wrote in the United States and not in Europe. Yet even in that prosperous country, and in England, are there not many who only keep the dark shadow of despair away by refusing to look in its direction?

However greatly modern man may abhor the traditional Christian doctrine of original sin, he is always liable, as was ancient man, to recognize something that he cannot explain. That fact may be illustrated by reference to the theologian who, perhaps more than any other influencial Christian thinker, tended to identify sin with ignorance.

Ritschl's teaching about sin—as about other matters—was too many-sided to be justly summarized in a few sentences. In much of his writing there is the truly biblical insight that sin is only recognized for what it is by the light of the Gospel. But his understanding of this truth brought him near to teaching that the only sin to be wholly condemned is the deliberate rejection of Christ.⁵ He distinguished between deliberate and ignorant sin, and taught that 'sin is judged by God as ignorance', since otherwise it would be unpardonable.⁶ As H. R. Mackintosh wrote, Ritschl 'turned

---

³ *The Nature and Destiny of Man*, I.11.

⁴ ibid., p. 9.

⁵ *Justification and Reconciliation*, III, Chap. 5. I have not thought it necessary to discuss the theory that sin is an illusionary concept, as set forth, for example, by Spinoza: 'The knowledge of evil is an inadequate knowledge.' 'If the human mind possessed only adequate ideas, it would form no conception of evil' (*Ethics*, iv). See discussion by F. R. Tennant, *Origin*, pp. 43ff.

⁶ Quoted by H. R. Mackintosh, *Types of Modern Theology*, p. 160.

the Augustinian doctrine of Original Sin out of doors',[7] and held that sin is a purely individual act, although men are influenced by a bad environment. Yet, is not the shadowy background also to be found in Ritschl? There remained for him the dark 'kingdom of sin', just as the spectre of radical evil lay behind Kant's good will.

There are hard, inescapable facts about sin for which no tidy theory can find room, facts which lie behind such terms as 'original and actual sin', 'corporate sin', 'solidarity in sin'. We may seek to treat Man as though he were merely either a voluntary wrong-doer or an ignorant wrong-doer. But as we meet Man, in ourselves or in others, we are compelled to ask whether he is not both an offender and a victim, and whether he is as independent of his neighbour's sin as he likes to think. There is something to be said for the theory that sin *is* ignorance, and I shall attempt to say it in later chapters; that it is the whole truth, or that it is a clue to the remedy for sin is (as Mackintosh said of Ritschl's belief that 'sin is judged by God as ignorance') 'not only . . . out of line with biblical thought and reminiscent rather of the Greek doctrine that virtue is knowledge, but it is an idea which it is impossible to hold before our minds in the hour of penitence'.[8] As will be stressed later, only the penitent sinner knows what sin is, and among the facts that he knows is the fact that he has often chosen to sin.

The belief that sin is ignorance, and knowledge virtue, and the dread of 'the dark shadow' have existed together in human thought about good and evil from ancient days to our own. A fascinating study could be made of the many diverse manifestations of these incompatible conceptions. In our own day they explain the confused mixture of optimism and despair, of boundless hope that mankind can discover and reach the good life, and despair that such knowledge and attainment is for ever beyond his reach.

In the biblical account of Man both the need for knowledge and the 'dark shadow' are recognized; by the emphasis upon the divine revelation and upon man's wilful disobedience to the declared will of God, and by the emphasis upon the inevitability of sin, the two truths are stressed in the Scriptures. In traditional Christian doctrine the part played by knowledge in the good life

[7] op. cit., p. 159.   [8] ibid., p. 160.

has often been described under the term *actual* sin, and the dark shadow has been described as *original* sin. We may no longer find those terms as illuminating as our fathers found them, but we must beware of the temptation to discard, along with the terms, the facts which they sought to interpret. The discussion in this chapter has brought us back again to the reality of both moral ignorance and moral impotence. Any attempt to limit sin to voluntary choice of what is known to be wrong is exposed, not only by the Bible, but even by the mistaken identification of sin with ignorance and by the dread of the dark shadow.

We must now turn, however, to a more recent attempt to interpret the 'dark shadow' and to explain sin in terms of that shadow itself.

IV. 'SIN IS UNCONSCIOUS'

Probably R. S. Moxon was the only Christian theologian of repute to attempt to explain sin in terms of the unconscious. Rarely can a stranger definition of sin have been offered than this: Sin 'is being influenced by the subconscious instincts, tendencies, desires and habits when the time has come to pass under the higher rule of reason and of conscience'.[9] 'Man', said Moxon, 'is in process of passing from the subconscious to the conscious—from the natural to the spiritual—from Adam to Christ.'

Here is an educative example of the danger of seeking to reinterpret familiar facts by too hasty confidence in presumed scientific certainties. Employing a psychological theory which nobody would now accept, Moxon was persuaded that he had found the true meaning of many biblical terms. The 'subconscious' (from which mankind is mysteriously 'passing') served to account, not only for the 'natural' and for Adam, but for the 'flesh', as distinct from 'the spirit'. 'The subconscious mind is the *flesh;* the conscious mind is the *spirit.* To subordinate the spirit to the flesh is to oppose the development of the conscious mind and to arrest the only course of evolution which now remains for man. . . .'[10] That is why, according to Moxon, we need a Gospel: 'Christianity is the very religion to assist this divine process. . . .'

It is not necessary, at this date, to submit this theory to any detailed examination, but it may serve to indicate that, if we refuse to follow the example of very many theologians who pay

[9] *The Doctrine of Sin* (1922), p. 229.   [10] ibid., pp. 234f.

no regard to the unconscious, we must be careful not to exaggerate its importance. I do not know of any contemporary Christian writer who would thus identify sin with the unconscious, although N. P. Williams, in his reinterpretation of original sin, briefly indicated a way of salvation very similar to Moxon's. He, too (in a brief passage), suggested that the only hope 'which does justice both to man's moral and to his intellectual experience', is in the limited power of consciousness 'of gradually modifying the contents of the preconscious and unconscious by voluntary "sublimation" '.[11]

This method of attributing moral evil to the lack of conscious control has much in common with the older explanation of sin in terms of the failure of *reason* to control the passions and desires. It is, therefore, not surprising to find that some Christian psychologists come very near to identifying sin with the unconscious and virtue with conscious awareness and control. I do not know of any Christian psychologist who explicitly makes that identification, but two examples of a tendency toward it may be cited.

Dr R. S. Lee, a Christian disciple of Freud, and Dr Ernest White, a medical psychiatrist who writes as a Christian, both give definitions of sin that limit sin to conscious choice. For Lee, sin is 'conduct by an individual contrary to what his conscience or moral judgement believes to be right';[12] White denies that anything can be termed sinful except 'conscious disobedience to what we know is right'.[13] Both writers make the distinction between sin and moral disease which will be discussed in Chapter 6. Yet it is difficult, as one reads these authors, to resist the conclusion that man's most serious *moral* trouble is not sin, but his own unconscious mind. Dr Lee's books are full of warnings about the need 'to be free as far as possible from bondage to the unconscious',[14] and about the harm done by the unconscious in the lives of Christians.[15] The analyst, rather than the 'confessor', would seem to be the chief moral helper of sinful men and women.[16]

Similarly, Dr White gives us a detailed description of the 'unconscious motives' at work in juvenile delinquents. We are told that 'from a psychological point of view sin is a misdirection of the

[11] *The Ideas of the Fall and of Original Sin*, p. 485.
[12] R. S. Lee, *Freud and Christianity*, p. 157.
[13] E. White, *Christian Life and the Unconscious* (1955), p. 158.
[14] op. cit., p. 85.   [15] ibid., p. 91f.
[16] cf. R. S. Lee, *Psychology and Worship*, p. 90; and pp. 67ff, *infra*.

'SIN *IS* IGNORANCE'

energies of man', and we are shown how this misdirection takes place *unconsciously* even in childhood.[17] Thus we find sin, by definition, removed from all that is unconscious, whilst moral evil remains inextricably bound up with the unconscious. It is all the more unfortunate that Dr White does not help us over this difficulty, because he himself gives[18] a specially lucid reminder of the danger of thinking of the unconscious in spatial terms, as though it were a lower or separate part of mind. The objection to attributing sin either to the conscious or the unconscious is not only that moral experience forbids us to do so, it is also that such attribution involves a psychologically false separation between two alleged parts of the psyche. That, as we shall see later, is one of the principal objections to the popular way of distinguishing sin from moral disease.

This brief digression into psychological matters further demonstrates that it is equally impossible to define sin in terms of ignorance (the unconscious) or of knowledge (consciousness). We may neither say, 'Sin is due to ignorance and unconscious motivation', nor, 'Sin is conscious, voluntary choice of what is known to be wrong'. This latter definition is the one that has dominated much recent theology, and it must therefore be more closely examined as it was set forth by its ablest advocate.

[17] op. cit., pp. 150ff.   [18] ibid., pp. 24ff.

CHAPTER FIVE

'SIN *OR* IGNORANCE'

IN direct opposition to theories which equate sin with ignorance is the theory that only human activities (including thoughts and words) which involve deliberate, conscious, voluntary disobedience to the known will of God can rightly be called sinful. It was F. R. Tennant who, over a period of many years, argued the merits of this theory with unsurpassed clarity and brilliance.[1] Since Tennant wrote, his view has been echoed, often quite uncritically, in a great number—probably the majority—of Christian contributions to the study of sin and evil.

Of course Tennant was not the inventor of this theory. It is difficult, for example, not to imagine that John Wesley had enjoyed the great advantage of being a pupil of the Cambridge theologian, when we read:

Nothing is sin, strictly speaking, but a voluntary transgression of a known law of God. Therefore, every voluntary breach of the law of love is sin; and nothing else, if we speak properly. To strain the matter farther is only to make way for Calvinism. There may be ten thousand wandering thoughts, and forgetful intervals, without any breach of love, though not without transgressing the Adamic law.[2]

Or, again: 'Not only sin, properly so called (that is, a voluntary transgression of a known law), but sin, improperly so called, (that is, an involuntary transgression of a divine law, known or unknown), needs the atoning blood.[3] This concept of sin underlay Wesley's theology, although incongruous ideas sometimes confused his teaching. The influence of this upon his doctrine of Christian Perfection has not yet been cleared from the minds of many of his followers, in spite of Dr R. Newton Flew's patient and bold exposition of Wesley's 'inadequate analysis of the nature of sin'.[4] It is probably Wesley's influence rather than

[1] See p. x for titles and abbreviations used below.
[2] Letter CCCCXIX, 16th June 1772. (*The Works of the Rev John Wesley*, Vol. XII (1856), p. 368; omitted from Sugden's *Standard Edition* of the letters.)
[3] *A Plain Account of Christian Perfection* (*Works*, XI.380).
[4] *The Idea of Perfection in Christian Theology*, p. 332.

Tennant's which causes so many Methodist scholars to cling to this definition of sin, as, for example, is seen in Dr N. Snaith's query: 'Is there really any other kind of sin than [premeditated and deliberate sin]? There are many who would deny that unpremeditated sin is really sin at all.'[5]

Dr Flew was a pioneer among Methodists in boldly retorting, to both Wesley and Tennant: 'Our worst sins are often those of which we are unconscious.'[6] (Wesley continually qualified his doctrine of perfection by referring to 'conscious' sins.) As Flew adds: 'The stress on the consciousness and deliberate intention of the agent is the most formidable defect in Wesley's doctrine of the ideal.' Yet so difficult, and perhaps so dangerous, does the denial of Wesley's definition appear that even Dr Flew, discussing our deliverance from sin,[7] having raised the question, 'Is salvation possible for the sub-conscious?', and having stressed both that this is 'the real question for the seeker after holiness in our time', and that 'the answer ought not to be in doubt, if the assurances of the New Testament are received', leaves us, at the end of his great work, with a tantalizing problem: 'The acknowledgement that our worst sins may be unconscious opens up a new problem, which cannot be fully discussed here.'[8]

There is little or no indication that Wesley deeply considered the difficulties in his own theory. Tennant, however, brought to this matter a remorselessly critical intellect; he well knew what he was doing, when he thus limited sin to conscious voluntary wrongdoing, and he knew why he did it. It is, therefore, best to devote some care to his theory rather than to later versions of it, such as we find in H. D. Lewis's *Morals and the New Theology*.

I. TENNANT'S DEFINITION

Probably the shortest definition of sin given by Tennant comes toward the end of the volume which is of most significance for our present inquiry: '... sin may be defined as moral imperfection for which an agent is, in God's sight, accountable.'[9] Thus stated the definition may not appear to say very much, but it at least implies that there is another kind of moral imperfection which cannot be termed sin. This, indeed, Tennant did teach; but it is well to

---
[5] *The Distinctive Ideas of the Old Testament*, p. 67, note 1.
[6] op. cit., p. 333. [7] ibid., p. 411. [8] ibid., p. 412, note 2. [9] *Concept*, p. 245.

note, at the outset, that although he sought to provide a logically perfect denotation for the term sin, he did not assert, as more superficial exponents of his view have sometimes suggested, that he provided an infallible method by which men can recognize their own or others' sins. In fact, in the chapter from which I have just quoted he gave a prolonged reminder that 'God alone can try the heart, decide where moral accountability begins and ends, or assign to any volition its absolute position in the scale of relative turpitude or goodness'.[10]

Tennant's clear assertion that his definition does not enable human beings to determine which actions are in fact sinful has often been forgotten by those who have echoed his definition. The fact that, given this definition, there are insuperable difficulties in judging the extent of other people's sinfulness is no objection from Tennant's own point of view; he, rightly, leaves such judgement to God. If, however, we demand that men and women shall recognize their sin, and if we claim the right (as Christian preachers, for example) to tell them that they are sinners, then the difficulties become of grave importance. We do not find in Tennant's writings the kind of insistence upon an acknowledgement of sin that we find, for example, in John Wesley. Tennant's concern was to find a definition of sin which allows us to understand what is sin from God's point of view. His reasons for seeking to do this will become plainer as we examine his definition in more detail.

In his first book on this subject Tennant wrote that *a sin*

is an activity of the will, expressed in thought, word or deed, contrary to the individual's conscience, to his notion of what is good or right, his knowledge of the moral law or the will of God.[11]

Subsequently he filled out this brief summary by arguing that certain conditions must be fulfilled before any human activity can rightly be called sinful.

Firstly, there must exist in the social environment of the sinner some objective or common law or moral standard. Secondly, the sinner must be aware of that law at the time of action; he must know both its content and its bindingness upon himself; he must be aware of himself as transgressing it. To these primary conditions must be added two others: (1) '. . . until virtue be won, there

---

[10] *Concept*, p. 242; cf. p. 105.   [11] *Origin*, p. 160.

must be two lines of conduct open to the actor, to each of which he is impelled by impulses of different intensity and moral value.' (2) 'The activity must be the outcome of intention, and of choice characterized by the freedom which the subject's will possesses.'[12] Thus we reach the fuller statement of the definition:

Sin will be imperfect compliance (in single volitional activity or in character resulting from such activities) with the moral ideal in so far as this is, in the sight of God, capable of apprehension by an agent at the moment of the activity in question, both as to its content and claim upon him; this imperfect compliance being consequent upon choice of ends of lower ethical worth when the adoption of ends of higher worth is possible, and being regarded in its religious aspect (which may in some cases be wanting).[13]

For this definition Tennant made the claim that it is 'logically perfect... constant and universal and also definite. It is the only one which can fully satisfy the implications of the most fundamental of Christian doctrines.'

Lengthy quotation has been necessary because Tennant sought to anticipate many criticisms which he knew would be made of his theory. He did not, as is sometimes presumed, neglect to allow for habitual sins, nor for judgement upon character as distinct from isolated acts. Nor, as we have seen, did he make the facile assertion that it is easy to identify particular sinful actions. What he sought to do was to provide a definition free from logical, psychological and ethical confusion, and to do this by clearly limiting the meaning of the term *sin*, and by ruling out any kind of moral imperfection that could not be thus defined. In particular he sought to dispel for ever the notions of 'unconscious sin' and 'unintentional sin' and the presumed attachment of 'guilt' to such.[14] In a criticism of Kant, he suggested that Kant's errors (and, by implication, much other false teaching) would be avoided 'if we do not assume volition to exist until we empirically find it, and impute guilt only where we see volition'.[15] Here, as throughout his work, Tennant was much more ready to tell us what is *not* sin, than, save in general terms, what *is* sin. He made pardon, in the legal sense of 'not guilty', comparatively easy and apparently just; he left little room for the diagnosis of actual sin.

In this connexion it is significant that he was very diffident

---

[12] *Concept*, p. 209. [13] ibid., p. 245. [14] ibid., p. 101. [15] *ERE*, IX.563b.

about asserting the universality of sin.[16] This was partly due to his fundamentally empirical approach (how can we know the facts?); it was in part due to his keen awareness that only God can judge mankind; but it was, I think, a necessary consequence of his own definition. If the scope of sin is limited to deliberate disobedience to a known and recognized law, or, to anticipate a later theme, if 'perfection' is limited to an avoidance of that kind of sin, then both sinfulness and sinlessness have very limited meanings.

In Tennant's attitude to sinning men and women there was the charity of a true Christian disciple; unlike some who have shared his concept of sin, he never made it an excuse for harsh and censorious judgement of his fellow creatures. But perhaps he missed the gravity of their condition. If he did, it was certainly not his intention so to do; he argued with some intensity that, on the contrary, it was only his interpretation which clearly exposed the dreadfulness of human evil.[17] To those of us who would excuse ourselves, and even our neighbours also, on the ground that we are merely victims of fate or misled by our ignorance, Tennant's words offer a necessary rebuke:

... when we have made every allowance that true charity suggests, and have pleaded every extenuating circumstance that knowledge can discover, there remains in much lawless conduct that occurs an element which is not to be explained away and which it is simply wicked to ignore: namely, the fact of deliberate choosing of the worse when a better course is both known and possible. This is to be called by no other name than sin. Here at least is something inexcusable, something vile and hateful; and it is neither charitable nor compassionate to speak of it in language less severe.[18]

That this is 'the worst' that can be said about us, may be true if we are thinking in terms of blame-worthiness; but is it 'the worst' in terms both of our need and of the consequences of our actions? I think not; I believe that the fully Christian meaning of sin embraces more than Tennant would permit, in spite of the ostensibly great advantages of his definition.

[16] *Concept*, Note C, pp. 263ff; and cf. p. 59, *infra*.
[17] ibid., pp. 245ff. Notes D and E.
[18] *Concept*, p. 247. Tennant, however, resolutely denied that a man can ever choose evil *because* it is evil.

II. DIFFICULTIES IN TENNANT'S DEFINITION

Should these pages be read by anybody who is not familiar with Tennant's writings, I must point out that I am not attempting a full summary of his teaching about sin, nor a complete *critique* of it. His approach to the whole subject was dominated by his inquiry into the *origin* of sin—a matter with which I am not here concerned and with which, I believe, the Scriptures are but slightly, if at all, concerned. It is what I call 'the Tennant-type' definition of sin that I seek to modify, but because nobody else has expounded it with like clarity and care, the difficulties inherent in the definition are best discussed with yet further reference to this scholar.

As I have already remarked, Tennant sought, and believed that he found, in his definition logical consistency, psychological exactitude, and ethical propriety. Let us now look at each of these in turn, first noting, however, the significance of this approach to the problem of sin.

It must never be forgotten that our author sought to interpret *Christian* truth, but in so doing he was resolute that such truth must be expressed in a way that would be judged respectable by Logic, Psychology, and Ethics. In this he was a typical member of his generation, and although there has been a reaction against this early twentieth-century desire to re-express Christian dogma in terms of current beliefs, we need to remember that nothing can be 'religiously' true which is contradicted by any knowledge that man possesses. That fact does not, however, imply that the vocabulary of religion and theology can be directly transplanted into the language of other disciplines. It is just that which Tennant, and those who agree with him, seek to do.

(*a*) *Logical consistency.* Everyone who wishes to communicate his ideas to other people would like to share with Humpty Dumpty the ability to make a word mean 'just what I choose it to mean, neither more nor less'. Any reader of Tennant's *Philosophical Theology* knows that no theologian has more fully claimed that privilege, nor more meticulously made use of it. Given patience to learn his vocabulary, his readers need never be in doubt as to what he means, which (as Tennant never wearied of showing) can rarely be said of even the greater philosophers and theologians.

But the Christian student must seek to interpret the complexities of human personality and behaviour in the light, not only of such general knowledge as mankind has acquired to date, but also of the understanding of mankind expressed in the very different thought-forms, as well as different languages, of the Bible. It is this latter task which is the primary obligation laid upon those who seek to interpret the Christian understanding of sin.

There are manifest advantages in making a word bear one, limited, easily recognized meaning. Tennant had no difficulty in showing that the word *sin*, as commonly used by Christians, has several meanings which, at least at first sight, are by no means wholly congruous. Sin is used (in traditional Christian language) to refer both to the deliberate choice of what is known to be wrong and to acts which are thought to be right but which are in fact wrong; both to the acts of individuals and to the corporate behaviour of groups and even of 'mankind'; both to an individual's behaviour considered as a series of actions and to the total character of the individual. Christians describe as sinful not only deeds which quite obviously deserve blame because, as even the offender recognizes, there was no excuse for them, but also aspects of character which appear, to observers as well as to the 'sinner' himself, to be largely the result of the wrong-doing of other people.

More troublesome still is the fact that the word *sin* always implies the word *guilt*, and we therefore seem to be faced with two unattractive alternatives: either we must say that man is guilty for what is not, or is not wholly, his own fault (and so offend against ethical propriety), or we must (without any verbal distinction) allow the term sin to cover both 'guilty-sin' and (absurd notion!) 'innocent sin'.[19]

These are the logical arguments in favour of this type of definition of sin and they are very strong. Every preacher or pastor must often have wished that he could refashion the language of the Gospel in this as in many other ways. The question is whether the apparently clear, precisely limited definition of sin is in fact merely a remaking of language or whether it involves a distortion of the actual meaning of that which *sin* describes.

That is the important question. It is also true, as Dr Flew[20] has pointed out, that 'the word sin has too long a history behind it for such a limitation to be anything but very' difficult. (Dr Flew

[19] See Chap. 10, *infra*.   [20] op. cit., p. 333.

'SIN OR IGNORANCE'

writes 'possible', but if Tennant or somebody else could convince us that this was the only proper meaning of sin, and also that it was, as Tennant believed true to the teaching of Christ, we ought to make the difficult effort.) But if (as I hope to demonstrate) this apparently simple definition omits, from the denotation of *sin*, some of the most important characteristics of sin itself, then we have gained logical clarity at the price of obscuring the truth—we have relieved men from linguistic difficulties at the cost of concealing much of their need. If we seek to make the word mean what we wish it to mean we may only prevent ourselves from discovering what sin truly is.

(*b*) *Psychological exactitude*. In accordance with his entire philosophical approach, Tennant sought in psychology the clue to an accurate description of sin. I have not hitherto attempted to summarize his, by now familiar, teaching about the *cause* of sinning. Expressed in many ways, throughout his writings, the essential features of his explanation are as follows.

Man shares with the animals certain instincts or propensities. Before there was volition, there was appetite; and prior to morality, there was volition. The propensities are neither volitional nor moral; but, when man attained the *capacity* to make volitional and moral use of his propensities, he failed thus to use them, and so he sinned; his 'fall' may, from one point of view, be described as a 'rise'. We sin when our natural, non-moral, animal propensities are not controlled and directed by reason. Quoting James Seth, Tennant described morality as 'subjecting "the seething and tumultuous life of natural tendency, of appetite and passion, affection and desire" to the moulding influence of reflective purpose'.[21]

The alleged universality of sin is thus easily explained: it is because 'the inherited appetitive propensities, natural and necessary for the animal life of our non-human ancestry, are entrenched in every one of us before the moral consciousness dawns, and require incessant coercion and voluntary direction through life', that no human being 'has absolutely avoided moral failure at some time and in some degree'.[22]

A complete discussion of this account of the origin of human sinning falls outside the scope of this book. I would suggest, however, that critics are too quick to take advantage of the fact that the

---
[21] *Origin*, p. 107. [22] *ERE*, IX.564b.; cf. *Concept*, pp. 151ff.

'Instinct' psychology of fifty years ago is now out-moded. Whether they be called propensities, drives, or by any other name, even if 'they' are interpreted as an 'it', there is no reason to deny the existence of 'natural tendency, appetite and passion', and there is no justification for minimizing the need for 'reflective thought' and the control of our innate propensities. A doctrine of salvation which requires from man none of the exercise of reason for which Tennant constantly appealed is as far from Christian truth as is Pelagianism. It is, rather, in certain other ways that Tennant's psychological basis seems to me to be faulty.

(1) So far from 'blaming' human passions for man's sinfulness Tennant fully appreciated the significance of the fact that it is just in the exercise of his 'reflective powers' that man is at most grievous fault. It is not fair to accuse Tennant (although the accusation could more justly be made of some of his supporters) of forgetting that man sins *with* his reason and not merely because he does not employ his reason but yields to appetite. Tennant never made the fatal error—made by so many people in recent generations—of identifying evil with sensuality, or even with sensation. The natural propensities are, for Tennant, non-moral and not evil. I do not think that Tennant's argument about the need for reason-controlled direction of our natural propensities can be rightly criticized as a description of *need*. It only proves itself inadequate when it is assumed that a description of need provides a causal explanation of sin and a clue to the remedy for sin.

The fact of human experience which all such description (true so far as it goes) ignores is that, in spite of all the achievements, in moral progress, as well as in knowledge-acquiring and in technical accomplishment, that man's reasoning power can secure, there is a point, quickly reached in this generation as in earlier generations, at which these powers prove inadequate to effect the moral control that Tennant rightly saw to be necessary. It is not that he may be delivered from the power of his reason that man needs a Saviour, but in order that he may rightly and fully use his reasoning faculties, not only as in his 'natural state' he can already do, but at the point where knowledge does 'fail with all its powers'.

For this reason, the doctrine that man's reason retains its 'divine' or uncorrupted nature whilst the rest of man's personality

'SIN OR IGNORANCE'

has fallen into sin is as dangerously far from the truth as is the notion that our intellectual powers are the cause of our sin and our salvation dependent upon their being destroyed or anaesthetized. 'Thou shalt love the Lord thy God with all thy mind'—but how? And I suspect, although I cannot prove, that one day it will become more manifest that the division of man's personality into reason and appetite, or into any other dichotomy, is putting asunder what God has joined together, so that in this, as in other ways, only a total salvation can meet what is in fact a total need.

(2) It is, however, in another way—or other ways—that the psychological presuppositions of Tennant's theory are faulty. At this point I must refer to a most searching criticism of Tennant, covering many points which I am not raising, made by Dr N. H. G. Robinson. Dr Robinson argues,[23] I believe rightly, that Tennant falls into *the atomistic conception of sin* of which he accused Pelagius, nevertheless a different kind of atomism. The three points at which Robinson sees Tennant breaking up what ought not to be separated are all important, although one or two of them take us beyond my immediate argument.

(i) Tennant, Robinson alleges, 'breaks up the one divine law so that it becomes many laws and each is apposite to some individual at some stage in his mortal career'. This is a well-made point, although Tennant was aware of the danger and sought to avoid it. But, if we are to hold that man sins only when he disobeys the known will of God, then we must admit that he will often sin when he does what other believers in God, and he himself at a different period of his life, believe to be right. (See Bertrand Russell's entertaining list of the contradictory 'sins' and 'virtues' of different religious beliefs.)[24]

(ii) Tennant, Robinson further suggests, 'breaks up the life of man into many different stages each standing by itself and requiring to be judged by its own appropriate ideal'. He did this by implication, I may add, in spite of the fact that he asserted that character—the result of past activity—is to be judged. I think Robinson is correct in saying that, if we are true to Tennant's teaching, we can only assess a person's character by considering each separate action throughout his life.

(iii) Tennant 'breaks up the society of men so that it becomes

---

[23] N. H. G. Robinson, *Faith and Duty* (1950), pp. 119ff; cf. *Origin*, p. 14.
[24] *Human Society in Ethics and Politics*, op. cit., p. 138.

little more than a mere accumulation of many units and many individuals'. Of course, Tennant resolutely sought to anticipate this criticism and to assert 'the solidarity of the race', but I believe that Robinson rightly shows that he leaves us with men and women who are very similar, rather than (to use my own and not Robinson's term) with men and women inextricably knit together in the bondage of sin. As Robinson adds: 'Moral solidarity varies greatly in degree at different levels, it is strongest precisely at that point where all men are pronounced sinful ... it is as sinners ... that all are completely unanimous.'[25] To which we must add, it is in our sinfulness that we unavoidably contaminate one another, so that my sin is always 'our sin', and 'their sin', mine.

Behind all these atomistic conceptions lies, I believe, the false start which Tennant made to his inquiry when he wrote: 'The starting-point for all definition with regard to the concept of sinfulness is, of course, the isolated single act of sin: *a sin.*'[26] In that 'of course' is to be found the shaky foundation upon which was built the elaborate and self-consistent structure of Tennant's concept of sin. In the strictest sense of the term there is no such thing as 'a sin'; sin is not an 'it', not a *thing*. To understand why and how his isolated acts are sinful we need to know why and how the man himself is a sinner. Sins are symptoms of sin, but, although useful to the diagnostician, they are not the disease.

There is, however, a fourth way in which Tennant's concept of sin involves atomizing, which Dr Robinson does not mention but which is most relevant to our present inquiry. Tennant (in common with all who share his view-point) treats human volition as though it consisted of isolated, fully conscious and deliberate acts. An act is not moral unless it is volitional; this statement, frequently made by Tennant and continually echoed by other authors, is obviously true if by 'volitional' we mean 'self-determined'. Unless we accept the fact of self-determination we cannot believe in morality. With what Tennant wrote about this we have no quarrel, however greatly we may disbelieve in the kind of 'free-will' which denies that our actions are self-*determined*. An action cannot be morally judged unless it is self-determined; the old illustration of the man helpless through alcohol may give place to more modern and dreadful examples from the use of modern scientific methods of brain-control. We may go farther and agree

[25] op. cit., p. 123. [26] *Origin*, p. 160.

'SIN OR IGNORANCE' 63

that, as Tennant often remarked, an act to be morally responsible must involve intention as well as volition.

But I can find no trace in Tennant's writings of a realization that the *self* which determines action is itself made up of conscious and unconscious aspects. As we have noted, this does not mean that there is a conscious 'part' of self, which can be morally judged, and an unconscious 'part' which may be considered amoral. The attempt to isolate human activities which are unaffected by any of the various mental processes summed up by the convenient, but not yet fully comprehended, term 'unconscious' is a vain attempt.

There is no escape from the apparently contradictory statements: we are what we do, we do what we are. If that suggests a vicious circle, it is the circle in which we actually live. Moreover, if this implies that we—our characters—are in part the result of previous actions the significance of which we did not comprehend; that our intentions, although indeed *ours*, are an inseparable mixture of conscious ideas and ideals and of unconscious motives and desires; that, in the most literal sense, sane as well as insane men often do not fully know why they do what they do, even though they know what they are doing; and that the most formative period of normal character (self) development is that of early childhood, before reflective thought and self-consciously directed action is possible; if such implications follow and are incompatible with the Tennant type of definition of sin, then we must ask whether, assuming our premises to be right and our implications properly drawn, that definition is at fault.

I do not intend to suggest that the concept of the unconscious (in any contemporary psychological theory) is sufficiently clear or strong to provide an *explanation* of sin, so that we can substitute an interpretation of sin in terms of the unconscious for one based on instincts. I do suggest that the, as yet largely unexplored, facts to which the term 'unconscious' draws attention are at least as significant for our understanding of sin as are the psychological facts to which Tennant drew attention, and I believe that they make invalid the definition which he offered.

(*c*) *Ethical propriety*. Ethics, according to Tennant, must be based not on metaphysical principles but upon the study of human nature through psychology and allied sciences, and therefore psychological considerations dominate his ethical discussions. Yet it is his purely ethical argument for his definition of sin which is probably the strongest point in its favour. He rebelled, as many have rebelled, against the double use of *sin* to describe both an individual's intentional disobedience to a moral standard, the authority and existence of which is recognized by that individual at the time of choice, and also actions which, unknown to the particular agent, are known (believed?) by others to be contrary to moral law. The former meaning of *sin* Tennant described as *subjective*, the latter as *objective*, so that (within his own terminology) the only proper use of the term *sin* is the subjective one.[27] (He also examined other less strict uses of ethical terms which need not occupy our attention now.)

There is no doubt, as Tennant repeatedly illustrated, that sin has normally carried these two meanings, however we describe them. We need look no farther than, to use Tennant's phrase,[28] 'the unfortunate example of St Paul' who 'sometimes allowed himself' to denote as sinful actions that were performed in ignorance. Elsewhere, Tennant claimed that Paul made a distinction in reference to *guilt* which thus differentiated the two meanings of sin, and in proof of this he quoted sentences from Paul (Romans 4^{15}, 5^{13}, 7^8)[29] which will be considered in Part 3 of this book. Without embarking at this stage upon an examination of Paul's meaning, it must be stressed that Tennant's objection to the wider or double meaning of sin is bound up with the meaning of guilt, rather than with that of sin itself. It is because sin involves guilt, and guilt, in both legal and moral contexts, involves blameworthiness, and blame-worthiness implies adequate knowledge and fully voluntary and conscious choice, that many agree with Tennant that it is necessary to restrict the meaning of sin, even although to do so means a break not only with Paul but with most Christian usage.

Although Tennant's most prolonged discussion of guilt is to be found toward the end of the last of his three books about sin, I think it is clear that his interpretation of sin was made with one eye, as it were, always on the nature of guilt. He did not hold, as some have done, that a man must know all that is to be known about goodness before he can commit evil—which of us then would be a sinner? But he did hold that guilt is only imputable

---

[27] *Concept*, p. 161.   [28] ibid., p. 233.
[29] *Origin*, p. 162; cf. *Fall*, Chap. 11.

'SIN OR IGNORANCE'

when 'an ethical standard which one *knows* to be binding upon oneself is *intentionally* transgressed'.[30] The italics are Tennant's own; but how many problems lie buried beneath them! At some of those problems we have already glanced; others we shall meet later, but it must be sufficient to ask now: Must we interpret sin in terms that will allow a ready-made concept of guilt to operate, or may it be necessary to reconsider what is the Christian meaning of guilt in the light (or under the shadow) of what we know to be our sinfulness?

That question can only be answered when closer attention has been given to the biblical account of sin. It is well, however, with Tennant's help, to recognize at once that the meanings of sin and guilt are, somehow, related, and that Tennant's definition sought to remove a very great difficulty, a difficulty which, as we shall see, is not removed by the expedient adopted by many contemporary writers, that of distinguishing between (actual) sin which carries guilt and (original) sin which does not involve guilt. If we are to speak of 'innocent sin' we are indeed doomed to play with words.

It is therefore, I believe, on ethical rather than on logical or psychological grounds that Tennant's definition makes its strongest appeal. We need very strong reasons if we are to continue to use the term *sin* in a way that may appear to be morally reprehensible, because it unjustly attributes guilt where no guilt is due. Nor can we ignore the plea that ambiguity can never serve spiritual ends. Tennant knew that his account of sin involved a break with much traditional Christian doctrine, including that of St Paul. He believed, however, that he was truly interpreting the mind of Christ. It will be best for us to consider that claim in a more general consideration of New Testament teaching (Chapter 8), but, first, there is another attempted solution to the problem of ignorance which calls for some consideration.

[30] *Concept*, p. 233.

CHAPTER SIX

'SIN OR MORAL DISEASE'

THOSE who exclude from the concept of sin all that is not conscious, voluntary disobedience to a known moral obligation must account for all moral imperfection which is not to be described as sin. Tennant himself frequently refers to such 'moral imperfection', and he explains it as being the result of the failure of moral, rational man to control his animal nature. It has already been indicated, and will be further argued, that this explanation misconceives both the character of man's moral failure and the nature of much of his moral choosing. Some, however, who share Tennant's understanding of sin are content to leave other forms of moral imperfection as a shadowy enemy of human well-being. They are eager to assert that man only *sins* when he knows that he is doing what is evil; they have little to say about the 'sins of ignorance'. Perhaps the most hopeful word that can then be said about this non-sinful moral imperfection is that we are not to be blamed for it.

It is not surprising, therefore, that there should be a welcome for any attempt to explain this aspect of human behaviour, and for any promise of a remedy for it. Such an explanation and offer is made by those who draw a clear-cut distinction between sin and mental disease. Whilst some prefer to speak of mental disease, or psychical disorder, others speak of *moral* disease, and then the remedy for such disease is differentiated from the remedy for sin.

I must stress that, in the following pages, I am not seeking to minimize the importance of psychiatric medicine, nor do I wish to deny the relationship between disease (both 'mental' and 'physical') and our thought and behaviour. I fully agree that much needless human suffering is inflicted by well-intentioned confusion between moral culpability and sickness of various types. I wish only to suggest that the belief that *sin* can be distinguished from psychical disorder, whether or not the term 'moral disease' is employed, *by the method of distinguishing what is conscious from what is unconscious* is false, and that the attempt to base either psychiatric or pastoral counsel upon such distinction is injurious to both. The belief that this distinction can and must be made is so strongly held today that several examples of the arguments given in favour of it must be cited.

I. THE ALLEGED DISTINCTION

I shall not refer to the beliefs of those who deny moral values, reject the Christian faith in salvation from sin, and substitute psychology for religion. It is the argument of Christian psychiatrists and students of psychology that concerns us here.

Firstly, then, we turn to a writer whose work in this field has won the gratitude of many members of the medical profession as well as of Christian ministers. Dr Leslie D. Weatherhead, speaking of 'the danger which modern psycho-therapy makes clear', writes:

Sin must always be understood as 'missing the mark' ($\dot{a}\mu a\rho\tau\iota a$) through the conscious choice of evil in the presence of the conscious recognition of good. A certain activity might be for one person sin, but for another moral disease. The latter is due to complexes repressed in the unconscious, and condemnation of their expression is most injurious and harmful.[1]

It is the first sentence in that quotation that I most wish to criticize, but it should be pointed out in passing that several debatable assumptions lie behind the subsequent sentences. That a certain activity might for one person be caused by sin, but for another by moral disease, suggests both that the causal concept is a clear one, and that every activity has a single 'cause'. Why should not an 'activity' of an individual have behind it both 'sin' and 'moral disease'? Again, it is, to say the least, arguable whether *all* moral disease is 'due to complexes repressed in the unconscious'. (I do not stress the point that many psychiatrists are suspicious of the whole concept of 'complexes'.) However, the main implication is clear: only what is consciously and deliberately chosen whilst known to be evil can be called sinful; all else in man's immoral behaviour falls outside the sphere of sin, and, as Weatherhead adds, 'psychotherapy, as such, has no relevant word to say about sin'.

A Roman Catholic writer, Father Victor White, makes this same distinction: 'Sin being essentially voluntary, is also essentially

[1] *Psychology, Religion and Healing* (1951), p. 451.

conscious, while it is of the very definition of any analytical psycho-therapy that it is concerned, at least no less, with the unconscious.'[2] Father White proceeds to distinguish between the concern of Sacramental confession 'with actual sins committed after baptism', and the interest of psycho-therapy which 'cannot confine itself to factors acquired in the patient's own lifetime, still less limit itself to any definite date in the patient's history. It can on no account neglect inherited factors and dispositions; least of all can any depth-analysis which, under whatever name, recognizes a "collective unconscious" as an important factor in mental health and sickness.'

White works, of course, with the accepted Roman Catholic definition of sin: 'A voluntary transgression of some moral law, of a law that imposes an obligation on the will.'[3] He also holds to a description of the unconscious which is much closer to that of Jung than of Freud, and in his discussion of the Idea of God and of several other important matters, he makes many illuminating comments about the significance of the unconscious for religion and theology. But sin, the work of the priest, and the purposes of the Sacraments have no relevance to the unconscious aspects of human personality.

In a slighter work, written by a Christian physician, the title of which demonstrates that it, too, is primarily concerned with the unconscious, we find this same acceptance of the Tennant-type definition. Dr Ernest White says: 'Sin is a matter of the will. It is conscious disobedience to what we know is right. It is transgression against God's laws.'[4] But the succeeding sentences are significant: 'The shadow self is part of our make-up. We cannot help it, we cannot obliterate it. If we allow it to rule us, if we bend our will to its influence and turn evil thoughts and desires into purpose and action, then we commit sin and harm ourselves and others.'

Dr White is not a theologian, and his book is more helpful for its medical than for its theological insight, but we must notice that whilst he does not blame the unconscious for 'causing' us to sin, he does imply that 'it' provides, as it were, material for sin. That is to say, he does not dissociate the unconscious entirely from

[2] *God and the Unconscious*, p. 166.
[3] Henry Davies, S.J., *Moral and Pastoral Theology*, p. 203.
[4] *Christian Life and the Unconscious*, p. 158.

the domain of sin. He suggests that it provides 'temptation', but, 'temptation is not sin'. With that last statement we must fully agree, but Dr White goes on to point out that 'the power to repress the shadow self', which man urgently needs, is greatly weakened in many individuals, often by factors for which they can in no way be judged morally responsible. We seem to have travelled a long way from an easily made identification of sin with wholly voluntary, conscious disobedience to what is known to be God's law. In fact, White, in common with Weatherhead and (for somewhat different reasons) with Tennant, is concerned primarily with the matter of *guilt*. (Further pages of both White's and Weatherhead's books make this apparent.) Their account of sin is set forth in order to rescue us from the apparent need to attribute guilt to unconsciously motivated or 'caused' behaviour.

As I have previously noted, I am postponing discussion of this crucial topic of guilt because I believe that our understanding of guilt (in relation to sin) must be made in terms of our comprehension of sin, and not vice versa. But this attempt to separate 'guilty sin' from mental infirmity was also made, with particular clarity, by a writer whose work pre-dates by many years the books already quoted in this chapter.

In a small volume, for which innumerable Methodist ministers must share my gratitude, Dr W. L. Northridge wrote much that was helpful concerning the notion of unconscious guilt,[5] he also gave a valuable criticism of the attempt to distinguish between mortal and venial sins.[6] But he, too, made a rigid separation between sin and moral disease. (Note his use of the term 'moral' rather than 'mental'.) He endorsed an earlier account of sin by Dr J. A. Hadfield: 'The full and efficient cause of a sin is a deliberate and conscious choice of the will moved by a false or wrong ideal.'[7] Hadfield, with Northridge's approval, amplified this familiar definition of sin in words which have been echoed by Weatherhead: 'Sin is due to wrong sentiments, moral disease is due to morbid complexes giving rise to uncontrollable impulses.... The sinner and the morally diseased both see the ideal; but whereas the former does not, the latter cannot, under ordinary circumstances, respond to it.'[8]

[5] *Psychology and Pastoral Practice* (1938, revised 1947), Chapter 6. See p. 144, *infra*.
[6] ibid., pp. 129ff.
[7] *Psychology and Morals*, p. 48; quoted by Northridge, op. cit., p. 137.   [8] ibid.

The necessary consequence of this statement is that we can no longer speak of 'helpless *sinners*'; the bondage of sin has given place to chains which only the psychiatrist can loose.

II. DIFFICULTIES IN THE DISTINCTION

Dr Northridge has so many true things to say in the last chapter of his book about the distinction between sin and moral disease from the point of view both of the pastor and of the sinner, and about the power of God Himself in relation to *both*, that I am loathe to make any criticism of his position. But I do not believe that the truths which he and others teach necessitate the formal distinction that is made.

Several questions are at once suggested by Northridge's quotation from Hadfield, cited above. Apart from the fact that most people would now be less confident in their use of the terms 'sentiments' and 'complexes' than were these authors, writing nearly a quarter of a century ago, one may ask: What is meant by the statement that sin is due to some cause? What, in actuality, is this causal process? Again, is it impossible, or even improbable that *sin* played its part (to make use of the 'it' conception of sin which our authors appear to hold) in the formation of morbid 'complexes'? Can we be certain that the sinner does both 'see the ideal', comprehend the true relation of his action to it, and possess the ability to do what he knows he ought to do? Probably nobody would deny that what has become an 'uncontrollable impulse' often began as a voluntary act, but does that possibility not carry implications for our sin-diagnosis?

Such questions give rise to the difficulties which I find in the distinction between sin and disease as it is commonly made. These difficulties I must try to formulate more clearly, but, first, I would point out that there is a considerable difference between the terms 'moral disease' and 'mental (or psychical) disease'. It may well prove that the only matter at issue between Dr Northridge and myself is whether evil in human life must be separated into 'disease' and 'sin', or whether (as I shall urge) all sinning involves both moral disease and moral responsibility. It must be remembered, however, that very many who make the kind of distinction now being examined prefer to speak of mental, or psychological, or (blessed cover for ignorance!) 'psychosomatic' disease, rather than of moral disease. Moreover, to say that we human beings can mark out the limits of sinfulness (in other people, if not in ourselves), distinguishing it both in our moral judgements and in our attitude to those whom we seek to help from moral disease, is to travel very much beyond Tennant's definition, which, as we have seen, was never set forth as a practical guide. It is in fact this further step that those whose point of view I have sought to describe desire to take. With their hope that, one day, the nature and cure of mental disease may be more fully understood, and with their desire for closer co-operation between the doctor and the minister, I have every sympathy,[9] but I do not believe that such goals are brought nearer by the suggested method of isolating *moral* disease from sin, however necessary it is to identify the mental or 'psychic' aspects of illness.

The main difficulty that I find in this theory is that I do not believe that it is in harmony with the understanding of our sinfulness which we gain from the Scriptures, nor with the actualities of the Christian experience of salvation; but that major criticism must be held in abeyance. The intrinsic limitations of what I may term 'the moral-disease theory' have much in common with the limitations in the Tennant-type definition of sin, which this moral-disease theory has assimilated. They appear to me to be the following:

(1) The attempt to make a clear distinction between moral disease and sin focuses attention upon human activities *in isolation from the totality of self or character*. A thought, word, or deed is judged to be, or not to be, sinful on the basis of the particular 'cause', 'reason for', or 'motivation of' that specific activity. For some purposes an examination of this kind is necessary, for example for some forms of psychiatric work and in some aspects of moral training; but it provides a poor clue to the Christian meaning of sin. Pursued with thoroughness this distinction is liable to lead us to a conclusion far removed from the intention of those Christian writers who urged us to use it; it is liable to make it very difficult to call any man a sinner.

More than one point is included in this criticism. Firstly, the causal concept, in relation to self-determined action, is by no means clear. All students of ethics are familiar with the difficulties inherent in the theory that our actions are determined by our

---

[9] See Weatherhead, op. cit., pp. 469ff.

strongest motives. Quasi-physical notions easily slip in; we are tempted to conceive of our 'motives' (conscious or unconscious) as existing apart from, or in some separate part of, the self; and we are all too apt, for the sake of simplification, to seek for one motive as the 'cause' of each action. From this it is easy to progress to the false belief that self-determination is something that happens to us, rather than a description of what we do and of what we are.

Secondly, it is not only neurotic behaviour which draws our attention to the problem of ignorance; a fuller study of the most deliberate and clearly understood human action—whether judged morally good or bad—will reveal elements for which the individual is not wholly responsible and aspects of which he himself is not fully aware. Psychological abnormality, and that which our authors describe as moral disease, are not the only phenomena that point to the unconscious, nor do they alone turn our attention to the fact that we human beings are members one of another. Activity that is believed to be psychologically healthy and morally good point in those same directions.

We may say with equal truth of the mentally sound and of the saint what Jan Ehrenwald says of 'the individual patient who lies on the therapist's couch': 'It is never [he] alone who lies [there]. Invariably his friends and relations and a long line of ancestors are arraigned behind him and are involved in his situation.'[10] Ehrenwald stresses that we need to take into account more than hereditary influences. 'We must realize that he may be equally affected by the interlacing patterns of illness and neurotic conflict that plague his next of kin, his friends and enemies *here and now*. . . like an ink-pot on blotting-paper, mental or neurotic disorder tends to spread in all directions—in the perspective of both time and space.' All this might also be written, with suitably changed nouns and adjectives, of the whole of our thinking and doing; it is not only 'mental or neurotic disorder' which 'is not confined to one isolated member of a family group'. As Ehrenwald adds: 'Mental health, like peace, is indivisible.' Psychology itself calls for the insight into the solidarity of sin, and demands the community in salvation, which are taught by both the Old and the New Testaments.

(2) The distinction between moral disease and sin encourages

[10] *New Dimensions of Deep Analysis* (1954), p. 294.

us to ignore *the moral factors that contribute to the formation of neuroses and of other mental disorders.*

It may, perhaps, be true that 'psycho-therapy, as such, has no relevant word to say about sin',[11] but if the further conclusion is drawn that the psycho-therapist should ignore moral factors, that conclusion must be challenged.[12] The picture of a poor neurotic sufferer, whose moral failures are entirely the result of influences beyond his control, would be by no means universally accepted as a true picture of all neurotics. Here, for example, is a very different portrait, painted by Erich Fromm:

> My experience as a practising psychoanalyst has confirmed my conviction that problems of ethics cannot be omitted from the study of personality, either theoretically or therapeutically. The value judgements we make determine our actions, and upon their validity rests our mental health and happiness. To consider evaluations only as so many rationalizations of unconscious, irrational desires—although they can be that too—narrows down and distorts our picture of the total personality. *Neurosis itself* is, *in the last analysis, a symptom of moral failure* (although adjustment is by no means a symptom of moral achievement).[13]

Fromm later stresses the way in which these value-judgements are formed in childhood, and reminds us of the significance of 'the friendly or unfriendly reactions of the significant people' in the child's life.[14]

The attempt to isolate actions which can rightly be termed sinful because they are free from all unconscious, hereditary and enviromental influences is psychologically impossible. There are many instances of actions which may safely be judged to be compulsive; there are actions where deliberate refusal to do what was known to be right will readily be admitted by the agent himself. There are types of mental disorder which, so far as we can possibly judge, render the patient incapable of moral choice; but the difficulties involved in the legal interpretation of 'irresistible impulse' is but one example of the difficulty involved in any attempt to decide

---

[11] Weatherhead, op. cit., p. 451.
[12] See p. 154, *infra.*
[13] *Man for Himself: An Inquiry into the Psychology of Ethics* (1949), pp. viiff. Any reader who may not be familiar with this author's work should be reminded that his purpose is very different from mine. Fromm seeks to emancipate ethics from theology and the development of moral character from religion.
[14] ibid., p. 10.

particular cases.[15] The staffs of theological colleges are often told that their students should 'at least' be able to distinguish between neuroses and psychoses, but that 'at least' conceals a problem of the utmost complexity.

The moral disease theory, therefore, imposes upon us the insuperably difficult task of ascertaining which actions may be described as sinful because they are free from psychotic, neurotic and other more-or-less carefully defined psychological characteristics. These *actions* are to be recognized as sin and to *these* actions the Divine judgement upon, and the Divine salvation for, sin are applicable. Thus our attention is drawn away from the judgement upon the person himself, the sum total of his character as well as his behaviour, and the way of Divine salvation is reduced to a dealing with particular types of moral behaviour.

(3) A further dangerous tendency in the moral-disease theory is that of ignoring or minimizing the *psychologically valuable characteristics of the unconscious itself*.

All too frequently, as I have previously remarked, we are given what may be termed 'a cesspool' picture of the unconscious aspect of the human mind. That picture is particularly prominent in many popular books, of the kind which the average minister of religion may be expected to read. A noteworthy exception is to be found in two chapters of G. N. M. Tyrrell's well-known 'Pelican', *The Personality of Man*, in which the significance of the hypothesis of the unconscious is described in relation to 'the higher reaches of personality', to genius, poetic 'inspiration' and mystical experience. But, so far as popular imagination is concerned, and (from all that is actually said) so far as not a few scholarly volumes suggest, 'the unconscious' would appear to be the depository of all moral filth and mental rubbish.

This false impression is, probably, in part the result of a too-exclusive consideration of the part played by *repression* in developing our unconscious motivation. Freud has captured public attention as Jung, with his emphasis upon other aspects of the unconscious, has not. In the work of some of Freud's disciples there is the further suggestion that we need to 'get free' from the unconscious. Such an ambition involves less than justice to Freud,

---

[15] cf. the illuminating discussion of this problem in W. Moberley, *Responsibility*, pp. 17ff.

'SIN OR MORAL DISEASE'

although (so far as I know) he contributed little amplification to his own significant remark: 'Not only what is lowest, but also what is highest in the Ego can be unconscious.'[16]

I must hasten to withdraw from complex psychological problems, but it should be noted that there are strong arguments for using the hypothesis of the unconscious to cover many facts about human life which are neither psychologically nor morally a hindrance to human welfare. The unconscious has this in common with sin—it is not a *thing*. Moreover, many would agree with Ehrenwald, himself interpreting Jung, that our unconscious activity 'far from being as chaotic and irrational as it had appeared at the beginning, is covered by peculiar laws of its own'.[17]

As Reinhold Niebuhr has said, 'There is . . . less freedom in the actual sin and more responsibility for the bias toward sin (original sin) than moralistic interpretations can understand.'[18] To this I would add, as a parallel statement but emphatically *not* as a synonymous one: There is more that is psychologically and morally healthy and more that is rational in the unconscious, and less in consciousness that is wholly rational and due to fully understood choice than this moral-disease theory implies.

(4) The attempt to distinguish moral disease from sin, by the method that we have been examining, is in part based upon the realization that diagnosis of mental illness and the making of moral judgements are totally different activities. With that fact we have no quarrel, but the theory under discussion also assumes that *moral judgement is the main purpose of a diagnosis of sin*. That assumption has already been questioned, and its validity will later be more explicitly denied. Psychologists such as have been quoted have, indeed, made clearer to many of us the relativity and inadequacy of all our moral judgements upon our fellows and even upon ourselves, but, in seeking to make such judgements more reliable, many of them have relied upon a psychologically controlled use of the Tennant-type of definition of sin, and, in so

---

[16] Freud, *The Ego and the Id* (London, 1935), p. 133; quoted by E. Fromm, op. cit., p. 33.

[17] op. cit., p. 126; cf. Fromm's salutary warning against the claim that psychoanalysis proves that conscious thought is insignificant, or that 'rationalization' is always inevitable (*Psychoanalysis and Religion*, pp. 63ff).

[18] *The Nature and Destiny of Man* (1941), p. 266.

doing, they have been less than true to their own *psychological* insights. For the purposes of sin-diagnosis they have treated consciousness as though it were a separate 'faculty', as they would not do in their own work, and they have disregarded those social influences which, in their own psychotherapeutic labours, they have themselves done much to illumine.

One consequence of this, if it may be said without disrespect, is that in the works by Christian writers quoted in this chapter we find very much clearer light shed upon 'moral disease' than upon 'sin'. Another, unintended, result of this distinction is found in the perplexity with which many Christian ministers now approach those who come to them for spiritual direction. It appears to be necessary, before such help can be offered, for the director to decide which thoughts and actions are to be classified as moral disease and which as sin, and the inquirer must (at least metaphorically) be directed in turn to the analyst's couch and to the penitent-stool or confessional.

Criticism of this kind will probably be judged obscurantist; it will be replied that much harm may be done by offering spiritual counsel to one who requires medical succour. There is much force in such a reply. All who engage in the task of spiritual direction need to be trained to recognize the more obvious symptoms of mental disorder, but, so difficult of diagnosis are many types of such disorder, and so insecure is present-day knowledge of the relationship between 'mental' and 'physical' disease, that there is urgent need for co-operation between ministers of religion and members of the medical profession. Few people are more dangerous than the amateur psychiatrist, unless it be the irreligious professional psychiatrist.

Risk there is that those who need a physician should be treated only as sinners, but a risk far less frequently recognized today is that the sinner should be treated as *merely* mentally afflicted. Such he may be—which of us is not? We have yet to explore to the full the resources of divine Grace for such sickness, as well as for the more apparently 'physical' types of disease. May it not be that the remedy for *sin* is also a remedy for much that is called moral disease, and, if that is so, is it not possible that, for so-called 'moral disease', as for all kinds of human sickness, all the manifold ways of healing must work together? That is, of course, the constantly reiterated plea of Christian psychologists, but I believe that many of them, in seeking to retain moral disease within their own sphere of work, misconceive both the nature of sin and the significance for 'moral disease' of sin itself.

Those who reject the whole Christian understanding of human life, whether or not they also deny the existence of moral—as distinct from mental—disease, cannot expect the unquestioning co-operation of Christian believers. The psychiatrist seeks to further the health of his patient; he, even more than the physician or surgeon whose concern is primarily with 'physical' ailments, is therefore influenced, to a greater degree than is sometimes admitted, by his own concept of human well-being. The Christian believes that man's true life is life lived in dependence upon the God whose nature has been revealed; he believes that sin is essentially *Gottwidrigkeit*, alienation of the total self from God. He must, therefore, believe that men and women are never truly *healthy*, never *normal* (by which he means living as God purposes) whilst they live, however happily and peacefully, in such sin. The psychiatrist has the right to claim the attention of all who seek to help their fellows to the results of his researches, but I see little evidence, even in the works of some Christian psychologists, of a readiness to listen in return to students of the Bible and of Christian doctrine.

If there is great need, today, for Christian *understanding* of developments in psychiatry, there is no less need for Christian *criticism* of such developments, particularly in the realm of physiological methods of personality control. Man cannot abandon his power to influence and, to a large measure, to control human nature; this, rather than his power over the rest of nature, is perhaps the human skill which is on the eve of most far-reaching progress. What man has a *moral* right to do to man depends upon what is the purpose of human existence.

Such considerations raise many problems beyond the scope of this book, but they also bring us back to the main criticism of the explanation of sin that has been discussed in this chapter. It ultimately fails, as do all theories that limit sin to conscious wrongdoing, because it fails to see that the fact of ignorance (to use that convenient term) lies at the heart of all sin. It does this because it looks to man's thought about the morality of his actions for an explanation of sin; it is characteristic of all such explanation that it has little to say about man's relationship to God. The fact that what is 'wrong' with man has to do with that relationship is both the clue to our recognition of sin and the proof that man often sins most deeply when he does not know that he is sinning. To see this fact of ignorance in the fact of sin we must turn to the Bible.

PART THREE

THE FACT OF IGNORANCE

CHAPTER SEVEN

THE OLD TESTAMENT AND THE FACT OF IGNORANCE

WHEN we bring to the Old Testament the difficulties that I have summarized under the term 'the problem of ignorance', our first impression is that the Old Testament suggests rather than answers our questions. In some instances this impression is made by what the writers say, in other instances by their silence. And this is especially so when we think about *ignorance* of *God*.

It has become platitudinous to say that the anthropology of the Old Testament is theocentric, and that the attitude of the Hebrew writers to the nature and destiny of man is summed up in the words:

> What is man that thou art mindful of him,
> and the son of man that thou dost care for him?
>
> (Psalm 8[4]).

But we dare not forget this fact; if we do so, we shall imagine that the authors of the Old Testament were, like ourselves, more interested in studying man than in fearing and obeying God. Historians and psalmists, prophets and priests, shared a common belief that God had disclosed His will and manifested His purpose, and that men and women disobeyed him and justly deserved His punishment.

Were we studying the history of Hebrew religion it might be necessary to examine the development of understanding that led to the simple, categorical statement, 'Against thee, thee only, have I sinned' (Psalm 51[4]), but that confession is dominant in the Old Testament as a whole. What Bishop Aulén (commenting on Psalm 51[4]) said about 'the viewpoint of Christian faith', may equally be said of Hebrew faith: 'It would be meaningless to divide sin into two classes: sins against God and sins against neighbour. There is no sin against neighbour which is not sin against God. . . . If we were to talk about some sins which are not sins against God, the concept of sin would have lost its meaning.'[1]

If it is necessary to bear in mind this God-ward emphasis in Hebrew thought about sin, it is equally essential to recall that, for every Jew, the people of Israel were in a peculiar relationship to God. They were the Covenant people. If we ignore the centrality of the covenant-concept in considering any aspect of Hebrew thought we distort facts and miss matters of supreme significance. So it is in regard to their view of sin. The familiar words of Amos (3^2) may serve as a summary of the relationship between *covenant* and *sin:* 'You only have I known of all the families of the earth; therefore I will punish you for all your iniquities.'

Again, as we consider Old Testament teaching about sin we must recollect that the strongly individualistic notions of sin and salvation, which have characterized the religion of very many Christians, were not shared by the Hebrews. For our present purpose there is no necessity to discuss when, and how, a sense of individual sin and responsibility developed, for, throughout the period covered by the Old Testament, the *corporate* emphasis is always strong. We tend to forget that the fiercest denunciation by the prophets was against *the people*. The Hebrew did not share our modern tendency to distinguish between personal and group morality. It is, for example, scarcely possible to determine whether the hortatory parts of Deuteronomy, although often addressed in the second person singular, were directed to the nation or the individual.

It is, therefore, obvious that we cannot expect direct answers from the Old Testament to many of our questions about sin, questions such as we have heard, in the first chapter, from Bertrand Russell. We cannot expect that the questions of a twentieth-century agnostic will be raised in the pages of the Bible. Again, when Amos preached he could rightly assume that his hearers ought to have remembered the Mosaic teaching; the missionary to an African tribe can scarcely condemn his hearers for that neglect. What is he to say, in the light of Old Testament teaching, when he finds that in trying to do what they have been taught is the will of God, they do that which, to the Hebrew and Christian, is evil?

What does teaching directed to the Covenant People mean when it is applied to England or to Russia? When we speak of

[1] G. Aulén, *The Faith of the Christian Church*, p. 261.

'the sin of a nation', what relation has this to individual moral responsibility? The Nuremburg trials press the question home. We shall not find answers to such questions by seeking *discussion of them* in the Old Testament. The New Testament more closely approaches such discussion, but perhaps some of the questions will need re-framing when we have come nearer to the Christian meaning of sin.

When we turn to the problem (or group of problems) that I have termed *ignorance of self*, the Old Testament writers appear to be more interested in our questions; they obviously have much to say about motives and intentions, about behaviour and character (e.g. Isaiah 1$^{12-17}$, Leviticus 19$^{11-18}$). But it is noticeable and significant that the four nouns that I have just used are English, with etymologies that do not go back to Hebrew. It may be that, in this matter too, we shall learn most by the words that the Hebrews did *not* use, and by the problems that they left unraised. Certainly we must expect to find very deep differences between their problems and our own.

A final word of introduction to this chapter must be added. I am not attempting the very difficult task of summarizing Old Testament ideas of sin. Such a task involves examination of many diverse teachings, for, as Gottfried Quell has remarked: 'The Old Testament offers no neat uniform doctrine of sin; qualifications are always necessary, and all sorts of subsidiary questions are involved in the general problem of sin.'[2] My limited purpose is to inquire how far the Old Testament sheds light upon that aspect of the general problem of sin which I have termed the problem of ignorance. In so doing I shall be especially dependent upon the scholarship of others; I hope that I shall sufficiently acknowledge my indebtedness and distinguish my conclusions from their information.

The three comments which I wish to make are as follows. (1) Whilst the complex and unfamiliar psychology of the Hebrews precludes us from making direct comparison between their ideas of human personality and our own, there was, in the Hebrew idea of man, recognition of facts which are of permanent importance for our thought about man and his sin. (2) When the teaching of the Old Testament is viewed *as a whole* (without the neglect of any main portion) it becomes plain that the *fact* of ignorance was by

[2] Kittel, p. 5 (see list of Abbreviations, p. x).

no means absent from the Hebrew understanding of sin. (3) The points at which the Jewish understanding of sin failed are themselves of much significance. In this, as in other ways, the Old Testament raises questions that it cannot answer; in this, as in other ways, its pages are like sign-posts pointing ahead.

I. HEBREW PSYCHOLOGY

Hebrew psychology is a notoriously difficult field of study and perhaps, at least in its more primitive forms, must remain outside the full comprehension of modern man. Yet many scholars have helped toward an elucidation of Hebrew psychological concepts and terms, and I think that even the difficulties that we find, when we attempt to think *with* the writers of the Old Testament, may be used to bring out the points that I wish to make. Three such difficulties call for mention.

(a) There is no direct, explicit equivalent for some of the words that we most commonly use, e.g. *will*,[3] *emotion, personality, character*, or, even, *self*. To find equivalents for such terms we must bring together several Hebrew words, and in so doing we may easily go astray. It is salutary for us to imagine ourselves discussing human nature, and, in particular, sin, without being able to use terms such as I have mentioned.

(b) Secondly, in order to understand what the Hebrew thought about what *we* call personality, or self-hood, we need to have in mind a wide variety of terminology. There are words which at once suggest to us mental or psychical concepts, such as *nephesh* (generally translated, soul), *ruach* (spirit), *lebh* (heart). There is also a large group of words describing what (to us) are bodily organs, such as eye, tongue, bowels, or words of more general physical reference, e.g. flesh, bones, blood.[4]

Two difficulties face the modern reader of the Bible when he attempts to grasp the significance of these terms. On the one hand, he quickly finds that the translation of *nephesh, ruach, lebh*, and similar psychical words, is not nearly so straightforward as might be expected. About the meaning of each of them countless pages have been written and the translations which I set in brackets are

---

[3] 'There does not appear to be any Hebrew verb that means "to will" without any reference to what is willed.' C. Ryder Smith, *The Bible Doctrine of Man* (1951), p. 27.

[4] See H. Wheeler Robinson, *The Christian Doctrine of Man* (1913), p. 12.

by no means the full story. But, secondly and most disturbingly of all, the Bible student finds that, if he is not to distort the Scriptures, he must be very careful about dividing the terms into two groups, psychical and physical. As Wheeler Robinson wrote, when giving what was, for many of us, our first enlightenment in these matters: 'The body, not the soul, is the characteristic element of Hebrew personality.'[5] We must hasten to add, however, that 'body' is itself an English word and a European concept.

It has become a commonplace in Old Testament literature to say that there is in it 'no ethical dualism of soul and body', and many writers have echoed what Wheeler Robinson wrote about this Hebrew attitude to what we call body and mind (soul): it 'affords a natural line of explanation of the ethical development of "flesh" in the Pauline epistles, without resort to any dualistic theory'.[6] It is, unfortunately, not true that this understanding has reached the ordinary Bible reader; nor is it easy for any of us to 'think ourselves into' the thought-forms of the Hebrew people, to whom our sharp-cut distinction between spiritual and physical, mind (or soul) and body was quite foreign. We must attempt to do this, however, when we study the Bible.

May we not also learn from the example of the Hebrews when we think about human personality itself? In these days use is so frequently made of the term *psycho-somatic*, that some of us are apt to forget that, however significant may be the hyphen in that term, the use of Greek has not solved what used to be called the problem of the mind-body relationship. I do not, of course, mean to imply that we should turn to the ancient Hebrew scriptures to find our answers to scientific problems; I do mean that we should today be more prepared than were some of our immediate forebears to think of human personality *as a whole*, and that we should be less quick to despise those who never treated man as though he were ethereal 'spirit' unfortunately imprisoned in a gross body.

Therefore we may conjecture that a 'man of the Old Testament' would have been much less surprised and indignant than are many Christians today by the relation of the 'physical' to the 'spiritual'. We are very prone to seek a definition of sin which implies that man is some kind of spiritual being who happens to possess a

[5] See H. Wheeler Robinson, *The Christian Doctrine of Man* (1913), p. 12.
[6] ibid., e.g. pp. 24f.

'body'. Then, when such disturbing facts as the effect of glandular disease on character, the influence of brain surgery on personality, or even the very simple and everyday facts about the influence of our physical condition upon our moral outlook and behaviour, are brought to our notice we are afraid that our whole concept of sin is in peril. A study of Hebrew understanding of human nature is not (it hardly need be said) a substitute for scientific investigation, but the conception of man's life *as a whole*, which characterizes both Testaments, is very far removed from many allegedly Christian ideas about sin and salvation that are current today.

(*c*) The third difficulty that we find, when we try to understand the Hebrew way of thinking, even more clearly illustrates their emphasis upon the totality and unity of human personality. I suppose that most of us today (apart from professional psychologists) still do our daily thinking with a vague psychological theory of the *faculty* type. We at least tend to think of thought, feeling, will, as though they were different *parts* of us. Even writers who, in their own territory, are informed and careful in expression, make references to *will*, for example, as though there were actually *something* that could be called 'a will'.

It is almost inevitable, therefore, that when we read the Old Testament we should look for counterparts to these 'faculties'. The most obvious example is the word *heart*. Even when we have learnt that *lebh* (as also *kardia* in the New Testament) does not mean feeling, or emotion, it is extremely difficult for us, when we meet the word *heart* in the Bible, not to read into the reference our notion of feeling (or emotion) as contrasted with reason (or thought). How many of us think of integrity of purpose when we pray, 'O God, make clean our hearts within us'? Scholars lay somewhat different emphases upon the degree to which *lebh* *included* reference to feeling, but all are agreed that its meaning was not limited to emotion.[7] Pederson says that it refers to 'the totality of the soul as a character and operating power, particular stress being laid upon its capacity'.[8] The main point, however, is

---

[7] e.g. H. W. Robinson (op. cit., p. 22), who includes in the 851 instances of *lebh*, *lebhabh*, 166 that imply varied emotional states. C. Ryder Smith (op. cit., p. 21) says that the Hebrew tended to use *nephesh* when feeling is uppermost, and *lebh*, *lebhabh*, when thought and will is uppermost.

[8] Johs. Pederson, *Israel* I-II (1926), p. 104; but cf. criticism in *TWB*, Art. 'Mind, heart.'

that even to inquire whether *heart* means thought *or* emotion is to misunderstand what it does mean; this division of personality into faculties is of our own making.

The point becomes especially significant when we think about the notion of *will* as a third faculty. We are apt to think of human volition as involving a series of more or less distinctive mental activities, performed by more or less separately functioning parts of our personality. We speak, for example, as though appetites and desires, motives and intentions, reflection and choice, preceded an action performed by the will. Often we think of these existing as a chain of causes, and then a host of psychological and ethical questions emerge which, for generations, have been the happy hunting-ground of scholars and of casuists.

It is possible to bring such questions to the Old Testament and to seek to wrest answers from it; but is that a task which is either worth-while or possible of achievement? I think not. Dr Ryder Smith, in *The Bible Doctrine of Sin*,[9] gave a five-fold analysis of human volition, using somewhat different terms from those used above. (Knowledge, desire, choice and will, plan, act). He comments that, for the Hebrew, 'sin began with choice. As might be expected with a practical people, sinfulness lay in the *will*.' Ryder Smith then puts to the Hebrew our modern question: 'Is there not something sinful in the desire to do wrong even though one does not yield to the desire?' And he adds: 'So far as any answer can be found in the Old Testament, the ordinary Hebrew answered "No", but *it is doubtful whether the question ever arose distinctly in his mind.*' Dr Smith's conjecture concerning 'the ordinary Hebrew' may well be correct, but is not the most significant point contained in the words that I have italicized?

Considerations such as have been briefly illustrated lead us to the conclusion that Hebrew thought did not *atomize* human volition as much European thinking has done. A few quotations from Pederson's description of the Hebrew concept of volition bring this fact to our attention.

It is not an isolated part of the man that acts, but the soul in its totality.... It is the soul that sins, not only in thoughts and passing feelings but in real acts.

For the Israelite ... the mental processes are not successive, but united in one, because the soul is always a unit, acting in one. But

[9] pp. 33ff.

no more are the action and its result to be distinguished from each other or from the mental activities; they are implied in the actual mental process. This is to be attributed to the fact that the soul is wholly present in all its works.

The man is responsible for his acts and their results, not only for his intentions. A distinction is impossible because there is no such thing as 'good intentions'. The intention or will is identical with the totality of the soul which creates action.[10]

Analysis will always be part of the function of the sciences, including the personal or social sciences, but if we are to understand sin it will not be by such analysis of human personality that we shall be helped to the discovery of our sinfulness. By the great variety of references to heart, thoughts, mind, soul, flesh and so on, the Scriptures focus our attention upon our total self and upon our total need.

A final example of this is provided by the dichotomy, often suggested in the previous chapters: *conscious* and *unconscious*. I believe that for *certain purposes* these concepts are necessary, however ambiguous and dangerous are the terms themselves. We must not read conceptions such as these into the Old Testament; yet there is much that is suggestive in the very *lack* of emphasis upon this subject. Once more to quote Pederson:

> We see that consciousness plays a subordinate part in the psychological basic conception. The question is what actually is in the soul, and *it may be there without our knowing it.*
>
> The decisive thing is what is the relation of the action to the acting soul; does it arise in the central will of the soul, or does it merely lie on the periphery of the soul.[11]

This biblical picture of the wholeness of mind and body and of the total, complex self must be the starting-point of all Christian thought about sin and its cure. Many pressing questions, posed both by our knowledge and by our ignorance, concerning mental and physical health and disease and about individual, moral responsibility, call for patient inquiry, but, however necessary specialized study and departmentalized thinking may be, I hazard the guess that to find the answers to all such questions we shall need to keep more clearly in mind the one-ness of personality. It

---

[10] op. cit., pp. 105, 128, 132.   [11] ibid., pp. 132 and 420. (My italics.)

is unquestionably true that we must do so when we think about sin.

The study of the stages by which the Hebrews came to the truth that man is *sinful*, as distinct from one who commits particular sins, is both difficult and fascinating. When, for example, Jeremiah, Ezekiel and the author of Psalm 51 passed beyond sins to *sin*, they passed (and knew that they passed), beyond anything that can be externally judged, to what is inward; beyond a description of sin that involved moralistic and legalistic assessment of degrees of responsibility to the unclean 'heart'; and beyond a description of sin to the unveiling of the desperate need of the sinner. It is Man, not part of him and not 'a man' in isolation from his fellows, who is unclean and needs cleansing (Ezekiel 36^{25}, Psalm 51$^{2, 7}$); who is sick and waits for healing (Jeremiah 17^{9f}). As Dr Ryder Smith wrote: 'Jeremiah's text, "The heart is insidious above all things, (verily) *it* is sick!; who knows it?"—with its answer, "Only God"—is the climax of the Prophet's doctrine of sinfulness (Jeremiah 17^{9f}). It is the counterpart of the oracle of the "new Heart" (Jeremiah 31^{31ff}).'[12]

We are thus brought near to one of the profoundest truths concerning the nature of sin: what it is can be recognized only by those who hope for its removal. When that hope is born, the *it-ness* of sin disappears, as the sinner waits before God.

II. THE VARIETY IN HEBREW THOUGHT ABOUT SIN

The previous section has served, I hope, to indicate that, whatever problems are set by our modern study of psychology, we cannot escape from those problems, as we seek a Scriptural account of sin, by *limiting* sin to the spheres of reason, conscious choice and 'will'. We turn now to the attempt to limit sin to deliberate disobedience to the known will of God.

It is, I believe, only when we take account of the variety in the Hebrew picture of sin, that we become sure that 'the fact of ignorance' is part of the picture. When we recall that Hebrew has 'no single word suitable for religious or theological purposes, like our word "sin" ',[13] and when we notice that the variety in terminology is somewhat concealed in our English versions, we are prepared to discover that it is impossible rightly to give an

---

[12] op. cit., p. 35.   [13] Kittel, p. 4.

Old Testament definition of sin. The attempt has often been made, and (so far as my reading and hearing have suggested) the most common definition is: 'Sin is missing the mark.'

The only possible justification for such a 'definition' is that the *dominant* verb, *chaṭa'*, with the nouns and adjectives derived from it, has this meaning. But as Wheeler Robinson pointed out (in the course of a discussion to which all subsequent students are indebted), this description of the effect of sin as deviation from a prescribed norm, 'tells us nothing that is definite about sin: it is the failure to do something or other, in relation . . . either to God or man'.[14] It is unfortunate that this point has so often been missed by Christians. There is, in Christian language as in Jewish, need for terms that speak of missing the mark, wandering away, going astray, turning aside from the will of God. But they describe what has happened; they shed no light upon how and why it happened; neither do they tell us anything about the sinner that can adequately help his restoration. Indeed, when they are used as a sufficient account of sin they lead to the mistaken optimism that characterized much later Jewish thought as it has marked every Pelagian-type of Christian thinking.[15]

A similar point needs to be made about all the words which describe *sins* with respect to their diverse characteristics and the different consequences to which they lead. Wheeler Robinson first gathered these into a class—words such as violence, destructiveness, trouble, folly, and the general term for evil (*ra'ah*)—and remarked that they call for little comment.[16] Useful for their purpose, such terms were not employed to *diagnose* sin.

There is, however, another type of word which, as Robinson put it, 'yields a positive idea of sin'.[17] This positive idea is that ot *rebellion* (the main term being *pesha'*), and Dr Norman Snaith has described it as being the *religious* meaning of *sin*, as distinct from the ethical notion of transgression of a code.[18] Snaith further coins a word for this concept—*theofugal*.

That man rebels against God was the characteristic message ot the eighth-century prophets, although it was, of course, by no means confined to their writings. In recent years it has become increasingly common for Christian theologians and preachers to

---

[14] H. W. Robinson, op. cit., p. 44; cf. Kittel, p. 8: 'The commonest expression for sin in Hebrew lacks the deep religious quality of our word.'
[15] See next Section.   [16] ibid., p. 45.   [17] ibid., p. 44.
[18] Norman H. Snaith, *The Distinctive Ideas of the Old Testament* (1944), p. 60.

add to the above-mentioned definition of sin ('missing the mark') an explanation of the *cause* of sin—rebellion against God. As we have noted such attempts in previous chapters it is therefore perhaps worth-while to make a slight digression at this point concerning this attempt to find a *cause* for sin.

The philosophical difficulties in the causal concept in general are familiar, but I imagine that not many are aware of the perceptiveness of the ancient Hebrew in this matter. According to Pederson it was one of great interest to us:

... it is not due to chance when the Israelite has no special term for what we call causal connexion, no more than he has a word which we may render by cause. He does not consider an action as something isolated, directly determined by the immediately preceding; he does not judge '*post hoc, ergo propter hoc*'. All that happens is to him a link in a comprehensive continuity, i.e. the character and capacity of the entire soul such as it is. A wicked act may wrack ruin upon its perpetrator; not because the one wicked deed must directly wreak ruin, for this is not always the case, but because a soul that perpetrates wicked deeds must also wreak ruin.[19]

If this interpretation is correct it is of considerable importance.

That the dominant Old Testament message about the meaning of sin is that it *involves* rebellion against God is so evident that I need only refer to Isaiah 1[2f]: 'Sons have I reared and brought up, but they have rebelled against me.' It is further clear to the most casual reader that such rebellion is said to deserve, and to receive, the punishment of God (e.g. Isaiah 1[20]). That *this* is what the sinner does, and that *this* is the result of his sin is Christian belief as well as Jewish. But when we add to this understanding of sin, *causal* notions, taken from somewhat vague notions of mechanistic causation, we change the whole meaning of the Scriptural account of sin.

It is, indeed, this search for causes—a very proper search in its right place—which has led to ideas about the origin of sin and its transmission which take us very far from the writings of the Old Testament. (This, of course, began to happen very quickly in Hebrew thought itself.) But our immediate concern is to notice that if we are to say to Everyman, 'You have deliberately chosen to rebel against God, and that rebellion has *caused* you to sin, and

[19] op. cit., p. 133.

that sin has *caused* this and that . . .', we are saying something quite different from what Isaiah meant. He was speaking, as a prophet, from God's point of view, *he was describing what in fact men and women do*. Rebellion does not cause them to sin; sin does not cause rebellion; in rebelling they sin.

But is there any possibility of rebellion of which the rebellious is not aware? Can there be, from the point of view of the Old Testament, *unwitting sin?* To that question (which brings us back to our main theme) no quick and easy answer is possible. Quite apart from the difficult task of dating the documents, we are faced with the danger, already mentioned, of reading our questions into the minds of authors to whom they were unknown; but a few observations must be attempted.

(*a*) It is very obvious that in the prophets, especially those of the eighth century, the main emphasis is upon deliberate disobedience. We should expect that to be so. We must recall that their message presupposed a revealed knowledge of God's will, a presupposition shared by the prophet and his hearers. Again, it is part of the function of a prophet (in the Old Testament sense) to awake repentance by denunciation. That is why terms that implied missing the mark, or going astray, or rebelling were so commonly used. As Quell says: 'If the religion of Israel recognized the will of God as the supreme and universal law, then it must try to bring home to men the fact of their separation from God, and hostility toward Him, by means of ideas which had binding force because they indicated the direction in which human life ought to move.'[20] Israel had disobeyed and rebelled, their sinning involved deliberate refusal to do what they recognized to be their duty.

(*b*) We must go farther and agree that a very large number of texts could be quoted, from all parts of the Scriptures, which stress deliberation and intent, and in which attention is drawn to the absence of the excuse of ignorance. Dr Ryder Smith, in the three books from which I have quoted, has examined the great majority of these passages. We may sum this point up in Quell's words: 'Although recognition of the irrational factor in sin is not lacking in Hebrew, as may be seen in *pesha'*, *marah*, and *shagah*, it must be admitted that, apart from *pesha'*, it does not play a predominant part.'[21] This again is what we should expect, for

[20] Kittel, p. 13.   [21] ibid., p. 13.

however actual be the fact of ignorance, it is by no means the chief fact about our transgression.

(c) This, however, is not the whole story as my quotation from Quell indicates. One example of the use of one of the terms which contain 'an irrational factor' must suffice. Commenting on the fact that *shagah* (err) is used of a straying sheep and of a meandering drunkard (Ezekiel 34[6], Isaiah 28[7]) Ryder Smith remarks[22] that a helpless drunkard 'is responsible for being drunk. Similarly a sheep may *choose* to go astray, though this idea does not happen to occur under this rare term (cf. Isaiah 13[14], 53[6]).' Not to raise the troublesome physiological and social problems concerning the responsibility of the drunkard, I will only say that I find it impossible to believe that, in a pastoral land, Hebrew prophets can have used the sheep-metaphor to imply rational and deliberate choice, or that their lack of reference to choice was purely accidental. Is it quite certain, as Ryder Smith suggests, that when Job cried, 'Teach me, and I will be silent; make me understand how I have erred' (6[24]), *err* 'implies that man culpably chooses to "go astray"'? Or, again, not all interpreters would agree with Dr Smith,[23] that in 19[12] the Psalmist meant: 'Acquit me of the "errors" that are "hidden" from me (for Thou knowest that *these* are not sins).' The word *sin*, as Ryder Smith points out, does not occur; but is not Oesterley nearer to the meaning of this passage when he translates, 'Errors—who discerneth them? from unintended sins keep me innocent; also from purposeful sins keep thy servant, let them not master me'?

I do not make these points merely to set one scholar against another, but because Dr Ryder Smith stresses to the utmost the Hebrew emphasis upon *knowledge* as a condition for the existence of sin. It seems needful also to appreciate that the farther the Hebrew saw into the *sinfulness* of sin, into its inwardness and far-reaching character, the more he recognized the irrational and unconscious aspects of sin, even though those concepts were themselves unknown to him. That fact is, I suggest, most fully seen, not by a selection of isolated texts capable of different interpretations, but by the Hebrew idea of *guilt*.

(d) According to Quell, we must add yet another to our mounting list of divergences between Hebrew thought and our own. 'It is evident', he writes, 'from their promiscuous use of terms that the

---

[22] *Bible Doctrine of Sin*, p. 18.   [23] ibid., p. 19f.

Hebrews attached little importance to the distinction between sin and guilt, the causal connexion being obvious between abnormal behaviour and an abnormal situation.'[24] He adds that the one root (*'shm*) which quite definitely expresses the idea of guilt is almost exclusively confined 'to matters of ritual law'.

That within the sacrificial system *guilt* implied uncleanness, and that such guilt could be incurred by those who were completely unaware of their sins, are facts illustrated by such a passage as Leviticus 4[13-22]. Sacrifices are to be offered

> if the whole congregation of Israel commits a sin unwittingly and the thing is hidden from the eyes of the assembly, and they do any one of the things which the Lord has commanded not to be done and are guilty. . . .

or

> when a ruler sins, doing unwittingly any one of all the things which the Lord his God has commanded not to be done, and is guilty. . . .[25]

There is, of course, much difference of opinion among Christians concerning the sacrifices of the Old Covenant; there are, for example, those who see in them only a perversion of true religion. But the supremely important question is whether the 'sacrificial system' was wrong in seeking *any* remedy for unwitting sin, or whether it failed to discover the true remedy?

I wish to urge—against much opinion[26]—that the latter alternative is the true one. It is, therefore, with much interest that I observe that at least some Old Testament scholars are correcting our impression of an unbridgeable gulf between the prophet and the priest, and reminding us that there were prophets and priests who alike saw the uncleanness of sin, and who were at one in the realization that only God could cleanse and deliver man from its leprosy.[27]

One must, however, go farther and say that if it *were* true that

---

[24] Kittel, p. 21.

[25] The question whether, as has often been stated, sacrifices were *only* for unpremeditated sins need not concern us here. See C. Ryder Smith, *The Bible Doctrine of Salvation* (Index 'Unwitting sins'), for criticism of the contention that there was no atonement for intentional sins, and contrast N. H. Snaith, op. cit., p. 67.

[26] cf. especially N. H. Snaith, op. cit., p. 67, note 1; cf. p. 53, *supra*.

[27] cf. an interesting review of *The Old Testament and Modern Study* (ed. H. H. Rowley, 1951) in the *Expository Times*, Vol. LXIII, pp. 33ff, where words of A. C. Welch are quoted: 'The difference between priest and prophet was one of tempo rather than principle.'

the prophets of Israel did not recognize the evil that men do unwittingly, nor appreciate that such evil-doing is inextricably woven together with their deliberate wrong-doing, nor understand that, far more urgent than any inquiry about the measure of our responsibility and the degree of punishment that will fit the crime, is the need that our whole *self* may be delivered from the burden of sin—then we should have to assert that the prophets had a superficial view of sin compared with that of the priests and the apocalyptists.

We are, however, not forced to such a conclusion. Can we imagine that Hosea had not sensed the dark mystery of human volition, or that to Jeremiah the 'priestly' idea of the taint of sin was merely 'a survival of the early *quodesh-mana* ideas where "Holiness" is equally to be got rid of as "uncleanness" '?[28] Isaiah was not unfamiliar with the stupefaction and unawareness with which man sins unwittingly (Isaiah $6^{5, 10}$, 29^9). Perhaps priest and prophet drew nearest to the truth, as well as to one another, when they recognized that inquity (*'awon*) is a burden too heavy for man to lift. Perhaps, also, it was when, 'through the application of legal ideas to the relationship between God and sinners',[29] the idea of sin was developed away from that of uncleanness and burden, that the deepest insight of the prophet and the profoundest vision of the priest were obscured. When He who came to the sick and not to the whole arrived, He came not only as the greatest of the prophets but also as the High Priest, and Christians can ill afford to forget either of His titles.

III. THE FAILURES OF HEBREW RELIGION

It was only after considerable reflection that I gave the above title to the concluding section of this Chapter. In these days, Christians are increasingly aware of the debt that the New Israel owes to the Old, and are ever mindful of the wickedness of much Christian treatment of Jews. We cannot, however, 'atone' for such evil by concealing our conviction that it was to meet the need of the Jews (as of us all) that the Saviour came. It therefore seems necessary, when we consider any aspect of Christian belief, to ask what the history of Judaism can teach us both by its achievements and by its failures.

The failures of the 'priestly religion' are made so plain to us

[28] N. H. Snaith, op. cit., p. 67.   [29] Kittel, p. 23.

within the Old Testament itself that there is no need for enlargement here. There was the tragic failure to discover the *true* way of 'atonement', of cleansing and of healing. The deep longing for a divine remedy for man's separation from God, for the removal of the taint of sin and for the healing of the disease of sin, is what gives both splendour and poignancy to the ancient Hebrew sacrifices. But along with frustrated hopes, and as part of the cause of that frustration, was the tendency to *depersonalize* sin, to think of sin as though it were merely some kind of quasiphysical corruption. It was against this misunderstanding, and not only against the character of the Hebrew sacrifices themselves, that other men of Israel prophesied.

If the priests were right in recognizing the irrational and unconscious aspects of human sinning, they, and those who thought with them, were ever in danger of forgetting the deliberate character of much wrong-doing, and the element of undeniable personal responsibility in man's sinning. Thus there was urgent need for insistence, as against them, upon the inescapable duty to God owed by both individuals and the nation, and upon the resolution and action which is required from us by our pardoning God.

Perhaps the failure of the prophets, or, at least, of those who received and taught but part of the message of the greater prophets, is not so universally recognized today. Dr Snaith[30] has criticized Oliver Quick's statement that 'the prophets did not fully realize the nature of sin, and regarded it too exclusively as the immediate choice of the individual will'.[31] Snaith has rightly shown that, among the prophetic utterances, were many reminders of man's inability to save himself. Nor was every prophet an individualist, unaware of the influence of environment and heredity (although it is important not to read modern notions of those influences into Hebrew, or early Christian, minds). But as a description of a tendency to which an *exclusively* 'prophetic' emphasis upon sin leads, Quick's criticism is just. In all spheres of human thought, men of opposite views have a habit of falling over the same precipice. Those who, for excellent reasons, lay all the emphasis upon reason, volition, and personal responsibility find themselves in the empty wastes of moralistic and legalistic concepts of sin; there they meet their opponents

[30] op. cit., pp. 65ff.   [31] *The Gospel of the New World* (1944), p. 46.

who regard sin only as a taint or burden, for both have lost sight of the sinner—the *real person*—in contemplation of his 'sin'.

To hasten away from simile and generalities, the failures of Hebrew religion are to be seen in the features of Judaism which Jesus exposed, and from which, as from all the perversions of all kinds of religion—not least of 'Christianity'—He alone can rescue men and women. It is, therefore, in the next chapter that we shall see more fully the contrasts between our Lord's view of sin and that of Judaism; but a few points call for notice here.

We find in later Judaism an increasing attempt to differentiate between different *kinds* of sins. This, as Stählin and Grundmann have pointed out, involved two tendencies which appear to be contradictory. 'On the one hand scribal casuistry regards all breaches of the law, however trivial, as sin; and on the other hand an effort is made to maintain the Old Testament differentiation between "sinning with a high hand" and sinning through ignorance.'[32]

The existence of these two opposite tendencies is, I think, very significant. When sin is primarily regarded as consisting in isolated breakings of rules, and when attention is focused upon the personal responsibility of the agent for such crimes, the immense variety of crimes becomes apparent, so that it becomes impossible to treat all *offences* as being alike; at the same time, degrees of personal responsibility are seen to be so diverse that it becomes impossible to treat all *persons* alike. In a desperate anxiety to classify and apportion blame, the deepest insight of Judaism, of both prophet and priest, is lost. In this connexion, it is interesting to note that an examination of the Septuagint translation of Hebrew terms for sin has led at least one scholar to the conclusion that a clear doctrinal purpose controlled the linguistic usage: 'Instead of splitting up human sinfulness into all sorts of separate sins, after the manner of late Judaism, it [i.e. the Septuagint] shows a tendency to get to the root of the matter, to that fundamental sin which separates man from God and is indomitable ... until he lets God save him.'[33]

---

[32] Kittel, p. 39; where, along with other illustrations, an interesting Rabbinic comment on Isaiah 58[1] is cited. 'My people' (says Bab. Baba Metzia) means those familiar with the Law, 'whose conscious mistakes are equivalent to deliberate sins', and 'the house of Jacob' means the unlearned masses 'whose deliberate sins are equivalent to unconscious mistakes'.

[33] Georg Bertram, in Kittel, p. 38.

This tendency away from the 'root of the matter' could be exemplified by several other characteristics of later Judaism, such as speculation into the *origin* of sin—a speculation strikingly absent from the Old Testament—and wearisome, confusing arguments concerning the 'good and evil tendencies' in human beings. N. P. Williams suggested, nearly thirty years ago, when discussing the *yetser ha-ra'*, that the Jewish writers, by describing the 'heart' as the seat of the evil impulse, 'meant at least to orientate their readers' attention in the direction of what we now know to be the "unconscious" '.[34] His argument was a detailed and powerful one, but I doubt whether many Hebrew scholars, or many psychologists, would now be convinced by it. It is true, however, that there was much Rabbinic argument about degrees of culpability, and about the difference between mistakes and deliberate sins. It is also important to remember that the *evil tendency* itself was believed (by some) to have been implanted in man by God Himself.

We have moved toward a very different way of thinking from that which characterizes the *dominant* message of the Old Testament, and we have done so because this is where moralistic and legalistic concepts of sin always lead. The attempt to measure degrees of human wickedness and to mark out the element of ignorance, excluding it from the sphere of sin, over-reaches itself, as all human attempts to play the part of God eventually do. Either we must make God responsible for our sin, and become fatalists; or we must comfort ourselves with optimistic hopes.

Some religions have inclined to the former alternative; not so Judaism, for which the optimistic escape was the only possible solution. Complicated and burdensome as was the attempt to sort out the multitudinous offences against innumerable laws, in the end all would be well, for men and women could avoid sinning, if they would.

Whatever *freedom* the Christian assigns to himself, whatever worth he ascribes to human personality, in view of the Cross he stands incapacitated, i.e. he cannot save *himself*. . . . But such is not the Jewish view. God indeed acts, but his action is conditioned by human behaviour.[35]

These words, with very many others that accompany them, are hard, and, it may seem, offensive words. They cannot be quoted

[34] *The Ideas of the Fall and of Original Sin* (1927), p. 65 (see also pp. 60ff.)
[35] Jacob Jocz, *The Jewish People and Jesus Christ* (1949), p. 272.

by a Christian without the sombre reflection that he, too, may have measured sin by a human yard-stick, because he has viewed his salvation as a human achievement. It has not been Jews, but Christians, who have transformed 'salvation by grace through faith' into salvation *by* a 'faith' of which man may be proud. With such 'faith', as with the blood of goats, we cannot believe that God is well pleased. Wherever it be found, a doctrine of sin that leads to a man-centred hope of salvation proves itself to be false.

In the canonical books of the Old Testament we may discover tendencies that lead toward legalistic moralism and toward semi-magical concepts of the removal of a quasi-physical taint through sacrificial ritual. But in those same books, as nowhere else in ancient literature, is to be found the recognition of sin as both deliberate wrong-doing and as unwitting wrong-doing. There, above all, we discover, in prophet and priest, in historian and psalmist alike the awareness that sin is a matter between men and God, and the longing for a remedy that can come only from God. The sin of Adam is exposed when the need of Adam is recognized: 'Make me a clean heart, O God, and renew a right spirit within me.'

CHAPTER EIGHT

THE NEW TESTAMENT AND THE FACT OF IGNORANCE

SOME of the difficulties that faced us as we brought our questions to the Old Testament disappear as we turn to the New. The long period of history, and the element of conflict between the prophetic and the priestly understanding of sin are replaced by the record of a comparatively brief history and by a relative homogeneity of thought. Traditional Christian language about sin is more closely related to the New Testament terminology, and, whereas in the previous chapter it was often necessary to stress that problems that occur to our minds did not occupy the attention of the Hebrew writers, some of our questions are directly suggested by the New Testament scriptures.

When, however, we consider the ways in which New Testament teaching have been interpreted it becomes plain that no quick and easy solution of our main problem is possible. From one point of view the New Testament itself raises the problem. One of the reasons why I selected F. R. Tennant's own presentation of what I have called the 'Tennant-type' definition of sin, rather than more recent expositions of it, was that he so clearly recognized that fact. He knew that he was breaking, not only with much orthodox Christian teaching, but also with that of St Paul himself. Paul certainly employed the term *sin* to cover more than Tennant's definition will allow—as is seen, for example, in Romans 5^{13} and $7^{7 \cdot 11}$. Whether or not the best way to describe Paul's meaning is to say, with Tennant, that he used *sin* to include 'unconscious and inevitable non-fulfilment of the Divine law',[1] there is no possible doubt that subsequent Christian teaching, which has refused to limit sin to deliberate disobedience to a known Divine law, can claim the authority of Paul. Tennant spoke of 'the unfortunate example of St Paul', and asserted that Paul's teaching about sin was, in this respect, in opposition

[1] *Concept*, p. 42.

to that of other 'first Christian writers', and of Christ Himself.[2]

Whilst I shall seek to disprove this opposition between the teaching of Paul and that of Jesus, the fact that so careful a scholar as Tennant can assert it, and claim biblical support for his position, shows that it is by no means easy to give an account of the fact of ignorance which is characteristic of the New Testament *as a whole*. That is partly because our understanding of the 'fact of ignorance' involves many presuppositions that were not shared by the first Christians—a point that has been repeatedly stressed in earlier pages; it is also due to the fact that no true comprehension of the meaning of sin in the New Testament can be gained if we limit our study to the word *sin* itself. The latter fact is of primary importance, and it has special, but not exclusive, reference to the Synoptic Gospels.

It is not, therefore, by a particular discussion of particular references to *sin* that this chapter will pursue its purpose. Our purpose is to ask whether the wider denotation of *sin*, found in Paul and in so much Christian teaching, must be rejected, or whether it must be retained if the essential truth about sin is to be kept in view. That the latter position is the true one can be demonstrated, I believe, only if we cast our net very widely and recall important facts about the teaching of the New Testament. There are five facts to which attention will be drawn; each of them has been the theme of many volumes of exposition, but—with the possible exception of the third—it may be safely assumed that they are both familiar to and accepted by any who are likely to read these pages. The statements, which I believe to be statements of fact, are as follows:

(1) There is a striking lack of reference to *sin* (or *sins*) in the teaching of Jesus as recorded in the Synoptic Gospels. (2) Our Lord's message—both as offer and as demand—was a *universal* one. (3) The word *forgiveness* has, within the New Testament, a meaning that is very limited in comparison with its meaning in later and, especially, in contemporary Christian usage. (4) The whole of the New Testament literature has an *eschatological* emphasis. (5) Jesus Himself and the writers of the Gospels and Epistles recognized that men were *victims* as well as offenders.

Let us examine the significance of these facts with reference to the limited theme of our inquiry.

[2] ibid., p. 233; cf. pp. 43 and 25ff.

I. JESUS AND THE WORD *SIN*

Many readers of the Synoptic Gospels are astonished when their attention is drawn to the rarity with which *sin* (or *sins*) is found among the words of Jesus. Nor does the Greek New Testament explain away this surprise. It has been estimated that the noun *hamartia*, the corresponding verb and adjectival noun, and the synonym *hamartema* occur 270 times in the New Testament (91 times in Paul alone.)[3] But, so far as the Synoptic records inform us, our Lord used the noun only on six occasions and the verb on three occasions.[4] *Paraptoma* (RV 'trespass') occurs only in the Lord's Prayer and in Mark 11^{25f}, and *kakos* in one Saying (Mark 7^{21}). *Poneros* is found rather more often, especially in Matthew, but with a variety of meanings.

The significant point is that the principal Greek word in the Christian tradition for *sin*, and therefore the corresponding Semitic expression, is seldom placed on the lips of Jesus. This is the word that is connected by etymology (both Greek and Hebrew) with 'missing the mark' and has subsequently been assumed by many to give the clue to the definition of sin. Yet, according to the synoptic evangelists Jesus very rarely used it, nor was there any other specific term that He preferred.[5]

Arguments based upon silence are notoriously dangerous, but we cannot ignore this remarkable fact. In view of all that is known about Rabbinical discussions concerning sin, and having regard to all that Paul's Epistles suggest to us about similar discussions that must have taken place in Christian circles long before the Gospels were written, it is most improbable that the limited occurrence of *hamartia*, or of any other specific term for sin, in the words of Jesus is merely due to accidental omission by the evangelists. There is no reasonable ground for assuming that it was the result of their deliberate suppression of the word; it is difficult not to believe that here we are indeed hearing the speech of Jesus

---

[3] C. Ryder Smith, *The Bible Doctrine of Sin*, p. 142.

[4] i.e. allowing for parallel accounts. See C. A. Scott, *New Testament Ethics* (1936), p. 27.

[5] Mr K. Grayston reminds me that Aramaic used *debt* as a characteristic metaphor for sin (M. Black, *An Aramaic Approach to the Gospels and Acts* (2nd edition), pp. 102, 270, note 2), but there are only three not very impressive uses in the Gospels: Matthew 6^{12}, 18^{24}, Luke 13^4.

Himself. It is tempting to conjecture that He deliberately avoided the frequent use of terms that had, for His contemporaries as for ours, many varied meanings, some of which were a hindrance to an understanding of the true nature of sin.

Such a conjecture must be tentative, although it is, I think, a reasonable one that is not without significance for our contemporary evangelism, but the fact remains, however it be explained, that were our Scriptures limited to the Synoptic Gospels, the word *sin* would not be as dominant as it is in the Christian vocabulary. Moreover, the lack of references to *sin* in Christ's teaching is related to several similar facts about the Synoptic record of His words.

He did not define sin; the Johannine report (Chapter 9) that He refused to be drawn into a particular type of current speculation about sin is in accord with the picture given to us by the other Evangelists. Luke 13[5] is an example of our Lord's refusal to countenance measuring of sins. Nor did He give any detailed, comprehensive list of sins or trespasses.[6] The defilement passage (Mark 7[14ff]) is not intended to be a complete enumeration of sins, and it is noteworthy that the word *sins* is not there used. When we speak about 'our Lord's attitude to different kinds of sin,' or about 'the sins that Jesus condemned' we are, in actuality, putting the *word* upon His lips. That may be a legitimate and necessary step to take; but—in so far as we attach any degree of accuracy to the Synoptic record—it is important to recognize that we are taking the step. So far as the Synoptic Gospels teach us, it is impossible to gain a clear and full picture of what sin meant to Jesus if we limit ourselves either to His use of that word or to His other references to trespasses, offences, and evils.

Yet every Christian would say that he has learnt more about the meaning of sin from Jesus than from any other teacher. I believe that we can only appreciate how that happens if we notice that it is by our Lord's dealing with *sinners* that we learn what He meant by *sin*. In order to develop that point the argument of the two following sections of this chapter is necessary. We must recognize that He treated all men and women as sharing a common *need;* the meaning of sin to our Lord can only be seen when we consider His *answer* to that need.

---

[6] *TWB*, 'Sin', etc., p. 228b, where it is suggested that Jesus only spoke about specific sins (*paraptomata*) in the community of his disciples.

II. THE UNIVERAL CHARACTER OF CHRIST'S INVITATION

John 3^{15f} and Acts 2^{21} truly reflect the universal scope of our Lord's message. He gave His life for *all;* His invitation was to whosoever would receive it; whatever were the demands that He made and the gifts that He offered, they were for all.[7]

To add that both the demands and the offers of Christ concerned the *sins* of human beings may appear to be obviously correct. So far as the Synoptic Gospels are concerned, however, in view of what has been said in the previous section, we cannot immediately make that additional assertion. There is, for example, no recorded saying of Jesus in which He explicitly connects His death with the forgiveness or remission of sins.[8] Of course the New Testament writers believed that they rightly interpreted the thoughts of Christ Himself when they taught that He sought to deliver men from *sin;* but, for the purpose of our immediate discussion it will be wise to use an ambiguous term. I shall use the word *trouble* (as we use it ambiguously in such phrases as, 'the trouble with you is . . .') to describe that which our Lord saw to be the need of men and women, the need which He offered to meet.

The most significant fact about this *trouble* is that, according to Jesus, it was shared by all alike. That fact is most strikingly evidenced precisely in the one apparent exception to it. It is in the contrast between our Lord's treatment of the Pharisees and Scribes and His treatment of other people that His recognition that all share the same trouble is most clearly manifested. It is also, I believe, only as we examine this diverse treatment of the same *trouble* that we begin to gain a right perspective upon the fact of ignorance.

Certain questions that loom large in most discussions about our Lord's attitude to the Pharisees need not occupy our attention. Whether or not St Matthew's Gospel makes Christ's words of condemnation more severe than they actually were, the main points of His criticism in Matthew are abundantly and unanimously clear in the three Gospels. Attempts to estimate the many

[7] For the grounds for holding that 'many' in Mark 10^{45} and 14^{24} means 'all', cf. J. Jeremias, *The Eucharistic Words of Jesus*, pp. 123ff, 148ff. For the universal reference of Christ's message, see T. W. Manson, *Jesus and the Non-Jews*.

[8] Vincent Taylor, *Forgiveness and Reconciliation* (1941), p. 13f. This statement assumes that Matthew 26^{28} is a comment by the evangelist.

virtues of many of the Pharisees are unnecessary for our purpose, because, as is too often forgotten, it is quite clear that our Lord recognized those 'virtues'. (See Luke 18^{11f}, where there is no suggestion that the Pharisee was giving a false account of his good works.) Nor is it necessary for us to attempt to list the sins of the Pharisees, contrasting them with the sins of others. The Pharisees were not *unique* in their 'sins'; they are not to be understood by noticing how they differ from the rest of us, but rather by recognizing that—in spite of all appearances to the contrary—they are essentially like the rest of us. It was, of course, just this that neither they nor those whom they called 'the sinners' could recognize; it is just this that much contemporary thought about the Pharisees fails to comprehend.

It has been suggested that the most profitable way of studying the concept of sin in the Synoptic Gospels is to examine the term *the sinners*, and the varied meanings of that term are all of importance if we would fill in the Synoptic picture of sin.[9] It must suffice here, however, to note that when Jesus said, 'I came not to call the righteous but sinners' (Matthew 9^{13}), His hearers must have listened to Him with a very clear picture in their minds of both 'the sinners' and 'the righteous'. To whichever class they believed themselves to belong, they were quite certain that there were two classes. The sinners knew that they were sinners; the righteous knew that they were righteous; they were equally unaware that they shared a common need. Because of that ignorance they were both alike ignorant of the true nature of their *trouble*.

This point is of outstanding importance for our whole understanding of the fact of ignorance, and accordingly more must be said about it, for it has unfortunately been obscured behind much confused thought concerning different types of sins. The often-made distinction between sins of the flesh and 'respectable' sins is a distortion of both the teaching of Jesus and that of the New Testament as a whole. The distinction between flesh and mind, which this classification involves, implies an understanding of the body-mind relationship which is as foreign to the New as to the Old Testament; the statement that our Lord treated lightly sexual and similar 'fleshly' offences is directly contrary to the facts.

[9] *TWB*, p. 228b, where different meanings of this term are analysed. I am indebted throughout these paragraphs to this article.

The distinctiveness of the Pharisee (and his fellow-traveller the Scribe) lay, not in the uniqueness of his 'sins' but in the fact that he manifested to a peculiar degree ignorance of what was the *trouble* with him. By treating him as in need of the condemnation which he himself made of 'the sinners', by demanding from him the repentance which was demanded from 'the sinners', by inviting him to the same kind of faith that was expected of 'the sinners', Jesus showed that the Pharisees' *trouble* was that of 'the sinners'. Hence we may now abandon this make-shift word *trouble* and speak of the *sin* of the Pharisee, which—in essence—is Everyman's sin.

The outstanding characteristic of the Pharisee is his *blindness*. The use of that metaphor in relation to the Pharisees suggests to us at once that, however it may be explained, the *fact of ignorance* lies at the heart of sin, according to our Lord's teaching. Yet, once again, we move on to a false track of thought if we assume that the Pharisee is unique in being blind. It is significant that the main discussion of sin in the Fourth Gospel is set within the context of a man born blind.[10] The Pharisee is the man who is certain that he is *not* blind; that is why the publicans and sinners go first into the Kingdom. The Fourth Gospel reflects an emphasis by Jesus upon 'blindness' which is fully in harmony with the teaching in the other Gospels, as, for example, in the reiteration of the word *blind* in the Woes of Matthew 23.

Tennant[11] and others have suggested that the Johannine words, 'If ye were blind, ye would have no sin: but now ye say, We see: your sin remaineth' (9^{41}, RV), implies that if the Pharisees could have pleaded blindness they could not have been sinners. This is to miss the irony of the words, and to snatch them from their context. The whole chapter is a picture of the work of Christ as the Light, and of *faith* as the response to that Light, resulting in the opening of blind eyes. St John summarizes the passage in the words: 'For judgement came I into this world, that they which see not may see; and that they which see may become blind' (9^{39}, RV). The blind man sees—sees what he could not see before; in saying, 'One thing I know, that whereas I was blind, now I see', he speaks for all 'the sinners' who, through Christ, have come to understand the nature of their blindness by receiving sight. The Pharisees by their claim to see prove that they have

---

[10] Chapter 19; cf. the preceding discourse, 8^{31}ff.   [11] *Concept*, p. 31

become blind. 'Those who enjoy the light of the Law are unwilling to leave it for more perfect illumination, and so become blind, losing the light they have.'[12] The very boast that they *see* discloses their sin. That this happens when they are confronted by Christ Himself is the most important point in the whole chapter, but that truth will be mentioned in a later section. My immediate concern is to stress that a passage which has been taken by many to deny the existence of unwitting sin is in fact one of the most emphatic reminders that at the root of all sin lies ignorance.

If we further examine our Lord's criticism of the Pharisees in detail, it becomes plain that their sin is typical of, rather than different from, the sin of all, and that there is an element of ignorance in all our sinning. Three points require attention.

(1) Our Lord charged the Pharisees with neglecting 'the weightier matters of the law, justice and mercy and faith' (Matthew 23[23]). Those who made a speciality of understanding the law are exposed as misunderstanding it. For our own comprehension of the teaching of Christ the character of this misunderstanding is of great significance, but for our present inquiry it raises the question of innocent and culpable error.

Tennant commented that the Pharisees knew the law, and that there is no certain instance of our Lord describing as *sin* 'any deviation from the objective right or good, in which the agent was, through no moral fault of his own, ignorant that he was contravening the law of God'.[13] It is hardly necessary to say once again that the *word* sin occurs so infrequently in the teaching of Jesus that, in the literal sense, Tennant's comment loses much of its force, but is it true that the Pharisees were culpably ignorant in the sense that Tennant asserts? I think not. It is arguable whether all individual Pharisees could be said to have consciously 'deceived themselves', and, indeed, it is difficult to know what such self-deception psychologically involves. It is inconceivable that our Lord can have meant that each Pharisee had with deliberate intent turned a blind eye to the 'weightier matters'. Ryder Smith remarks that the Pharisees were hypocrites in the sense that they first deceived themselves and then went on to deceive others.[14] But this statement fails to recognize the character of self-deception,

---

[12] C. K. Barrett, *The Gospel According to Saint John* (1955), p. 303; cf. p. 293, and C. H. Dodd, *The Fourth Gospel* (1953), p. 358.
[13] *Concept*, p. 29. [14] op. cit., p. 153.

the painstaking and zealous 'blinded sincerity' that was characteristic of the Pharisee.

Nor must we forget that those whom the Pharisees instructed were, as Christ emphasized, misled by them, yet there is no suggestion from Jesus that those who were thus misled were 'innocent'. He never implied that 'the sinners' were not sinners. In short the question about degrees of culpability is submerged by His penetrating criticism of the Pharisees' *ignorance* of the very Law that they seek to obey.

(2) Christ's second major criticism of the Pharisees concerned the *externalism* of their moral and religious attitude. This criticism is so familiar that quotation is needless, the similes of the whitened sepulchre and the cup dirty within are sufficient reminder of much of Christ's teaching on this matter. It is at this point that we begin to see clearly that there was nothing unique about the Pharisees' manner of sinning; there is nothing in the reported words of Jesus to them which is more than an application of Matthew 5[21ff], in which Jesus emphasized inward morality and focused attention upon motive and intention rather than exclusively upon behaviour.

This *inwardness* of our Lord's description of moral evil was in sharp contrast to the externalism of much Rabbinical moral teaching and to the externalism of the conception of defilement by what is 'from outside' (Mark 7[18]). It is, therefore, in this way that Jesus Himself focuses our attention upon the aspect of ignorance which I have termed ignorance of *self*. All our questions about unconscious motivation and the like rise up in our minds as we consider this important aspect of Christ's message. It is *comparatively* easy to measure personal responsibility if we concentrate our attention upon individual actions; it is impossible to assess personal responsibility for motives and intentions, for desires and for that totality of personality which is described by Jesus as 'within' or as 'the heart' (Mark 7[21]).

Questions about degrees of personal responsibility rise in our minds—but are they raised by the Gospels themselves? That query only needs to be raised to receive at once a negative answer; this is but one of innumerable ways in which the Scriptures are silent about our questions. When St Paul came within sight of our question about motivation, as he did in Romans 7[15ff], he did not in fact ask it, for that passage is as much a statement of fact as is the defilement passage in Mark 7, even though later readers have mistaken it as a discussion of divided personality employing modern psychological concepts.[15]

Our contemporary anxiety to mark out the limits of individual responsibility for motives, desires and the whole inner life of man is foreign to the New Testament. On the contrary there is much in New Testament teaching to suggest that man does not know the truth about his own intentions and about his own personality. Although *personality* and *self* are not biblical concepts, we do not distort New Testament teaching if we say that it is our self—our whole self—that *acts*, and that our knowledge of that self is seriously limited and imperfect.

There are two major points involved in the statement that has just been made. The New Testament, like the Old, is remarkably free from the kind of faculty psychology to which I have previously referred, and which still bedevils so much discussion about free will and moral responsibility. A host of questions that enter into such discussion become irrelevant if we remain true to the biblical picture of man—questions, for example, which involve thinking of *the will* as a separate part of man that is somehow separated from other parts of him. If this remark has been made with wearisome repetition, the repetition may perhaps be justified by the anxiety of many Christian teachers to draw a sharp distinction between 'thoughts' and 'acts of will'.

The moral teacher and the pastor have, indeed, occasion to remind troubled people that there is a difference between evil thoughts and desires that enter 'the mind' and the holding to such thoughts or the carrying of such desires into action. But when it is said that thoughts only become sinful when they become intentions and so 'proceed out of the man'[16], or that temptation only becomes 'sin when the self is identified with it',[17] we are, I believe, passing beyond New Testament psychology. Moreover such

---

[15] cf. A. Nygren, *Commentary on Romans* (1949), p. 292ff, for a criticism of the 'divided will' interpretation. K. Barth comments on Romans 7[20]: 'It is one man that wills and does not perform; one man that does not will and yet performs; within the four walls of the house of sin dwells but one man' (*Epistle to the Romans*, trans. E. C. Hoskyns, p. 266).

[16] C. Ryder Smith, op. cit., p. 163. The author, remarking that 'evil thoughts' is an inadequate translation of *dialogismoi*, says that such thoughts 'baulked within a man' do not 'proceed out of him', whereas evil *intentions* do so proceed. But 'evil thoughts' which do not become consciously recognized intentions are one aspect of unconscious motivation—however they may be described.

[17] W. E. Sangster, *The Pure in Heart* (1954), p. 234. cf. pp. 167ff, *infra*.

statements are by no means unambiguous; they at least suggest that we always know when our 'thoughts' have become intentions, and that *self* is identical with *self-consciousness*. It is precisely the 'desires' of which we are not aware which most powerfully influence our conscious thought and our behaviour. It is 'out of the heart' (the whole of our inner life is in that word) that both desires and actions come. It should be noticed that the list in Mark 7[21ff]) includes 'desires' and 'actions' indiscriminately. The 'I' of which Paul speaks, in Roman 7 and elsewhere, is the total 'I'; to parody a familiar Negro song, 'It's not my "will", it's not my "emotions", it's not a part of me, it's *me*, Lord, that's standing in the need of prayer.'

Just as the Pharisee is the man who devotes himself to the understanding of the Law and fails to understand it, so he is the man who seeks, with unremitting zeal, to understand himself and to measure his own innocence and guilt; nobody can be more full of ashamed remorse than can the Pharisee. But he fails to understand himself, as he fails to understand the Torah. It is most often concerning the Pharisees and Scribes that we are reminded that Jesus 'knew their thoughts'. Is it possible to doubt that this implies that He understood the truth about them which they themselves were incapable of comprehending? There is one passage in particular which provides more than a hint of our Lord's attitude to what would now, by many people, be regarded as evidence of unconscious mental processes.

It would be anachronistic to see in the reference to 'careless (idle, *argos*) words', in Matthew 12[36], a foreshadowing of what is said about slips-of-the-tongue in Freud's *The Psychopathology of Everyday Life;* but Christ's emphatic reminder that 'careless words' reveal the true character, which is hidden both from ourselves and from those who see only our actions, is constantly brought to mind by anyone who, over a period of many years, makes use of Freud's description. I do not wish to impose upon these words of Jesus an elaborate psychological theory, but, especially when they are read, as Matthew sets them, within the context of the healing of a blind and dumb man, they are a further indication that Christ's concern was to unveil the 'hidden depths of many a heart'. 'The evil man out of his evil treasure brings forth evil' (Matthew 12[35]).

It is, then, the *hardness* of the Pharisee, not his uniqueness, that lead to the severity in the attitude of Jesus; it is his inability to recognize his blindness, not that he alone is blind, that places him in peculiar peril. All men are ignorant, but he thinks himself wise. In him the sin of Adam is made clear; he, if any man, has snatched at the tree of the knowledge of good and evil, and amongst the consequences of his action is the paradoxical fact that the man who 'knows' most about good and evil, about innocence and guilt, knows least. As Dietrich Bonhoeffer wrote: 'Only the overcoming of the knowledge of good and evil can bring about the conversion of the entire existence of the Pharisee; only Jesus can overthrow the authority of the Pharisee which is founded upon the knowledge of good and evil.'[18]

(3) Even yet, however, we have not come within sight of the supreme ground for our Lord's chastisement of the Pharisees, nor have we reached the point at which, alone, the depth of ignorance in human sinning can be recognized.

The Pharisee was as unlike the Good Pagan, to use Miss Rosalind Murray's descriptive term, as it is possible for natural man to be. His whole life was devoted to the business of being *right with God;* he was confident that he knew, not only the will of God, but also the nature (the Name) of God. Yet he totally misunderstood the Divine nature because he believed that rightness-with-God could be achieved through the faithful performance of moral and religious duties.

The whole doctrine of justification is to be found in germ in the parable of the publican and the Pharisee (Luke $18^{9\text{ff}}$). Nothing more devastating could be said about the Pharisee than that it was not he that went home 'justified'. In a sense, an important sense, he spoke truly when he said that he was 'not like this publican' (this 'sinner'); the law and the prophets and the ritual of synagogue and temple had at least enabled him to say that with a measure of truth. It is not true, as is sometimes claimed by eager evangelists, that a man cannot follow a strict moral code unless he is 'saved' in the Christian sense; it is not true that only Christians can worship God. The righteousness that the Pharisee lacked, the righteousness that comes by faith, does not preclude us from recognizing moral worth in the Pharisee nor cause us to term his ways of worship 'hypocrisy' in the modern sense of that word.

The trouble with the Pharisee (as with the rest of men) is that

---

[18] *Ethics* (1955), p. 156. Bonhoeffer makes a most penetrating study of the significance of our Lord's attitude to the Pharisees for the whole Christian Gospel.

he does not know the true meaning of righteousness; and failing to know *that*, he fails to know the deepest meaning of sin. It is precisely his 'knowledge' of God that is the proof of his abysmal ignorance. That ignorance, however, is best examined by turning our attention from the particular instance of the Pharisee, and from this brief study of what our Lord saw to be 'wrong' in men and women, to a consideration of the *remedy* that he offered to Pharisees and 'sinners' alike.

III. THE MEANING OF *FORGIVENESS* IN THE N.T.

Dr Vincent Taylor, in *Forgiveness and Reconciliation*, demonstrated the remarkable difference between the concept of *forgiveness* in the pages of the New Testament and the meaning of that term in later, and especially in contemporary, Christian usage.[19] It is neither possible nor necessary for me to summarize Dr Taylor's argument, which amounts to proof of the fact that the now prevailing use of *forgiveness* to include the whole reconciling act of God is in strong contrast to the language of the New Testament as a whole and to that of Jesus Himself in particular. That the term is now used with this all-embracing significance will not be questioned; that usage has not grown less since Dr Taylor's work first appeared, and he himself, after full discussion of the question, suggested that we could not return to a strictly New Testament usage.

Whilst it is true that, throughout the New Testament, forgiveness means the covering, or cancelling, or removal of the barriers to reconciliation, rather than reconciliation itself, it was (as Taylor noted) Jesus Himself, in the parable of the Prodigal Son—in which there is no explicit reference to forgiveness—who was 'directly responsible for the enlargement of the idea of forgiveness'.[20] That fact does not imply, however, that the more limited New Testament concept of forgiveness can be forgotten in any careful thought about the Work of Christ; it is very relevant to our present theme.

Only when we recognize that forgiveness is a necessary prelude to the ultimate purpose of God, only when we see that forgiveness is both distinguishable from and inseparably related to reconciliation or at-one-ment, does it become clear that men must both confess and plead guilty to the offences of which they become

---

[19] op. cit., Chapter I, where *aphesis*, *aphiemi* and *charizomai* are examined in detail.
[20] ibid., p. 23.

cognizant and must accept a salvation the need of which was unknown to them. That double-necessity is implied in the meaning of *metanoia*, repentance. Whilst repentance is not mere remorse, but a complete 'reorientation of personality' through 'the active acceptance of God's gift of faith',[21] a true and lively contrition for all our misdeeds is involved in repentance. Yet repentance, as John Wesley said, is but the 'porch of religion', and (I may add) penitence for sins past is but a step into that porch.

Therefore, although for very different reasons and with very diverse conclusions, I find myself in agreement with Tennant in his denial that 'the forgiveableness of sin is constitutive or regulative of the Christian idea of sin'.[22] For Tennant this meant that 'sin is sin whether God can pardon it or not', and he emphasized that conditions for divine forgiveness are clearly laid down in the Scriptures. But Tennant, and those who have followed his example, have, perhaps unintentionally, helped to show us that the meaning of sin cannot be discovered merely by an examination of Scriptural references to the *forgiveness* of sins. We know the meaning of anything only when we know its *end*—that, at least, we may accept from Aristotle. The *end* of forgiveness is reconciliation; the true nature of the sin that is forgiven, or, to speak more truly, of the *sinner* who is forgiven, is only revealed when he is 'made right with God'.

In much exposition of Christian doctrine, both by academic theologians and by preachers, there is an uneasy tension between the legalistic and the personal metaphors that are found in the New Testament. Fashions change in theology, as in all other spheres of thought, and for a considerable period the judicial element in the Scriptural account of human sin has been out of favour. In effect the Divine pardon has been submerged beneath emphasis upon the accomplished reconciliation. To some extent this tendency has been the inevitable outcome of a return, by Christian thought, to the eschatological point of view of the early Church—we stand in the day before the Final Judgement. (Of this more will be said in the following section of this chapter.) Moreover, the Divine forgiveness is not the so-called 'pardon' which declares innocence; the restoration of the prodigal son transforms the concept of forgiveness, although the term itself is not used in the parable. Yet, in that parable itself, the need

[21] *TWB*, p. 191f.   [22] *Concept*, p. 36.

for penitence is demonstrated by the words and actions of the prodigal, and the elder brother is 'outside', recognizing nothing of which he need be ashamed.

Thus we arrive at one of the double-truths which characterize every aspect of the Christian Gospel. The Pardoning God requires contrition, although in the Gospels there is remarkably little support for the detailed self-analysis and cataloguing of 'sins' which both moralists and many spiritual directors demand. Yet—and this is the second part of the double-truth—the true plight of the sinner cannot be confessed in advance of his forgiveness. The prodigal understands what his sin has been only when his desire to be counted a servant is discovered to be itself an indication of the lost sonship that was both the beginning and the consequence of his sinning. *Now* he recognizes that 'sin' is not what he did, but what he *was*; he can only know this when he has discovered what he *is*—'this my son'. To return to non-Scriptural terminology, he only begins to understand his *sins* when he recognizes his *sin*—his self-estrangement from the Father. Then he knows that his previous contrition, necessary and sincere as it was, was comparable to the confessed blindness of the man who has never seen; it is the man whose eyes are opened who can say, with entirely fresh understanding, 'This one thing I know, whereas I was blind . . .'.

It is by no accident that the Lucan parable of the Father and his two sons has captured the imagination of all readers of the New Testament. Almost everything is in it—except the Gospel. Taken by itself it gives little hope for most men and women, for there are far more 'elder brothers' than 'prodigals', and when the parable finishes, the elder brother is outside. A ray of hope is conveyed in the fact that the Father, who saw the prodigal afar off, is Himself 'outside' with the elder brother. In this we have a glimpse of the Gospel of that Divine intervention which we describe as Incarnation and Atonement, but, so obtuse is the ignorance of the elder brother, that, were our study of sin to be limited to this parable, we might well despair that all men can be saved. Nobody, having carefully considered this parable, or that of the Pharisee and publican, or very much else both in the New Testament and in his own experience of life, can expect that men and women will easily recognize their own sinfulness.

Much of the discussion concerning acts of willing, unconscious

NEW TESTAMENT AND THE FACT OF IGNORANCE

motivation, and similar problems that have occupied our attention in previous pages, becomes relatively insignificant when once it is acknowledged that the true nature of man's sin can be known only when he 'gets right with God'. We shall not be surprised that the Bible—in both Old and New Testaments—has much more to say about God making himself known to man than about our questions concerning man's knowledge of God. Even that suggested contrast is liable to misrepresent the Scriptural point of view, for, as Dr J. Burnaby has reminded us,[23] the knowledge of God of which both Testaments speak can be compared only with that 'knowledge which by its very nature cannot belong to a single knower: it is an exchange, a sharing, by which two human lives are in some measure joined together, giving and receiving'. As Dr Burnaby adds, the knowledge of God by Israel, as taught by the prophets, 'rests upon the covenant relationship' (cf. Amos 3^2, Hosea 2^{20}, Isaiah 1^3). Moreover,

it is the same covenant-idea which makes St Paul turn more than once from the thought of knowing God to that of being known by God. 'Now', he tells his converts, 'ye have known God, or rather are known by God' (Galatians 4^9). 'Now I know in part, but then shall I know even as also I am known' (1 Corinthians 13^{12}).

This kind of knowledge of God cannot *precede* faith. It is equally important to remember that such knowledge of God cannot be preceded by knowledge of the true nature of our sin; that is why *sin* needed to be manifested, revealed as what it is. This was one of the works of the law. 'If it had not been for the law, I should not have known sin' (Romans 7^7). The law was also 'our custodian until Christ came' (Galatians 3^{24}). But in and through Christ, 'God has done what the law, weakened by the flesh could not do' (Romans 8^3). Not only was the power to keep the law made available by Christ, but also the ignorance of sin was finally dispersed by His coming.

IV. THE ESCHATOLOGICAL CHARACTER OF THE CHRISTIAN MESSAGE

I use the word 'eschatological' to embrace the double truth that *Christ has come* and that *Christ will come;* in other words I assume that there is in the New Testament both 'realized eschatology' and

---
[23] *Christian Words and Christian Meanings* (1955), p. 24.

'the future hope', so that Christians know that men stand today in the age that is both the New Age and yet not the End.

Many of the questions that now occupy much of the attention of thoughtful Christians concerning this subject do not affect my present purpose, which is to draw attention to the significance of this double-truth for our understanding of sin. The entire teaching about sin in the New Testament is put out of focus if we forget either the difference that Christ has made to our knowledge of our condition, or the fact that the Day of Judgement is not yet—there is still *time* to repent.

It was because of both the confidence and the urgency which such a perspective gave that the writers of the New Testament paid little attention to many questions that worry our minds. There is, in their writings, none of the calm and detached exploration of human mental processes, and of individual moral responsibility, which characterizes much ethical, psychological and theological discussion. This does not prove that such discussion is reprehensible or useless; it does suggest that we shall not see the facts to which the Scriptures point if we look elsewhere. The impression made upon us by the opening chapters of Romans is not that of a writer who is confused, but of a man who is in no doubt about what he wants to say and who is conscious that it must be said with urgency. He is a man who knows that '*Now* He commands all men everywhere to repent, because He has fixed a day on which he will judge the world . . .' (Acts 17^{20}). This is no time for talking about 'the times of ignorance' as though we still lived in them.

The Scripture passages which are most commonly quoted in support of the thesis that sin must be exclusively conceived as deliberate and fully conscious choice of a known evil are Romans 5^{13}, 7^8, and John $15^{22, 24}$. Thus to interpret them involves separating these statements from their essentially eschatological context.

Commenting on Romans 5^{13}—'until the law sin was in the world: but sin is not imputed where there is no law'—Dr Ryder Smith writes: 'For instance sin would not be counted against Abraham when he committed the "sin" of polygamy for he did not know that it *was* sin.' Further, concerning Romans 7^8 ('Apart from the law sin is dead') Dr Smith remarks that Paul means that sin can do nothing against a man until the man *knows* that it *is* sin. In other words, the Apostle believes that 'anything contrary to God's will' *is* sin, but that when God comes to deal with a sinner He takes count of the sins that *the man knew* to be sins. *For the purpose of judgement* the definition of sin is not 'anything contrary to God's will', but anything *known* to be contrary to His will.[24]

If sin is thus to have two different definitions, according to whether or not it is defined for the *purpose of judgement*, then we may well agree with Tennant (who also cites this text) that we should cease to follow 'the unhappy example' of St Paul. But what is meant by the statement that 'sin can do nothing against a man until he knows it is sin'? Can this be reconciled with the assertion: 'All who have sinned without the law will also perish without the law'? (Romans 2^{12}). When Paul distinguishes those 'without the law' from those who, having sinned under the law, will be 'judged by the law' he is indeed stating that men who have not known the law cannot be judged guilty of actual rejection of that law; but did he also mean that 'sin can do nothing against them'? When he taught that the wages of sin is death (Romans 6^{23}), he was not thinking exclusively of those who were under the Law. Throughout the opening chapter of Romans Paul was writing primarily about his own sins and about those of his readers, and to make his words a psychological or philosophical discourse is to distort them.

Two facts gave urgency to his message: (1) Firstly those who had received the *Law* had received what is 'holy and just and good' (7^{12}); they could no longer sleep in their sins, no longer enjoy ignorance; the Law had both taken away their ignorance and become itself an incitement to sin, exercising a horrible fascination upon them. As Calvin commented on Romans 5^{13}: 'Without the law reproving us, we in a manner sleep in our sins and though we are not ignorant that we do evil, we yet suppress as much as we can the knowledge. . . . While the law reproves and chides us, it awakens us by its stimulating power . . . to God's judgement.'[25] If this could be said of Jews of the Old Covenant how much more could it be said of those who lived under the New Covenant? Paul was addressing himself to 'the Jews first and the Gentiles'. (1^{16}, 2^{10}). This fact that the last excuse for ignorance has been removed by the coming of the Son of God is the first truth that

[24] op. cit., p. 147. (Author's italics.)   [25] *Commentary on Romans.*

dominates Paul's thought, as it dominated that of all New Testament writers.

He confronts those who have received both the Law and the Christ with the Gentiles. In an illuminating note on the meaning of 'the Gentiles' in Romans 1^{18}-2^{20}, Professor Markus Barth has convincingly argued that Paul was not writing about the 'natural religion' of some 'splendid heathen', but about all who 'truly obey God and who, like the Ninevites in Matthew 12^{41f}, stand up in the last day and condemn 'this generation'.[26] Probably Paul had specially in mind the Gentile *Christians* whose justification must scandalize the Pharisee.

It is this same emphasis upon the removal of ignorance by the appearance of Christ that we find in John 15^{22}: 'If I had not come and spoken to them they would not have sin; but now they have no excuse for their sin.' It is a travesty of exposition that takes this to mean that only those who had met Jesus could be termed sinners. These words from the Fourth Gospel, in common with the teaching of Romans, are but echoes of the saying recorded in the Synoptic Gospels: 'It shall be more tolerable on the day of Judgement for Tyre and Sidon than for you.' This is also the explanation of the 'unforgivable sin', which is deliberate rejection of Christ when His work is recognized to be that of God.[27] The one man who cannot be forgiven is the man whose blindness has in fact been removed, who sees the Light and who calls the Light Darkness. Perhaps it was this same truth that lay behind the severity with which the early Church treated apostasy; what hope was left for those who had once recognized the Saviour and then denied Him? They had already known both the meaning of salvation and the meaning of their sin.

(2) The second ground for the urgency of Paul's message in Romans was the certainty that the way of salvation, as well as the reality of sin, had been made plain by Christ. We can never comprehend what Paul wrote concerning any of the enemies of mankind—sin, death, the law, the flesh, the powers of evil and the Wrath—if we forget that they are, for him, *defeated* enemies. As Markus Barth says, in the article previously quoted, Romans 1-3 is *good news*, announcing the victory of God over those who

---

[26] *Scottish Journal of Theology* (September 1955), pp. 280ff.
[27] cf. C. K. Barrett, *The Holy Spirit and the Gospel Tradition*, pp. 103ff, and Kittel, op. cit., p. 68.

have revolted against Him, and declaring His righteousness. If Paul was there describing the total character of human sin, he did so only because he was declaring the completeness of the Gospel.

The Christian can be glad—he need not 'be ashamed'—to recognize and declare either the blindness or the totality of sin; for he knows its remedy. He can, to quote Markus Barth once more, speak of sin in *gratitude*. God, in His mercy has manifested sin—*that*, rather than an attempt to prove that all men know what sin means, is the purpose both of Romans and of the New Testament as a whole. 'The light shines in the darkness; and the darkness has not overcome it' (John 1⁵). What the Law could not accomplish, Christ has done.

So the psychologist is right when he teaches that we need to know ourselves, and the moralist is right when he says that we must recognize and confess our faults, and the legalist is right when he says that offences merit punishment. But the Gospel declares that it is only the *restored sinner* who knows the deepest truth about himself, who recognizes the gravity of his faults and the nature of the punishment which is the consequence of his sins, and who knows all this through having ceased to be the slave of sin and having become the slave of righteousness as the child of God.

The fact to which the argument of this chapter has now brought us is that the understanding of the nature of sin which we owe to Christ Himself makes inevitable the use of the term sin with the comprehensive meaning that it had for Paul. Although the Synoptic records do not justify us in saying much about the way in which our Lord used the word itself, it is from His teaching and, still more, from the results of His work that this wider denotation becomes imperative. Strong as the arguments may be for distinguishing actions to which direct and unquestionable individual responsibility can be attributed from actions of a different kind, and necessary as such distinction may be for certain purposes, the attempt to make such a distinction obscures the desperate human need which is met by the Divine offer of salvation. To focus attention upon particular thoughts or deeds, because they are clear examples of deliberate choice of what is evil, to attempt to separate motives that are fully comprehended and 'accepted' by consciousness from other motives, and to emphasize the degree of

I

opportunity that a sinner has had of knowing the commandments of God, is to lose sight of the one important fact that Man (Everyman) is in fact alienated from God, with consequences that affect every part of his life. Nor have we explored the depths of sin when we have described the particular consequences of man's estrangement from God in terms of the unhappiness and suffering that has been brought upon himself and his neighbours. The supreme consequence of sin is—*sin;* it is to be estranged from God. The consequence of sin is not merely an instance of the fact that 'crime does not pay'; no careful adjustment of penalty to offence is here at work. To be a sinner is to be 'out of friends' with God, and the Scriptural name for this is *death.*

There is, indeed, much in the New Testament that permits us to be confident that when God judges this estrangement from Himself He takes into account the opportunity that men have had of recognizing the truth about God. But we who live in the *true* 'Age of Enlightenment' dare not presume upon that fact: '... now he commands all men everywhere to repent, because he has fixed a day on which he will judge the world in righteousness by a man whom he has appointed' (Acts 17^{30f}). We must leave to the wisdom and mercy of God those who, whether before Christ came or since, have had least opportunity to know the God against whom they rebelled, knowing that 'death reigned from Adam to Moses, even over those whose sins were not like the transgression of Adam' (Romans 5^{14}); we cannot hope to understand what it means for them that Christ 'descended into Hell', although we shall not think it strange if He who came to preach deliverance to the captive should have 'preached to the spirits in prison, who formerly did not obey' (1 Peter 3^{28}).[28]

We have not, however, yet exhausted the New Testament evidence for the inadequacy of the definition of sin that is rejected in this book. There are further reasons why *sin* cannot be used merely to describe personal activity that is solely the outcome of witting choice of a known evil.

V. THE SINNER A VICTIM AS WELL AS AN OFFENDER

If it be granted that *sin* describes that from which Christ came to save men and women, it is difficult to see how any Christian can

---

[28] See C. E. B. Cranfield, *The First Epistle of Peter*, p. 85, where much New Testament support for this belief is cited.

think of sin *wholly* in terms of individual moral responsibility, as such responsibility is normally conceived.

Throughout the New Testament man is shown to be both a victim and an offender. He who came to 'call the sick' announced His mission with a quotation from Isaiah which could not more clearly emphasize that He came to rescue, to deliver. It was to the poor, the captives, the blind, and the oppressed, that He proclaimed the acceptable year of the Lord (Luke 4^{18f}). The remarkable feature of this declaration is that it makes no reference to offenders.

Again, it is in the New Testament, not in the Old, that emphasis is laid upon Satan and upon the powers of evil. It is impossible to remove this emphasis without tearing the New Testament to shreds. As E. Stauffer has put it: 'In primitive Christianity there is no christology without demonology.'[29] However we may demythologize the demons, we cannot turn them into examples of 'intentional sins'. There is, however, a remarkable contrast between the attitude to other-than-human evil agents of the New Testament and that of moral and metaphysical dualists of all ages. This difference is due both to the belief in Creation and to the assurance that all the powers of evil are doomed—'His doom is writ, a word shall quickly slay him'. Whether it will ever be possible for men to comprehend more than we now do about supra-human personal evil we do not know, but it may well be that the human desire to claim complete responsibility for evil is but another manifestation of 'the sin of Adam'. It is as though, by some perverted ambition, we hope that even if we cannot control goodness we can control evil, so that even the Christian who trusts only to grace for his salvation seeks to find comfort in the fact that he alone was responsible for his sin.

Nor need we look so far as 'powers of evil in heavenly places' to expose this penultimate boast of human pride. (The ultimate boast is pride in *faith*.) What is commonly termed 'the solidarity of evil' is a reminder that we are not able even to sin in isolation. More will be said about this matter in a later chapter, but it is not necessary to impose upon the New Testament later notions of the mass-mind nor the somewhat confused analysis of group-psychology; there is, indeed, little trace of such concepts in the New Testament. Jesus spoke of a 'foolish and perverse generation', and

[29] *New Testament Theology* (1955), p. 67.

there is not a little New Testament teaching about 'the peoples' and about 'the world' (in the sense of mankind), but it is truer to say that the popular modern alternative, Individual *or* Society, is not found in the New Testament. 'The Bible presents no conception of individual man as existing in and for himself, nor does it know an abstract universalism. . . . Man and society are not opposing concepts but are involved in one another.'[30]

We may safely say that no contemporary knowledge about the influence of environment, especially human environment, upon individual character, or about hereditary influences, or about the behaviour of groups would cause any New Testament writer to revise his account of sin. There is room for all such knowledge within the faith that proclaims: 'In Adam *all* die; in Christ *all* shall be made alive.' There is much that is already known, and much more that remains to be discovered, about the relation between the individual and society, which is and will be of the utmost importance for human welfare; when we say that *all are sinners* we need neither deny nor attempt to anticipate such knowledge.

This New Testament understanding of sin as that which involves not only the whole individual, but also the whole human race, inevitably excludes the possibility of limiting the term *sin* by the Tennant-type of definition. That impossibility is further illustrated by another characteristic of Paul's treatment of *hamartia*.

In Romans 5-7, 'sin is regarded almost as a personified power external to man which reigns over him (5^{21}, 6^{12}) and enslaves him ($6^{17, 20}$) so that he experiences conflict between his own inclinations and the power by which he is possessed.'[31]

Man is 'under sin' (*huph' hamartian*)—sin lords it over him, rules over him, takes him captive; he is the slave of sin. This personification of sin may readily be interpreted to imply that concept of sin as a *thing* which I have previously criticized. But Paul does not

---

[30] G. E. Wright, *The Biblical Doctrine of Man in Society* (1954), pp. 47 and 51.

[31] *TWB*, p. 229a; cf. Nygren, *Romans*, p. 241, who comments that throughout Chapter 6 Paul always speaks of sin as a power or ruler over man. My colleague, the Rev. K. Grayston, has kindly made the following calculations for me. Of 60 references to *hamartia* by Paul (excluding Ephesians and Pastoral Epistles) only 8 are plural (i.e. acts of sin). There are perhaps 3 instances of the singular for an 'act of sin'. Of these 11 uses, 4 are Old Testament quotations (Rom 4^{7f}, 11^{27}, 1 Thess 2^{16}) 4 are primitive Christian formulæ (1 Cor $15^{3, 17}$, Gal 1^4, Col 1^{14}), 2 are probably used in the classical sense of 'error' (Rom 14^{23}, 2 Cor 11^7). The exception is Romans 7^5. Thus the overwhelming usage of *hamartia* is distinguishable from Paul's many ways of referring to particular actions.

refer to something *in* man, such as an evil part of his nature; the man himself is under enemy domination. This understanding of sin must be considered in relation both to the other enemies of mankind (see p. 118, *supra*) and to the main concern that controls all Paul's references to sin. His purpose is to proclaim deliverance through Jesus Christ. Just as his references to Adam are seriously misrepresented unless they be read in the light of his references to Christ, so his teaching about bondage to sin can only be rightly understood in contrast with his message about slavery to Christ. Subsequent generations of Christians have, perhaps inevitably, followed Paul's example in speaking of sin as *something* that holds man in bondage, and, whilst in so doing they have not retained the language of Jesus (as recorded in the Synoptic Gospels), they have been true to the example of the Good Physician who healed body and soul, the Shepherd who came to rescue the lost sheep, the Saviour who saw Satan fall as lightning from Heaven.

'All men have sinned [missed the mark] and fall short of the glory of God' (Romans 3^{23})—that is the grim fact upon which the light of the Gospel shines; but, just because it is light, it reveals that which otherwise would be unknown. It is a strange paradox that part of the 'good news' is the revelation of the true meaning of sin. The fact of ignorance, therefore, does lie at the root of the fact of sin. As the Epistle to the Hebrews reminds us, those who had offered 'gifts and sacrifices for sins' (5^1), who had hoped, through such sacrifices, to 'perfect the conscience of the worshipper' (9^9) and to obtain cleansing from the defilement of sin ($10^{2\text{ff}}$), had been seeking that which the Great High Priest came to make possible. The 'priests' as well as the 'prophets' knew much about sin; they, too, saw, as from far off and in shadows, the remedy that was needed. What they saw and did not see, what they knew and did not know was made known by Him who came not to destroy but to fulfil.

When he said . . . 'Thou hast neither desired nor taken pleasure in sacrifices and offerings and burnt offerings and sin-offerings' (these are offered according to the law), then he added: 'Lo, I have come to do thy will.' He abolishes the first in order to establish the second (Hebrews $10^{8\text{f}}$).

If, then, according to the New Testament, man needs to receive knowledge about sin as well as about salvation, if the 'fact of ignorance' is thus inextricably part of the fact of sin, can the more traditional meaning of *sin* be rejected? The answer to that question has been in part anticipated, but it can only be more adequately seen and examined by a consideration of the charges brought against the wider meaning. These charges concern *moral* concepts in general and the idea of *guilt* in particular, and to these matters we turn our attention in the following two chapters.

CHAPTER NINE

SIN AND MORALITY

I. THE PROBLEM

THE relationship between the Christian doctrine of sin and generally accepted ethical concepts has been increasingly discussed during the years that have passed since Tennant wrote. The subject was posed in trenchant words by H. D. Lewis:

> There appears, in fact, to be no point of contact between the doctrine of 'the equality of sin' and any recognizable ethical thinking. Can we empty the consciousness of sin in this way of ethical import? Does the word 'sin' stand for something altogether different from the immorality of this or that person, the evil-doing which we condemn in others and for which we feel the pangs of remorse in our own case? If that is so . . . let it be allowed that we are coining a new language . . .'[1]

It would not be irrelevant to comment that the term 'any recognizable ethical thinking' covers a multitude of diverse ethical theories and presuppositions, and that many in our day raise Lewis's questions with very different intent from his, seeking to liberate ethics from theology, morality from religion, and *evil* from all association with *sin*. But there is far too much point in this comment to permit superficial discussion. It is, moreover, a problem very present to the mind of the plain man, to whom regard was paid in the first chapter, but whom, as is the custom of theologians, we have almost forgotten. The relation between sin and morality puzzles many who do not think in terms of theoretical ethics and technical theology. It is most often seen as the problem of 'the good non-Christian and the bad Christian' and there is very much, both in Christian teaching and in Christian people, to justify this bewilderment.

The problem need not be stated in deliberately provocative words, such as these of Brunner which have been previously cited:

[1] *Morals and the New Theology*, p. 64.

'It is perfectly possible to combine being a sinner with being "good" in the ethical sense; indeed, in the last resort the fact of being or not being a sinner has nothing to do with the difference between the morally "good" and the morally "evil".'[2]

The more measured words of Aulén represent both a frequent Christian statement and, as I believe, an essential Christian truth: 'Since the religious conception of sin refers to man as a whole, and since the judgement of God is unconditional, it follows that from a religious point of view there can be no degrees of guilt.'[3]

These two quotations illustrate how difficult it is to isolate the relation of sin to morality from the relation of sin to guilt. Impossible as it is wholly to make this separation, we must endeavour to do so in this and the following chapter, not only because, by so doing, we may avoid wasting space by dealing with certain irrelevant questions about guilt that would otherwise arise, but, still more, because it is the attempt to understand sin in terms of guilt and punishment—rather than in terms of salvation from sin —which renders impossible any solution to the problem of the relation between sin and morality. Aulén, who draws attention to the fact that Luther used *forgiveness* with the wider meaning mentioned in the last chapter (p. 112, *supra*), reminds us: 'According to the testimony of the history of Christian thought the principal danger is that forgiveness might be interpreted negatively as simply a remission of punishment.'[4] When that is attempted, sin, as well as forgiveness, is distorted. Therefore, this intrusive problem of guilt must be yet further postponed, although it is bound up with the more strictly ethical problem.

That problem centres in the apparent contradiction between the Christian understanding of sin and the commonly accepted ethical distinction between 'the greater and the less'. The question at issue has been well expressed by N. H. G. Robinson: 'Is, then, the total sinfulness of man in which our understanding of the Christian faith constrains us to believe something which has no essential connection whatever with any degree of moral perfection or imperfection?'[5] In relation to our particular interest in this book we have to ask whether we must add to all the rest of the 'ignorance' that we have discussed a total *moral* ignorance in

[2] *Man in Revolt*, p. 154. [3] *The Faith of the Christian Church*, p. 280.
[4] ibid., p. 291. [5] *Faith and Duty*, p. 142.

unredeemed men and women, so that we must regard all his convictions that some men are better than others, some offences worse than others, as illusory.

II. SOME ATTEMPTED SOLUTIONS

Several attempts have been made to solve the problem of the relationship between sin and immorality, either by denying the reality of the problem or by marking out the respective spheres of the religious affirmation of sin and the ethical exposure of moral evil. The more important of these attempts merit brief discussion.

(a) Tennant's writings typify the desire to get rid of the problem by preventing its emergence. In treating sin as being exclusively moral imperfection for which man is, in God's sight, accountable, Tennant asserted, as we have noted, that there is other moral imperfection which is not sin. I need not repeat my arguments against this separation. The attractiveness of the definition is that it purports to equate sin with normal ethical judgement of moral culpability; it binds sin to immorality, so that the Christian and the moralist—whatever his religious beliefs—can speak the same language. But if, as I have tried to demonstrate, it does this by emptying *sin* of essential meanings, the gain is only apparent. Christian doctrine must capitulate to ethical theory in order to make itself respectable. In this matter, Tennant explained away rather than explained.

(b) A more traditional way of marking out the respective spheres of ethics and of religion—or of 'grace' and 'morality'—is by use of the distinction between *actual* and *original* sin. This distinction, often made by Protestant writers today, is virtually the same as the Catholic distinctions between *formal* and material sin, and between the *reatus* (guilt) and the *vitium* of sin. We thus obtain a series of contrasting terms that may be set down as follows:

A	B
Original	Actual
Material	Formal
Vitium	*Reatus*

Group A is sin which is inevitable, but to which no personal guilt can be attached, and which, therefore, is neither subject to ethical judgement nor capable of being dealt with by moral action. Group B is sin that is avoidable (wilful choice of what is known to be wrong), and is therefore sin to which guilt must be attributed and concerning which ethical judgements can be made. Divine co-operating grace is necessary in order that sin of this latter kind may be avoided, but it is to the removal of this kind of sin, rather than that described under A, that moral effort must be directed.

It may be noted, in passing, that one of the consequences of this rigid distinction is much misunderstanding between 'catholics' and 'protestants'. To the latter it often appears that the 'catholic' is seeking a way of salvation by good works, after the removal of original sin through Sacramental grace; to the 'catholic', the 'protestant' often seems to assume that evangelical conversion, having removed the root of sin, has relieved the 'saved man' from any moral task and from the need to grapple with actual (*formal*) sin. That either charge can be legitimately made of Christians at their best may well be denied, but we Christians are rarely 'at our best', and it is important to notice that, in this as in so many other matters, the differences between 'catholics' and 'protestants' conceal a deeper similarity. An artificial separation between original and actual sin lies behind the faults that each so quickly sees in the other.

It is against this artificial separation that Brunner protested in *Man in Revolt*,[6] reminding us that the analogy of the tree and its fruits may easily be falsely expounded. Original sin, as Brunner shows, must not be explained in terms of a logical-consecutive relationship to actual sin, so that we can set down a syllogism of which 'man is a sinner' is the major term and 'all his acts are sinful' the conclusion; nor must it be explained as a kind of 'physico-causal' phenomenon so that there is *something* in man that *makes* him sin.

It can hardly be denied that such misconceptions of original sin have plagued Christian thinking, nor can we be surprised that many Christians would wish to have done with the entire notion. Yet the term remains with us and serves as a reminder of one part of the double-truth which the New Testament holds, without (as Brunner remarks) even holding the two parts in a relation of tension: Man is a sinner, and man sins; man is a slave of sin, and every sin is an actual decision. I believe that Brunner is

[6] p. 147.

right in holding to this double-truth and in refusing to turn it into two separate truths. His own method of exposition is to speak of the *Contradiction*—the contradiction between Creation and Sin, between man as he is intended to be and man as he actually is. But this is not a contradiction that exists *in* man, it is a contradiction in which man *is*. 'This contradiction is not "something in" the actual man; *it is himself*.'[7]

It is, of course, only from faith, only from the vantage-point that comes through reconciliation to God, that man can recognize that this is what he *is*. This knowledge of sin transforms his whole attitude to morality, and radically affects both his moral judgements and his pursuit of the good life. It does not, however, enable him to forget about 'original' sin, nor make it possible for him to treat 'actual' sin as though it were 'merely a matter of ethics'. When the Christian falls back into sinning he falls back into 'original' sin. The failure to recognize that fact helps to explain why many Christians find it impossible to believe that Romans 7[13ff] can refer to post-conversion experience. They forget that justification is an act of grace that can never be spoken about retrospectively, as though it were over and done with. If I say, 'I *was* justified', I must, in the same breath, say, 'I *am* justified'. We may rejoice that we *were* reconciled to God, yet, 'not only so, but we also rejoice in God through our Lord Jesus Christ, through whom we have *now* our reconciliation' (Romans 5[11]). Sin, like the other enemies of which Paul speaks, always lurks in wait whilst this Age lasts. 'Moment by moment I'm kept by His love', or I fall away, not into a mere transgression, but into that egocentric unbelief which is the root of all sinning.

It is, in fact, to deal with the problem of *guilt* that the distinction between formal and material sin is most commonly made, and therefore further reference must be made to it in the following chapter. In anticipation it must now be stated that we cannot escape from the guilt-problem by treating 'original' sin as a matter that falls outside the sphere of moral judgement. It is the seeming element of *necessity* in original sin which itself presents the problem of guilt to our minds.

(*c*) A more promising solution to the relation between religion and morality is offered by the Catholic distinction between *theological* and *natural* virtues. Just as this offers a way of

[7] E. Brunner, op. cit., p. 478 (my italics).

distinguishing between natural and revealed ethical beliefs, so it offers to hand over to ethics certain virtues (and, by presumption, the avoidance of certain vices) in exchange for autonomy over other virtues (and, presumably, the corresponding vices). It appears as a plausible way of dividing the work of priest and moralist. But the offer is an empty one for, as N. H. G. Robinson says about this division between theological and natural virtues, 'here again is an artificial division bringing an academic abstraction in its trail; and moreover, any account of man's moral nature which leaves him subject to a plurality of moral standards is finally untenable.'[8]

(d) Can we escape from the whole problem by asserting that there are *two different points of view*—the ethical and the religious? There is much that is attractive about such a course, especially in these days when we are all learning to distinguish vocabularies that belong to one sphere from those that belong to others. It appears to harmonize with the suggestion that there is a scientific, a historical, and a religious view-point, not to mention other alleged vantage points. I can only ask here how far this way of thinking helps the particular problem we are discussing.

It is strongly advocated by Aulén,[9] who follows Luther in distinguishing between the religious point of view (man *coram deo*) and the moral (man *coram hominibus*). (The distinction is also exexpressed as that between man *in loco justificationis* and man *in naturalibus*.) Aulén rejects the manifestly unacceptable explanation of this distinction in terms of 'religious' concern with the *person* (disposition), contrasted with 'moral' concern with *conduct*. He favours the distinction between religious interest in man's relation to *God* and ethical concern with man's relation to *society*. His own immediate use for the distinction is in reference to guilt; he suggests that from the moral point of view 'to some extent the degree of guilt can be measured by the quality of the act', whilst from the religious point of view so such measurement is possible.

Whilst Aulén is careful to deny that he is delimiting two separate spheres or areas of human life—the religious and the moral—and states that he is only describing two points of view, his method of distinction cannot be judged wholly satisfactory. With respect to the religious point of view, it separates duty to God from duty to neighbour in a way that is irreconcilable with

[8] op. cit., p. 143.   [9] op. cit., p. 287f.

the teaching of Christ; the religious point of view, no less than the moral, regards 'man's relation to society'. Moreover, if the religious view is right in its emphasis upon 'man's relation to God', how can *any* moral view of man be anything but a distorted view, if it *excludes* that relation?

This question is brought even more clearly to our notice by a recent restatement of the *coram hominibus, coram deo* distinction by means of the simile of *dimensions*. N. H. G. Robinson,[10] describes natural man, confronted by the claim of duty, in a 'merely two-dimensional situation comprehending the claims of himself and his neighbour'. As a description of secular ethics, of moral man without God, this is a useful simile, and Robinson's brief description of the ways in which 'natural humanity fails to maintain its two-dimensional moral situation in independence' emphasizes both the achievements and the ultimate failure of morality without faith in God. But how far does it help the problem which is our present concern, the apparent contradiction between the 'more or less' of moral judgement and the Christian doctrine of sin? I suggest that it does no more than demonstrate the inadequacy of the 'two-dimensional' point of view. If the 'three-dimensional' view be a true one, any other view of morality is illusory.

Robinson rightly rejects a tempting solution to all our problems about sin and morality, namely that of denying that the two viewpoints are related. He adds: 'The truth lies no more with a non-moral view of sin than it does with a merely moral view of sin. The true conception carries an essential reference to morality; and yet sin cannot be properly identified with moral imperfection, partial or complete.' I believe this to be the truth of the matter.

A 'non-moral view' would make it necessary to empty the term *sin* of all moral content and to draw a clear distinction between sin and moral evil. Attractive as this would be to those who desire to preserve the autonomy of ethics, freed from theological 'bias', it is just this which the Christian, or any Theist, must forbid. If sin were a *thing* we could say that sin causes moral evil, but sin is not a *thing* to which the power of causation may be attributed. With Dr Robinson we must recognize both the 'essential reference to morality' and the inadequacy of a purely ethical interpretation of sin, and in order so to do we must return to a consideration of sin as *sin against God*.

[10] op. cit., pp. 143ff.

III. SIN AND GOD

The truth which Brunner overstated, in the words quoted on page 126, is that all descriptions of moral evil that exclude reference to man's attitude to God fail to describe *sin*. It is that fact which in much present-day Christian usage is set forth as a distinction between 'sin' and 'sins'. This terminology seeks to associate moral offences (sins) with the basic, or fundamental sin; and it is useful shorthand for those who employ it, but conveys little meaning to those who read or hear it without explanation.

The Jewish-Christian faith is that at the root of all moral imperfection lies man's rejection of God as God. Out of this rejection spring all kind of moral offences, not (as we have seen) by some kind of quasi-physical causation—as though sin were a *thing*, but because the man who sins is the man who 'does' all these other actions that are called *sins*. This happens whether or not the sinner consciously disobeys God. That all-important truth is most clearly seen when we bring together the two supreme biblical 'stories' about sin in Genesis 3 and Luke 15.

In the Myth of Adam and Eve there is deliberate disobedience to the command of God, and there is conscious acceptance of the temptation to be 'as God'. This must not, however, be taken as a description of the sin of every human being from the point of view of conscious awareness. Every man 'sins' as Adam sinned, but there have been 'sinners whose sins were not like the transgressions of Adam' (Romans 5^{14}).[11] The other great story about sin, Luke 15^{11ff}, is, as we have seen, a vivid reminder of the diverse consequences of the rejection of the Heavenly Father, and it makes clear that the prodigal was more ready to recognize what in fact he has done than was the elder brother. Even the prodigal only understood in part, for he came home hoping to be a slave and not knowing that he needed to be a son; the elder brother had no notion that he was a sinner. Adam's sin, then, is the explanation of what sinning is; it is falsely interpreted as an account of what sinning always means in the consciousness of the sinner.

It is, then, in this conscious or unconscious rejection of God as God that sinning consists. The common description of this as 'rebellion' too strongly suggests emphasis upon *deliberate* rebellion.

---

[11] cf. C. H. Dodd, *The Epistle to the Romans*, p. 82.

There are those who can rightly say: 'I did not intend anything against God'; they need to be brought to see that *what* they have rebelled against is God. (How far their action must be thought of as deliberate, in the sense that they knew what they were doing although they were unaware of their relation to God, is part of the problem of guilt.). It must be repeated that this awareness that sinning is always sinning against God is known only to faith; and therefore it is only faith that knows that moral evil is one manifestation of the godless-man, or, as it would perhaps be more true to say, that all moral evil *is* egocentric unbelief.

Aulén describes sin as being 'negatively unbelief and positively egocentricity'.[12] The term 'egocentricity' is, I believe, much more appropriate than the term 'pride' which is now employed by many Christian writers as a description of the basic sin. Pride, as much as sensuality, is the fruit rather than the root of sin. Reinhold Niebuhr gave, in the first volume of *The Nature and Destiny of Man*, a memorable analysis of the diverse forms of pride and of the manifold outworkings of sensuality. There is perhaps nothing that may be called 'moral evil' which cannot be subsumed under one or other of these grim titles. But they both issue from the egocentricity of man who worships self—including the extension of himself in various forms of greed and lust—instead of God.

It is in terms of this egocentricity and unbelief that the *total* character of sin must be understood. If the doctrine of total depravity implied the absence of all moral virtues in natural man it could be easily disproved from the recorded teaching of Jesus Himself. Moreover, in an often repeated phrase of Dr John Baillie's, 'total wickedness is a self-destroying conception'. But if total depravity is interpreted as true egocentricity over against God, 'total wickedness' is not asserted. 'Total' refers to the whole *ego*. The whole self, which was created to respond in loving obedience to God, is, as it were, turned in on itself. Hence all human thought and behaviour is deprived of its true character. The natural man indeed possesses many virtues, and manifests them in behaviour, including unselfish behaviour to his neighbour. But he does not see his neighbour as God's child, and in so doing he does not treat his neighbour *as what he is;* he does not see himself as God's child, and so he does not treat himself as what *he is;* he does

[12] op. cit., p. 260. Aulén is, of course, reaffirming one of the dominant aspects of Luther's teaching; see Philip S. Watson, *Let God be God!*, pp. 38ff, 59ff, etc.

not see the world as God's world, and so he does not treat the world as what *it is*. Most of all he does not see God as what *He is*, and that is why 'sin' is most fully manifested in religious sin.

This account of Man does not exclude the concept of 'greater or less'—for what it is worth. It is by no means impossible to say that some men more strongly, or whole-heartedly, manifest egocentric unbelief than do others; but no man can measure this in other people, and no man will seek thus to measure himself from the vantage point of faith. The sinner has lived as though he were not a child of God, whether he is the prodigal in 'the far country', or the elder brother who demonstrates that 'an alien heart can make a far country of the fields of the father's farm and the floor of the father's house'. The man who knows that he has been 'out of friends' with God does not measure the extent of his self-alienation. It is, of course, true that we can attempt to measure the relative gravity of particular moral offences, and more must be said about that subject in the next chapter. But, as Aulén has commented: 'However "small" a sin may appear according to a human estimate, to the religious consciousness awakened by the divine judgement it gives evidence of that disposition which is hostile to God's loving will and renders us worthy to be cast away from his presence.'[13]

This insistence upon the universality of sin and this refusal to differentiate between degrees of sin do not involve us in rejection of either moral philosophy or ethical study. There remains for the moral philosopher both the very necessary task of examining ethical language, and (we may confidently hope) his time-honoured, but temporarily over-shadowed, share in the whole philosophical inquiry of man into the nature of things. There also remains for the science of ethics much to accomplish: the examination of existing ethical standards and theories, which is part of man's duty to know facts; the continuance of the attempt to adjudicate between rival ethical theories; and the unpopular but needful task of casuistry. But the Christian cannot be expected to agree that either the moral philosopher or the ethical student, when pursuing the two latter duties mentioned above, can arrive at the truth if he 'leaves out God'.

It is, of course, exactly this claim of ethics to be autonomous which is being made with increasing forcefulness today. Any

[13] op. cit., p. 285.

attempt to deny its validity will be accused of bigotry and intolerance. We Christians all too often earn that opprobrium by our personal attitude to those who disagree with us; we must not shrink from receiving it concerning our faith. If the Christian interpretation of sin is true, there cannot be two authentic 'viewpoints' upon morality—one that is centred in man's relation to God and one that ignores or denies such relationship; one or other of these points of view must be a point of blindness. That assertion does not deny that many who have professed no faith in God have been nearer to understanding of His ways than have some who make such profession.

At this point we, at long last, return to the 'problem of ignorance.' Part of the account of man that Christian faith gives is the account of moral man who is *ignorant of the true nature of morality*. The Pharisee-in-us-all resents this part of Christian affirmation more than any other; at least, we claim, we know about right and wrong. So deep is this mistaken conviction—the sin of Adam as it is—that it returns to corrupt even the 'man in Christ', as is shown by the history of antinomianism and by the frequent neglect of both Christian ethics and the need for sanctification. Perhaps the moralist who forgets God is nearer to the Kingdom of God than is the 'religious' man who forgets the moral duties that are laid upon him.

IV. THE GOSPEL AND THE LAW

It is not, as is sometimes suggested, an insatiable search for paradoxes that leads many contemporary Protestant theologians to emphasize the difference between sin and moral evil, and that between salvation and moral goodness. There is much in Christian history, from very early times, to make us wary of identifying salvation with morality and sinfulness with immoral behaviour. If there is, on the one hand, the spectre of antinomianism, with its indifference to morality, there is, on the other hand, the fear of destroying the Gospel by returning to a way of salvation through 'works'. Much Protestant thought has been, and is, peculiarly sensitive to this latter peril, so that any suggestion that there is a *way* of holiness, as distinct from a *gift* of holiness is suspect.

R. Bultmann has given a fully documented reminder of the way in which, in the Church of the first centuries, the understanding both of sin and of Christian life itself quickly strayed from the insights of Jesus Himself, of Paul and of John. Bultmann argues that, except in Ignatius, the understanding of sin that is found in Paul and John was 'lost in moralistic-legalistic thinking—essentially under the influence of the synagogical tradition'.[14] Those who are still unashamed to call themselves heirs of the Protestant Reformers will not want to return to similar tendencies which existed in the Church of the Middle Ages.

But there is also, as Dr C. H. Dodd has remarked, 'a strong bias against any understanding of Christianity as a new law',[15] and this bias, characteristic of much contemporary Protestantism, has, I believe, serious consequences that are relevant to our present theme. Those who hold that man is made 'right with God' by justifying grace alone, and who teach that the power of sin is broken, and the guilt of sin cancelled, by this unmerited grace, are apt to forget the moral and spiritual journey that awaits the sinner who has been pardoned and restored. Then the ethical content of salvation is overshadowed, and the moral duties of the saved are minimized. Thus it becomes possible, even within a Christian community that speaks much about holiness, for there to be all too little actual concern about personal and social morality. The sins of the unconverted become a matter of deep and even excessive interest, whilst the New Law of the Gospel, and the necessity for growth in holiness, tend to be forgotten by those who rejoice in the liberty of the children of God.

I have been describing tendencies rather than fully-realized actualities, but I doubt whether any who are familiar with Church-life today can doubt that these tendencies exist within Protestantism. These tendencies are manifested in the moral and spiritual immaturity of many who have been truly converted, in the widespread indifference to moral problems, particularly those of a social and political character, and in the neglect of what B. H. Streeter called, 'the most neglected of all duties, the duty of finding out what our duty is'.

All this springs from a fatal readiness to identify justification with sanctification, and to assume that freedom to keep the Law, and deliverance from the *bondage* of the Law, are accompanied by some kind of instinctive knowledge of what the Law is, and by an

---

[14] R. Bultmann, *Theology of the New Testament* (1955), II.207.
[15] C. H. Dodd, *Gospel and Law* (1951), p. 65.

automatic guarantee that the 'saved' man will in fact obey the Law. It is not only the unrepentant sinner who is ignorant of the true nature of his sinning; the man who has been justified by grace, and who, therefore, knows the essential character of his sinning to have been his false relationship with God, still needs to comprehend the many manifestations of sin, and the manifold duties laid upon him in his new life. These duties are no less duties because now the power to fulfil them is offered to him, and because the grace to discharge them, joyfully and from love, rather than from fear, has been made available to him.

Pursuit of this subject would soon take us far beyond the scope of this book, but its importance is very great if we are not to be in grave danger by our acceptance of the fact that man is ignorant of the meaning of his sin until he knows its meaning from the viewpoint of the forgiven sinner. What he then begins to know is the truth about God and himself, about the relationship between himself and God; what he must not claim to have, is knowledge of the ways of good and evil.

This truth is shown in two related ways in the New Testament itself. It is demonstrated, firstly, by the amount of attention devoted by all the New Testament writers, and by Jesus Himself, to ethical teaching. It is brought to our attention, secondly, by the New Testament teaching concerning the relation between justification and sanctification.

(1) Much important New Testament study, all too little assimilated into the life of the Church, has been recently devoted to the ethical teaching of the New Testament. Since Archbishop Carrington's book, *The Primitive Christian Catechism*, appeared, other writers have continued examination of the clear traces, in the New Testament, of definite instruction, including detailed teaching about vices and virtues, which was given to those who, having received the *Kerygma*, needed to be taught the Christian Way.[16] The time has come, I suggest, when much more attention needs to be paid to this element in the New Testament. My point may most briefly be made by reference to the work of

---

[16] The most detailed study of this teaching is in E. G. Selwyn, *The First Epistle of Peter* (1946), Essay II, pp. 363ff; cf. G. Phillips, *The Transmission of the Faith*, in which the application of this teaching in different areas of the world is discussed. See also B. Reicke, A Synopsis of Early Christian Preaching, in *The Root of the Vine* (A. Fridrichsen and others, 1953), pp. 128-160. Cf., however, criticism of Selwyn by C. L. Mitton, J.T.S. (New Series), I, part 1, pp. 67ff.

Dr C. H. Dodd. Perhaps no book has more greatly influenced the message of the Churches in the last twenty-five years than has his *The Apostolic Preaching and Its Development*. This book, with its rediscovery of the primitive Gospel, helped to bring to an end the type of preaching which, thirty years and more ago, was described as 'merely ethical'. I see little sign, however, that the more recent book by Dr Dodd, *The Gospel and the Law*, has begun to supplement our preaching.

In the New Testament, as Dodd reminds us in this latter work, there is *Didache* as well as *Kerygma*. The Church cannot come into existence save through *Kerygma*, but it cannot continue in existence (nor grow, which is part of the meaning of its existence) without *Didache*. This teaching includes instruction in many matters other than the purely ethical—in the whole way of Christian living through the means of grace; but it does include detailed examination of moral duty. Bultmann, in the volume previously mentioned,[17] has suggested that even within later books of the New Testament there are the first signs of the formulation of a fixed moral code, of an ascetic conception of holiness, and of a 'double' morality. He shows, without difficulty, how such tendencies developed in the years immediately following the period covered by New Testament writings. But awareness of such distortions of primitive Christianity may make us unduly afraid of any emphasis upon the moral life.

Those non-Christian and non-theistic moralists who accuse Christians of lacking moral sensitivity, especially in regard to matters outside very private, personal behaviour, are not entirely without justification for their accusation. We have not fully answered them when we reply that they have forgotten the grace of God, and that we are remembering the need for the gifts of the Spirit. As Dr Dodd wrote: 'The Christian ethic ... can as little make itself good in the world apart from the Gospel as the Gospel can be understood apart from its ethical implications.'[18] The two truths hold together. If it is true that ethical theory can never lead us to the knowledge of sin, it is also true that the knowledge of what sin is lays upon us the duty of finding out what good and evil are.

We do well to heed Bultmann's reminder[19] of the way in which righteousness (*dikaiosyne*) tended to lose its Pauline meaning—the

[17] op. cit., Chapter 8.   [18] op. cit., p. 85.   [19] op. cit., p. 212f.

righteousness of God—and came to denote *only* 'moral uprightness', so that 'an ideal of moralistic piety' began to replace 'the eschatological consciousness and endowment with spiritual gifts'. The lists of virtues and vices, of that which must be 'put on' and that which must be 'put off', given by St Paul may easily be transformed into a Christianized Jewish code of morality. But this is not the only danger which the Church has met and still meets.

There is, indeed, much in Church life, especially among many who emphasize the doctrines of the Reformation, to suggest that the contemporary peril is neglect of 'the ethical implications of the Gospel'. In practice this neglect manifests itself as an impatience with any assertion that the interpretation of Christian morality calls for hard thought and resolute action, so that the work of a Christian Citizenship Department of a denomination, or of a Council of Churches, is viewed, by many devout Church members, as being slightly 'off-centre' from the fundamentals of Christian life. Behind this unhappy aspect of much 'evangelical' religion lies a theological error of the gravest magnitude.

(2) When justifying grace is divorced from sanctifying grace the whole perspective of Christian understanding is lost. Nobody more clearly recognized that fact than did John Wesley. G. C. Cell, in *The Rediscovery of John Wesley*,[20] affirmed that Wesley made a synthesis between the protestant emphasis upon justification and the catholic emphasis upon sanctification. In stating his thesis in this way Cell, unfortunately, made it possible for the truth of that thesis to be obscured by discussion of the degree to which, in fact, the Reformers themselves neglected sanctification and the more significant catholic teachers failed to understand justification. If, however, we attend, not to that very debateable issue, but rather to the positive synthesis in Wesley's own teaching, Cell's argument is of abiding value.

In a more recent, and more fully documented study, *Wesley and Sanctification*, Harald Lindström has fully demonstrated the dominant place occupied in Wesley's thought by sanctification and by *growth* in holiness.[21] Unhappily, many of Wesley's followers, whilst recalling his delight in sudden conversions, have largely forgotten his emphasis upon the need for growth. Yet the whole pattern of the corporate life of the Societies and of the Connexion was determined by the need to provide for this moral and spiritual growth.

[20] Pubd. 1935; pp. 341ff.   [21] Pubd. 1946; especially Chapters 2 and 3.

Wesley never confounded justification with sanctification, but neither would he allow them to be isolated.

By justification we are saved from the guilt of sin and restored to the favour of God; by sanctification we are saved from the power and root of sin and restored to the image of God. All experience as well as Scripture shows this salvation to be both instantaneous and gradual.[22]

Moreover, he taught that justification is itself the beginning of the work of the same Spirit who sanctifies: 'At the same time that we are justified . . . in that instant we are born again, born from above, born of the Spirit.'[23] 'Our main doctrines, which include all the rest, are three—that of Repentance, of Faith, and of Holiness. The first of these we account, as it were, the porch of religion, the next the door, the third Religion itself.'[24]

When the 'porch' and the 'door' are confused with 'religion itself', and when justification is identified with conversion-experiences subjectively considered, then the need for growth in holiness is forgotten. Moreover, when holiness is emptied of its moral quality, or when that moral quality is not identified with love (*agape*), it becomes possible for those who glory in the saving grace of God to take little interest in individual and social ethics. Yet again, it is all too easy to substitute fruitless discussion about the nature and 'degrees' of perfection for the pursuit of holiness. Those who make justification by grace through faith the foundation of their religion destroy that foundation if they imagine that their goal has been reached, forget that justification is *for* sanctification, and ignore the truth that love is both the gift of the Spirit and the fulfilling of the Law.

The conclusion of this somewhat discursive chapter may be best made by a return to its starting-point. The apparent contradiction between the Christian message about sin and much 'ethical thinking' is in part due to the essential difference between the meanings of *sin* and of *moral offence*, for, as we have seen, the nature of my sinning cannot be discovered by an examination of the different kinds of 'wrong things' that I do. But the *apparent* contradiction is sometimes made into an *actual* contradiction by a minimizing of the ethical content both of sin and salvation. Against this danger the Christian must always be on guard, not least when

---

[22] Sermon 85.   [23] J. Wesley, *Works*, VI.42.   [24] *Letters*, II. 268f.

he comes in contact with those who, having no faith in God, have deep moral concern. He must ever be ready to learn from them, as well as to 'evangelize' them; for to many of these he will rightly apply the words of his Master: 'He that is not against us is for us.'

Christians cannot compromise upon ethical opinions which they believe to be implications of the Gospel, but they must ever be ready to re-fashion their understanding of that Gospel and of those moral opinions. They will not be ashamed to follow the example of Paul in distinguishing between what is certainly the 'mind of the Lord', and what is the opinion of Christian disciples. They will not confuse deliverance from the bondage of the Law with escape from its precepts, nor the freedom to do the will of God with omniscience concerning that will.

Christians cannot, however, share the hope of many that moral evil can be removed from the lives of men by any other remedy than the pardon and remaking of man which the Gospel offers. And when they speak in terms of *guilt*, rather than of offence, much must be said which cannot but puzzle, and even offend, many of those whose moral concern is not in question.

CHAPTER TEN

SIN AND GUILT

I. THE PROBLEM OF GUILT

THROUGHOUT the previous chapters the problem of guilt has constantly appeared and been pushed aside. It has arisen because the Christian understanding of sin seems to be in conflict with generally accepted notions of moral responsibility. We have seen many examples of the way in which the meaning of sin has been reinterpreted in order that it may be accommodated to such ethical beliefs. In other words, we have noted ways in which sin is explained in terms of guilt, and it has been repeatedly implied, in earlier pages of this book, that we need to reverse the process and to interpret guilt in terms of sin.

I say 'interpret', that is, state what guilt *is*, rather than 'explain', for, just as there is no Christian theodicy which does not leave part of the meaning of evil hidden from human explanation, so it may well be with any attempt to explain guilt. Indeed, we may further suggest that only a full explanation of evil could make possible a complete explanation of guilt. The Christian who is content with the light that the Gospel sheds upon evil, even although he cannot answer the question, Why should there *be* evil? may not be surprised if that Gospel tells him more about what guilt is, and about how it may be removed, than concerning other questions that he asks.

What then is the *problem* about guilt? It is a problem which only presents itself to one who both believes in the God and Father of our Lord Jesus Christ and in the account of sin as human denial of creatureliness, that is, as egocentricity and unbelief. This problem—which for brevity I will call the *religious* problem of guilt—must not be confused with the problems of the non-believer. The non-believer may (and does) ask: 'How can I be blamed for what is not wholly, or even mainly, my own deliberate choice of evil? How can I be blamed, for example, for not believing in God?' But he cannot mean by such questions what the believer means. Just as the problem discussed in a theodicy is a problem that only weighs upon the theist, so the religious problem of guilt is a problem that only concerns the believer in God. Moreover, as is often forgotten in religious discussions, the shape our problems take depends upon the *kind* of God in whom we believe; we are concerned here only with Christian belief in God. It is therefore worth devoting a little space to a more careful examination of the *guilt* which we are to discuss.

(*a*) As I have already indicated, we are only concerned here with guilt *toward God*. It must never be forgotten that *guilt* has no meaning apart from reference to *that* toward which guilt exists. Endless confusion has been caused by ignoring this fact, as also by neglecting to notice that if we are to consider what *moral responsibility* means we must first ask the question: responsible to what or whom? Hence guilt may have many meanings.

There is, for example, guilt in respect to the law of the particular community to which the guilty person belongs. It is a platitude in British Courts of justice that moral and legal guilt are not synonymous. All that can be said here about the highly complex meaning of *legal* guilt is that, from the Christian point of view, all such guilt must be considered in relation to the individual's duty to the society of which he is part and to the 'rulers' of that society, whilst, at the same time, all human judgement must be recognized to be subordinate to the judgement of God. Niebuhr has rightly reminded us that 'without a judgement upon even the best judicial process from a higher level of judgement, the best becomes the worst', and he has further suggested that this is perhaps the significance of Isaiah's words—'He maketh the judges of the earth as vanity' (40^{23}).[1]

Again, guilt may be conceived in reference to a moral standard (which itself may be conceived in a variety of ways), or to a specific moral code, or to 'the general intuitions of mankind'—in short, in reference to any of the multitudinous ethical theories. We should not assume that guilt will have precisely the same meaning in all these references. Most of all, we should not assume that we can discover the *Christian* meaning of guilt unless we keep our attention firmly fixed on the fact that it is of guilt toward *God* that we are speaking.

(*b*) Secondly, if we are not to wander in a maze of avoidable

---

[1] *The Nature and Destiny of Man*, I.274.

perplexities, we must sharply separate *guilt* from *sense of guilt*. Psychologists, whose proper interest is primarily with the latter, are especially prone to identify guilt-feelings with guilt. A typical example is provided in Dr L. D. Weatherhead's suggestion that it is 'valuable . . . to divide guilt into three classifications: (1) Normal guilt. (2) Exaggerated conscious guilt. (3) Repressed or unconscious guilt.'[2]

It cannot be too strongly stressed that there is no such phenomenon as conscious—or unconscious—guilt. Guilt is an objective fact, not a subjective feeling. What Weatherhead terms 'exaggerated conscious guilt' is very much what moral theology has, for many centuries, known as *scrupulosity*. 'Repressed or unconscious guilt' is a term not infrequently used by psychologists[3] to describe an unconscious mental process which they believe to be the explanation of certain neuroses. I am not disputing this theory, but I am seeking to point out that a sense, or feeling, or consciousness of guilt must never be confused with actual guilt. Obvious as this fact appears, when once it is stated, failure to remember it makes precarious any attempt to gain that theological understanding of guilt which Dr Weatherhead states that he seeks no less than psychological understanding..

Psychology has much of great significance to say about guilt-feelings; it has nothing whatsoever to say about the guilt toward God which Christian theology studies. This is no mere matter of terminology. The preacher and the pastor, no less than the theologian and psychologist, must ever keep this distinction clear. The *acknowledgement* of guilt—which the Gospel demands—is a very different matter from many types of guilt-feelings, and not least from that 'buried' sense of guilt which can only be described by the somewhat contradictory term *unconscious feeling* of guilt.

(c) If guilt toward God must be differentiated from any other guilt, and objective guilt from the sense of guilt, no less must the concept of guilt be distinguished from that of *punishment*. In law, a man is punished if he is found guilty; in morals, a man is blamed if he is judged guilty. But guilt and punishment are separate facts; many who are in fact legally guilty go unpunished, and many are morally blamed who, in the sight of God, are not guilty of the offence for which they are condemned. Therefore we must not

---
[2] *Psychology, Religion and Healing*, p. 322.
[3] e.g. W. L. Northridge, *Psychology and Pastoral Practice*, Chapter 6.

attempt to understand the religious problem of guilt in terms of a legalistic concept of punishment or a moralistic understanding of blame. 'Guilt' and 'punishment' are separate facts, and it would be well if we could consider guilt without any reference to punishment. Punishment does not determine guilt, guilt determines punishment, and the attitude of mind that says, 'It is only a small punishment therefore it must be only a little guilt that I bear', is irrelevant when sin is in question.

It is just this conception of God meeting out punishment to fit the crime, a little punishment for a small offence and heavy punishment for a grave one, that lies behind much of the moral indignation that is aroused by the Christian affirmation: 'There is no distinction; since all have sinned and fall short of the glory of God' (Romans 3^{21}). Yet it is only if we imagine a future life in which differentiation is made between sinners bearing diverse degrees of guilt, and in which punishment is graded according to the deserts of different types of sinner, that any such relation between guilt and degrees of punishment can be associated with sin. Certainly it cannot be affirmed that in this earthly life there is this kind of co-relation between sin and punishment. Unless such a saying as, 'It shall be more tolerable on the day of judgement for Tyre and Sidon than for you' (Matthew 11^{23}), or a parabolic reference to many and few stripes (Luke 12^{47f}), be pressed beyond their meaning any such concept of divine punishment must be rejected. When our Lord spoke of the destiny of the wicked it was in terms of 'outer darkness', not of graded prisons. And for St Paul the wages of sin is *death*, not varying degrees or durations of punishment.

In short, so long as we regard sin merely from the point of view of secondary consequences—the unhappiness and suffering that sinning often brings in this life and is believed to bring in the next—we have not begun to see what sin is. The final consequence of sin is *sin;* the meaning of sin is also the meaning of the punishment of sin—self-alienation from God. So man either is or is not a sinner; he is or is not guilty; he suffers or does not suffer the only punishment, or consequence, of sin which is worthy of mention: 'Depart from Me.' If that were all that the Christian had to say about sin, his would be a message the pessimism of which would surpass the darkest gloom in non-Christian thought. That is not all that he says, but this he must say, and he says it with an *eternal* reference, although that reference has been strangely forgotten by recent generations who, in this respect, have been unlike all their Christian forebears.

II. THE FACT OF GUILT

It is now possible to see why the attempt to solve the Christian problem concerning guilt by means of the differentiation between *original* and *actual* sin fails. The attempt to hold to some kind of doctrine of original sin whilst denying 'original guilt' (whatever that may mean) breaks down even if we substitute for the term 'original' the notion of an 'irrational' element in sin which is 'inexplicable'. Dr J. S. Whale, who makes this attempt,[4] simply restates the fact that man both is a sinner and chooses to sin—the fact which the term 'original' sin served to state. (The interpretation of original sin as being the sin of our ancestors for which we are blamed, which Dr Whale seems to describe as 'the classical doctrine', is but the most unfortunate of many attempts to account for original sin). Even if we agree with Dr Whale that 'any alleged explanation of the fact that all men sin is only a new determinism' we must still recognize the fact, as he himself does. It is the fact— not any particular explanation of it—which raises the problem concerning guilt.

Nor is the problem eased by returning to the scholastic distinction between *formal* and *material* sin, to which reference was made in the previous chapter. Because of the prominence of this and allied distinctions in all moral theology that is deeply influenced by Aquinas, and because the purpose of such moral theology is to differentiate degrees of guilt, more must now be said on this theme.

The way in which the *formal, material* division is used in reference to guilt is well exemplified by Dr R. C. Mortimer when he states that 'the judge who conscientiously holds it his duty to send a prisoner to the rack is guilty of the material sin of cruelty, but not of the formal sin'.[5] This equating of formal sin with acts performed 'conscientiously', besides involving us in unbiblical notions of conscience, involves us in extraordinarily bewildering moral judgements; there is probably no crime that has not been, on occasion, committed conscientiously. We are at once involved in the most complex analysis of individual moral actions.

Perhaps nobody has ever made an analysis of human actions

[4] *Christian Doctrine* (1942), pp. 49f.   [5] *The Elements of Moral Theology*, p. 62.

with greater fullness than did Aquinas, and Dr Mortimer, in the commentary to which I have previously referred, has summarized, with a wealth of illustrative examples, most that can be said about the object at which an action aims, the circumstances under which it is done, and the motive and intention that prompt it. The weakness in much Protestant moral theology is that it pays too little attention to the moral quality of different actions, and so I do not wish to suggest that there is no place for an examination of this kind. There may, for example, be need for more instruction, by those whose task it is to give public and private Christian counsel, concerning the relation between motives and actions. But I believe that this kind of classification of 'sins' obscures, rather than illuminates, the meaning of sin. Once again, the example of the Pharisees provides a salutary reminder.

The necessity to mark out degrees of guilt in this way is suggested to us by the example of criminal law. Whether, in an ideal community, it would be necessary to relate punishment directly to the gravity of the offence, or whether such punishment should be determined by the needs of the offender for correction and reformation is a familiar subject of debate. It may, at least, be asserted that any attempt to measure character, as distinct from isolated actions, is a task beyond the skill of man. That is, perhaps, part of the meaning of the remark, often made by British judges, that our courts of law are not courts of morals.

When a further distinction is made between *mortal* and *venial* sins, yet greater damage is done to the understanding of sin. There is no sin which is not *mortal:* the wages of sin is death. The reference in 1 John 5[16f] to 'sin which is mortal', as contrasted with that which is 'not mortal', is best understood, as by C. H. Dodd in his Commentary on this Epistle, as an expression of the attitude of the early Church to 'high-handed' sin, to 'loving darkness' on the part of those who have seen the light, that is to say, to apostasy (cf. Hebrews 10[26]). This teaching cannot be allowed to negate the general New Testament emphasis upon the deadliness of all sin, nor the promise of the Gospel that the divine forgiveness is offered to all men.

The use of the distinction between formal and material sin, as a solution of the religious problem of guilt, reaches its climax in the assertion that the *reatus* (guilt) of sin is attached only to formal sin. This, as I have already sought to indicate, involves treating the blemish or imperfection (*vitium*) of material sin as something that has no *personal* meaning. It is then, almost inevitably, treated as a quasi-physical defilement, removed by the washing of Baptism. The double-truth that man is by (fallen) nature one who sins and also one who chooses (consents) to sin is then reduced to the concept of some kind of taint that has no relationship to the individual's thoughts and actions, and the sacrament in which the baptized is initiated into the family of God is in danger of being transformed into a rite that has little to do with the relationship between man and God.

The desire to associate guilt only with so-called formal sin is a very natural one; that we should suffer for 'sins not our own' appears to be unjust. To this only two replies can be made. Firstly, if we abandon notions of the enumeration of particular sins and of degrees of punishment, and think of the punishment of sin as estrangement from God, it is little comfort to be told that certain 'sins' will not be taken into account. Secondly, the Gospel is that man can be saved from both the *reatus* and the *vitium* of sin. O. C. Quick has stressed that the recognition of the *vitium* of sin was an insight of the Hebrew apocalyptists and of the priestly religion of sacrifice. Moreover, as Quick added, the penitential psalmists—especially Psalm 51—were 'almost Christians before Christ in their deep insight into God's attitude toward sin and His power to save not only from its *reatus* but also from its *vitium*—"its guilt and power", as Toplady put it.'[6]

We may, indeed, be relieved that we are not compelled to isolate *formal* sins before we can acknowledge our guilt before God. The facts which were noted in the opening chapters of this book must not be forgotten. Unconscious motivation, hereditary and environmental influences, mistaken ideals and false ethical teaching authoritatively given and innocently received, all these are facts about human experience. So, also, the manifold complexities of motive and intention, of choice and of opportunity are actual complexities, not inventions by academic minds. It is not merely that we human beings cannot judge other men as God judges them; we cannot judge ourselves. When we consider ourselves most un-free we are often most free, and vice versa. There is almost no action that we perform for which we cannot make some excuse, by saying either that *that* was not what we intended to do,

[6] *The Gospel of the New World*, p. 49; cf. pp. 94ff, *supra*.

or that we were 'not ourselves' when we did it, or that we were not wholly responsible for thinking the wrong action right or for being the kind of person who could act in that way. There will be a greater or less measure of truth in all such statements, and the realism of the Bible is such that it recognizes, without seeking to define or to delimit, that measure of truth. Those who would compel us to limit guilt to actions performed with full knowledge both of their wrongness and of their disobedience to God's will are asking what may appear ethically attractive but is certainly psychologically obscure. Nor is it worth-while trying to surmount the difficulties, for no isolating of such actions will bring us in sight of our essential guilt.

Therefore, to gain light upon the religious problem of guilt we must look yet again at the nature of sin. In so doing, reference will be made to sin as the sinner *acknowledges* it, but this is not to make the mistake, against which warning was offered at the outset of this chapter, of interpreting guilt by the *sense* of guilt. It is not to any feeling or sense of guiltiness that we now turn our attention. ('Consciousness' is an ambiguous word which *may* be used for acknowledgement, but which is more often used for some kind of emotional feeling detached from thought.) It is, I repeat, not by regarding his feeling of guilt, but by *seeing his sinfulness* that man discovers his guilt toward God. Even that is too brief a statement, for it should rather be said that it is by knowing himself pardoned and restored that, at long length, man says without qualification or excuse: 'I am guilty.'

It is not by looking at his own guilt-feelings, nor by comparing himself with some ideal of his own that man is able to acknowledge his sin and guilt. It is when his self-centredness and unbelief are broken down by the judgement of God which is also His mercy, and by the mercy of God which is also His judgement, that he says: 'Father, I have sinned against heaven and before you; I am no longer worthy to be called your son' (Luke 15^{18f}).[7]

III. THE ACKNOWLEDGEMENT OF GUILT

It is only as we think of the guilt that the repentant sinner acknowledges that we can begin to comprehend why the 'religious'

---

[7] cf. G. Aulén, op. cit., p. 281. 'The consciousness of guilt implies that man knows and submits to *God's* judgement.' Aulén uses 'consciousness' where I use 'acknowledgement', but he emphasizes that he does not refer to 'conscience' or to any 'feeling'.

problem of guilt is precisely the problem which does not—or should not—weigh upon the Christian.

What do I see, when I see myself a sinner? I recognize that I have thought, spoken and behaved as *though God were not*. Most probably I know that I have sometimes done this deliberately, I have pushed God away; more often I have pretended to myself that God is not; most often of all I have totally ignored or forgotten Him. This fact, as it comes home to me, is a fact about many particular actions which I can now see to be the consequences of this God-rejection—the manifold 'sins' of pride and of covetousness and of sensuality. But I see more than that; I recognize that I have most completely forgotten God in my 'good works'; even my virtue has been *my* virtue, my religion *my* religion, my 'God' *my* idol. Above all, I see that I have been most in opposition to God when I have been *most myself*; it is not what I have done but what I have *been* that I now confess.

Let us pause in this attempt to describe the acknowledgement of sin, to which many have come with startling suddenness, others by gradual stages. *Part* of the meaning of my sinfulness is this inescapable awareness of the *me* that is the sinner. That is why questions about the particular degree of 'responsibility' for particular actions becomes irrelevant. There comes a point when I can no longer say, 'I was not myself', when I recognize that I always *am* myself.

Nor can we remove the problem of guilt by explaining it in terms of the solidarity of sin. N. H. G. Robinson argues that it is possible to posit the universality of sin and man's responsibility because of this solidarity, because, as he puts it, 'the world is an absolutely joint enterprise'.[8] Dr Robinson's exposition of the moral solidarity of the race, and his reply to those who confuse this with legal responsibility is of the greatest value. But in the acknowledgement of *my* guilt, this most important truth that I am bound up with the sin of the world cannot be used as an excuse. The recognition of sin involves the recognition of my sinful solitariness. I, who was made for fellowship with God and with my fellows, have isolated myself; the acknowledgement of sin involves this awareness of the dreadful aloneness of the sinner.

---

[8] *Faith and Duty*, op. cit., pp. 132ff; cf. G. Aulén, op. cit., p. 282: 'The consciousness of guilt cannot be made dependent upon the relation between individual sinfulness and the solitary relationship of sin.'

Yet that is only part of the truth, for the recognition of the 'I' that is a sinner is at the same time the recognition of the 'I' that is 'not I, but sin' (Romans 7^{17}). This is the unavoidable paradox which lies at the very centre of the Christian view of sin, and this is the truth about man which would be unbearable but for the paradox of grace: 'I, and yet not I, but Christ.' The final egotism of the sinner is to think that he is both unique and wholly responsible for his sin.

That he is not unique is a comparatively small matter which he may readily learn; that he is not the master even of his own sinning is the hardest of all lessons to learn. Man craves a *freedom* that he does not possess, he claims freedom from himself. This indeterminism, as contrasted with self-determinism, is a psychological will-o'-the-wisp the search for which has consumed a vast amount of human energy, but it is not through psychology that man can discover the 'not I, but sin'. He may indeed think himself a *slave*, but he only recognizes that this slavery is to *himself* when he is confronted by the God whom he has rejected but who has not rejected him. Then he knows that he has been most himself when he has been not the self that God created him to be, but the self who is in opposition to the Creator. It is only then that all questions about 'responsibility' become empty questions. As Bonhoeffer wrote, concerning those who have learnt from Christ the true nature of their sin:

> They confess their guilt without any side-long glance at their fellow offenders.... Wherever there is still a weighing-up and calculation of guilt, there the sterile morality of self-justification usurps the place of the confession of guilt which is made in the presence of the form of Christ.[9]

This acknowledgement of guilt is not an interpretation of our feelings, nor a logical conclusion drawn from an argument about ourselves, nor an awareness that we have broken some laws and failed to reach to some ideals. It is, to quote Bonhoeffer again, the sight of Christ's grace that 'blots out entirely the sight of the guilt of other men and compels a man to fall upon his knees before Christ and to confess *mea culpa, mea maxima culpa*'. Hence the Hebrew insight that saw no need for a specific word for guilt as contrasted with sin was a true insight. When I am guilty for being what I *am*, and when what I *am* is a sinner, the two terms,

[9] *Ethics*, p. 47.

sin and guilt, become synonyms. So, too, the dislike of Luther for any use of the word 'freedom' in relation to sin is understandable. Whatever 'freedom' natural man possesses he uses wrongly; thus he is both a slave to sin and one who "consents" to sin.[10] The fact that the self which has thus sinned is a self that is bound up with all other men, and the fact that this self's motives have often been 'unconscious', are but part of the ignominy of sin. It is only when the last vestige of pride is stripped from us that we can be saved, and the last vestige of pride is the illusion that we are the 'captains' of our own souls.

If it be said that this identification of sin with guilt destroys the normal meaning of guilt, then two replies must be made. Firstly *sin* is not *like* anything else, not even like crime, and we should, therefore, not be surprised if any word used in connexion with sin has a unique meaning in that context. We have found it necessary, as was anticipated, to interpret *religious* guilt in terms of sin rather than the reverse. Secondly, there are at least two ways in which the *uses* of the term guilt in other contexts are not needed when we are speaking of sin.

In the first place, in relation to crime, or to ordinary moral judgements about particular actions, we need to be able to say 'guilty', or, 'not guilty'. But *we have no need for the term 'not-guilty' in regard to sin*. Nobody is 'not guilty'; the forgiven sinner is not declared innocent, his guilt is cancelled; the guilty is pardoned. This is part (but not all) of the meaning of *justus et peccator*. In the second place, we need the word 'guilty' in other contexts in order that the judge may pronounce sentence; the Christian needs the word 'guilty' in order to declare that *the sentence need never be pronounced*. This is a matter of supreme importance. We are told that our Lord 'came not to judge the world' (John 12[47]). We live not in the Day of Judgement, but in the day before the Judgement; yet we live in the day in which, in another sense, judgement has already come (John 12[31]). If once we forget the work of Christ either as the unveiler of sin or as the redeemer, the whole New Testament account of sin and guilt becomes incomprehensible; it also becomes a message of despair.

The question that weighs upon many sincere Christians, concerning those who have had no opportunity to hear the Gospel, is

[10] See p. 37, *supra*.

one upon which a little light is shed in the New Testament. We are emboldened to believe that 'it will be more tolerable' for them than for those of us who have 'seen Christ'. Little is to be gained by speculation concerning the lot of those who have been without the Gospel; we may safely trust them to the wisdom and mercy of God. But we must not allow that trust in God to make us content that men should 'sleep' in their sins, nor must we forget that, over an ever-increasing part of the world, any discussion of 'before Christ' is an anachronism. It is not our business to judge other people, nor to appoint their destiny. If God has committed to His Church the task of addressing men as sinners, it is because He has commanded the declaration of 'the absolution and remission of sins' and given the Holy Spirit who alone can convict of sin. Therefore we must remorselessly refrain both from making excuse for other people's sin and from taking upon ourselves the right to condemn. The task of the Church is to offer Christ to men and women, not in order that they may know that they are sinners, but in order that they may know that they have been redeemed and may enter into their inheritance.[11]

It is through Christ that the knowledge of sin and the guilt of sin comes in the experience of forgiveness and restoration. In previous chapters attention has been drawn to the fact that *sin* is recognized when salvation is at hand; it now becomes clear that *guilt* (the guilt of *sin*) is only acknowledged fully when the Saviour is in sight. This is not to deny that, from the point of view of introspection, many Christians can recall a period of deep remorse prior to the acceptance of divine grace. But remorse is not *metanoia*, repentance, and our real guilt is not known by remorse.

IV. GUILT-FEELINGS

Guilt-feelings must be clearly distinguished from the acknowledgement of our true guilt for two reasons. Firstly, as has already been indicated, it is not by means of such guilt-feelings that man can recognize his sin; secondly, there are many different kinds of 'feeling' of guilt, many of which are hindrances to the acknowledgement of the guilt of *sin*. No attempt can be made here to explore the labyrinth of man's guilt-feelings; rather an attempt must be made to indicate the kind of inquiry that needs to be

---

[11] The implications of this truth for evangelism are discussed below, pp. 181ff.

carried farther, and the relationship between such inquiry and the Christian Gospel of divine salvation.

The most obvious part of the inquiry concerns the difference between conscious and repressed guilt-feeling. Dr Weatherhead's long discussion of this matter raises many highly debateable theological issues, but his graphic description of scrupulosity and of the influence of repressed guilt-feeling upon psychosomatic health provides a forceful reminder of the way in which misguided zeal, on the part of Christians, may serve but to increase this repressed sense of guilt, and thereby increase mental and physical suffering. This peril has been stressed by Dr Weatherhead and by many other experts.

But there is another danger, perhaps even greater, of which less is said today. It is the danger of lulling men and women into a *false* sense of freedom from guilt; it is the danger of ignoring the existence of that deep *anxiety*, that dissatisfaction with oneself, which is the consequence of man's self-alienation from God. It must be stressed, once again, that the work of the psychiatrist, as of all who seek to help men and women toward health and well-being, is shaped by their understanding of what that well-being is. I am aware that some psychiatrists would deny that fact and would say that it is no part of their duty to help men toward a pre-determined goal of personality and character; they would conceive their task as simply to help each to be *himself*. But it must be retorted that even this conception of their task involves a theory about what man ought to be, even if it is a theory that he ought just to be what he is when freed from mental and physical abnormality. Even to believe in abnormality we must believe in the normal. The dreadful and inescapable responsibility of any human being who, in any way, influences his fellow men is that he is influencing them to be what, before such influence, they are not.

This digression was necessary in order that it may be stressed that the Christian, who believes that man was *made for* a life that is 'right with God', cannot acquiesce in any attempt to treat *all* human discontent, guilt-feeling and anxiety as 'much ado about nothing', or as neurotic symptoms that only need to be removed. It is interesting to find that certain writers who are not Christians are recognizing this danger. Mr Arthur Koestler, for example, raises the question whether one is ever justified in dismissing guilt-feelings—however unwarranted they may appear—as merely 'neurotic symptoms'. I am inclined to think that explanations which trace the subjective origins of guilt to an exacting super-ego acquired in early childhood are more or less correct as far as they go, but that they beg the question of the ethical significance of guilt, and of its creative aspect. Regarding the latter, I believe that if properly canalized, the consciousness of guilt may become a powerful and constructive driving force; and that the anguish which accompanies it should be regarded as income tax paid in emotional currency.[12]

The Freudian account of the origin of conscience is too well known to require repetition; however great divergence of opinion there may be about the details of this theory, it is, I think, impossible to doubt that much that we term 'conscience' is the result of fear of various authorities, fear that is buried within us. Erich Fromm, however, has suggested that in addition to this 'authoritarian conscience', there is a 'humanistic conscience', by which he means 'the reaction of our total personality to its proper functioning or dysfunctioning'.[13] Fromm, as a rationalist, believes that this 'conscience' is not only 'a reaction of ourselves to ourselves', but is also that which, if not suppressed, can be the stimulus to that self-salvation of which Fromm believes man to be capable.

Although the Christian cannot share Fromm's hopes of a godless solution to man's problems, there is much that he can learn from this penetrating study of the kind of guilt-feeling which is man's awareness that he is not what he should be, and of Fromm's description of the way in which this is often buried beneath the 'authoritarian conscience'. But whereas Fromm sees in this only man's guilt-feeling for 'not living up to his own expectations of himself',[14] the Christian believes that it springs from his failure to love, honour and obey God. It is just because man is not what he is *created* to be that he has this anxiety. There is much in common between Fromm's 'humanistic conscience' and Kierkegaard's study of *Angst* (Dread) and Despair. There is even more in common with Tillich's profound study of Anxiety.[15]

Perhaps, then, it is only when we consider the guilt-feeling which is better described as Anxiety that we become most aware

---

[12] *The Invisible Writing* (1954), p. 360.   [13] *Man for Himself* (1949), p. 158.
[14] ibid., p. 165. As Fromm notes (pp. 167ff.), Kafka's *The Trial* is a study of these two types of 'conscience'.
[15] Paul Tillich, *The Courage to Be* (1952).

of the danger to which I have referred, the danger of artificially removing all traces of this from man's conscious, and even (if that be possible) from his unconscious life. A too-ready assumption that neurotic symptoms must be removed *at all costs* is a dangerous aspect of some contemporary psychotherapeutic work. Tillich suggests that it was the profound anxiety produced, by the presence of Jesus, in the 'demoniacs' that revealed to them His messianic character, and he adds: 'The history of human culture proves that again and again neurotic anxiety breaks through the walls of ordinary self-affirmation and opens up the levels of reality which are normally hidden.'[16]

Yet the demoniacs, whether they be called neurotics, psychotics or by any other name, need to be helped. The peril, as well as the opportunity, is that, in our generation, so many, in so varied ways, are seeking to mend human minds. Freudian analysts and those who work with quite different psychological theories, physiological experimenters practising brain surgery, drug-treatment and the like, social welfare workers and political advocates of social security, are all at work seeking to dispel men's anxieties and fears and to give the troubled mind and conscience peace. All such ministries must be matters of deep concern to the Christian. It is not sufficient to say that individual Christians should be engaged in all such work; there is urgent need for corporate Christian thought about the true nature of anxiety and guilt-feelings. In this, as in all things, the Christian must be prepared to learn *facts* from those who do not share his faith, but the Christian cannot for one moment imagine that what he believes about God's purpose for man can be ignored without disaster to those whom we should all seek to help. The problem of how far man is helped to be what *God* means him to be by merely removing from him all sense of insecurity, guilt and anxiety is only part of a much larger problem that concerns all interference with human personality. But it is a fundamental part of the problem.

There are many false escapes from the kind of guilt-feeling that is now under discussion. There is the escape through self-justification (the Pharisee); there is the escape through collectivism, in which the individual delights in his guilt, whilst in another sense knowing his innocence, which is one of the most terrifying aspects

[16] Paul Tillich, p. 68. In the following paragraphs I am further indebted to this book.

of contemporary totalitarianism; there is the escape through the 'scapegoat' which may take many shapes; and (more difficult to express in words), there is the escape through surrender to one's guilt, which is part of the meaning of Nihilism and atheistic existentialism. There are, doubtless, many other avenues of escape from true guilt which we human beings seek and follow. The worst that can be said about these ways of escape is that they can be successful. That is why the Pharisee, with all his companions who seek the same end by varied routes, is in supreme peril. Not even God can save a man who refuses to recognize his need.

The old-fashioned notion of 'divine discontent' is by no means out-worn. Yet man is not delivered by despair, nor rescued by anxiety; it is not by introspecting his guilt-feeling that a man may come to spiritual health. There is, however, a guilt-feeling, an existential anxiety, which is perhaps the *point of contact* between God and man for which some contemporary theologians have sought. There is little that is flattering to man about this point of contact; it would indeed be more encouraging to his self-respect to find that point in his 'reason', or his virtues, or a religious 'instinct', rather than in his need. Yet it is his sense of *responsibility*, a sense which may be so deeply buried that we can only call it an 'unconscious' sense, manifesting itself in meaningless anxiety, which is the sign (if only he knew) that he was made 'in the image and likeness of God' and made to have fellowship with Him. It is little wonder that all men, and especially sophisticated, psychological, ethical men, seek to explain, or to explain away, this responsibility. Yet it is the life-line to his destiny. As William Temple used to say, man has nothing to contribute toward his salvation save his sins. But *that* he must contribute. Therefore, however greatly needed are all means of removing false guilt-feelings, the deepest need of man is to acknowledge his guilt.

v. 'THE BLESSED SENSE OF GUILT IMPART'

The conviction that we can discover, and thereby remove, our own guilt is part of the illusion that we are 'our own' and not God's. Therefore no peering into our guilt-feelings can explain them to us; nor, as we have previously seen, can any measuring of our offences disclose our sin to us. That is the seeming hopelessness of mankind; if knowledge were virtue, how different it would be for man! The problem of ignorance is no phantasy; sometimes the opponents of Christian truth recognize that problem more clearly than do some Christians. As in the days of His flesh, the enemies of Jesus still strangely understand Him even whilst they misunderstand.

There is no way that *man* can take out of this predicament. What he is meant to be, he cannot see, for it is exactly *that* which he is not. 'Sinful man is not "the real man" at all. The real man is the sinner who participates in God's grace.'[17] Yet it is when we confess our sins that God forgives us; how can we confess that which we know not?

The *good* news is that God can enable us to acknowledge our guilt. The most complete understanding of this fact is revealed in one of Charles Wesley's hymns, from which I cannot forbear lengthy quotation:

> *Give us ourselves and Thee to know,*
> *In this our gracious day;*
> *Repentance unto life bestow,*
> *And take our sins away.*
>
> *Conclude us first in unbelief,*
> *And freely then release;*
> *Fill every soul with sacred grief,*
> *And then with sacred peace.*
>
> *Impoverish, Lord, and then relieve,*
> *And then enrich the poor;*
> *The knowledge of our sickness give,*
> *The knowledge of our cure.*
>
> *That* blessèd *sense of guilt impart,*
> *And then remove the load* . . . (MHB 347).

Every word of that poem is chosen with consummate skill and with Wesley's characteristic Scriptural undertones. The questions which rise into all our minds, some of which have been the theme of this book—questions concerning our ignorance of God and of ourselves, our 'responsibility' and our 'free-will'—can never wholly be answered. If they are silenced without being answered, they only add to the weight of that deep self-pity which is itself a

[17] K. Barth, *Kirchliche Dogmatik*, III.2, 36.

SIN AND GUILT

symptom of our fallen manhood. But the questions can be transformed into the prayer: Give us ourselves and Thee to know.

Without the doctrine of the Holy Spirit, who convicts of sin, and of righteousness and of judgement, the Christian account of guilt is unintelligible; without the doctrine of redemption the Christian account of sin is incomprehensible. Bertrand Russell, with whose remarks this study began, was perfectly right in saying that the concept of *sin* is obscure; it is meaningless if we attempt to interpret it, as Russell does, in non-theological terms. It was with characteristic intellectual honesty that Russell expressed his doubt whether 'in my own view, there is a valid concept deserving to be called "sin" '. Neither was his logic at fault when, criticizing Tennant's definition of sin, he added: 'If "sin" means "disobedience to the known will of God" then clearly sin is impossible for those who do not believe in God or do not think that they know His will.'[18] The knowledge of sin is God's gift, as certainly as is His forgiveness.

In Chapter 8 no reference was made to the Words from the Cross: 'Father, forgive them, for they know not what they do' (Luke 23[34]). This silence was not due to doubt concerning the authenticity of this Saying,[19] but rather to a sense of the unfittingness of seeking to establish a theological theory upon words spoken by the dying Saviour. Yet those words cannot be forgotten. We cannot limit the purport of our Lord's petition to the soldiers and others who *least* understood what they were doing,[20] nor can we be content to find in them a proof 'that ignorance enters, as a palliating factor, into many sins, perhaps into all'.[21] Is it not the bitter truth that nobody knew what he was doing when he contributed to the death of Jesus, 'For if they had, they would not have crucified the Lord of glory' (1 Corinthians 2[8])?

None of us knows what he does when he sins; none, except the Christian who falls back into sin—*that* is the difference between 'Christian' sin and all other. God has innumerable ways of bringing his children in sight of Himself, so that they may become

---

[18] *Human Society in Ethics and Politics*, pp. 94f.
[19] The textual authority and the opinions of commentators upon this saying have been summarized by A. R. George, *Communion with God* (1953), pp. 47f. Mr George concludes: 'It seems more likely to be due to His insight than to that of the early Church.'
[20] F. R. Tennant, *Concept*, pp. 30f.
[21] H. R. Mackintosh, *The Christian Experience of Forgiveness*, p. 56.

able to recognize their guilt; but these ways are no more than a *preparation for the Gospel*, for the *Word* who is the Son of God. In the record of Calvary there is only one human being who discovered the truth about himself—a crucified thief who cried: 'Remember me!' Set within the drama of human redemption is that miniature, that play within the play, wherein is seen the Divine answer to man's desperate search for self-knowledge, as well as his deliverance from 'the trouble' that he has vainly tried to understand and remedy. Man calls that *'trouble'* by many names: Fate, Necessity, Ignorance, Finiteness, and many more. He learns that its name is *Sin* when the remedy is in sight. God, in His infinite mercy, does not allow his children to see their true guilt before the Saviour is in their view. (That is why we should not expect to find a fully Christian understanding of sin even in the Old Testament.)

> *Give us ourselves and Thee to know.*
> *In this our gracious day . . .*

Yet, even on that 'gracious day' God will not coerce us; he leaves us free to accept the horror of our sin whilst refusing the Saviour, he leaves us free *to be sinners*. But He never ceases to 'seek and to save them that are lost'. He makes the knowledge of our guilty sin available to us, and He says, as Jesus said: 'What do *you* think?'

CHAPTER ELEVEN

ACCEPTANCE OF THE FACT OF IGNORANCE

WE began this study by considering a number of related problems concerning our ignorance about ourselves, our neighbours and God. Our inquiry has brought us to the conclusion that ignorance is involved in all our sinning; we have seen that men lack the knowledge of what sin is, and that it is precisely this lack which the Gospel remedies. If this conclusion is true, it is no matter of detached, academic interest; it concerns the welfare and destiny of every human being, and it has consequences for every aspect of the Church's life and mission.

In these closing chapters we shall be concerned with some of those consequences, to which only passing reference has been previously made. It has often been said that a true theology is one that can be preached; it is equally true that no theological statement is without implicit reference to the daily life of mankind. What, then, is implied by the statement that we need to *learn* that we are sinners? It implies, in the first place, that Christians, and especially those who hold positions of leadership in the Church, must, without reservation, *accept* the fact of ignorance. I proceed to illustrate that need with reference to ourselves, to other people and to God.

I. IGNORANCE ABOUT MYSELF

Modern depth psychology has but served to increase our awareness of the limitations of introspection and our recognition that 'the heart is deceitful'. In earlier chapters, however, examples have been given of ways in which some Christian theologians tend to minimize the importance of these facts. That error, as we have seen, is encouraged by an ambiguous use of the term *voluntary*.

When it is claimed that only voluntary action can be judged sinful, it is often, quite wrongly, assumed that 'voluntary' implies both self-understanding and freedom from any kind of determination of the self other than that which is the result of past sins. Those past sins must, according to this theory, have themselves been 'voluntary', save in so far as they, too, were influenced by previous sins. We are thus involved in a regress which, if it is not artificially halted, takes us back to the experiences of infancy, in which the desired 'voluntariness' is conspicuously absent. At the root of this type of theory about sin lies a belief in indeterminism or libertarianism which must be totally abandoned. That necessity has been demonstrated, with freshness and humour, by Mr P. H. Nowell-Smith in his book, *Ethics*, in the 'Pelican' series. As he remarks, 'being self-determined implies only that a man acts freely in the ordinary sense of "freely" which the libertarian rejects as inadequate in the special case of moral choice'. 'I choose what I choose because my desires are what they are; and they have been moulded by countless influences from my birth or earlier.'[1] As Nowell-Smith rightly insists, those who would make *moral* choice an exception to this fact must prove their claim.

The traditional Christian belief in the bondage of the will, and those aspects of the idea of *original* sin which have to do with hereditary and environmental influences, are in harmony with this fact of *self*-determination; a theology which substitutes for such beliefs a doctrine of libertarianism is as psychologically false as it is theologically unsound. It is this *total* self of which we must think when we refer to self-determination, and much of it is hidden from my own observation. An interpretation of sin which focuses my attention only upon those aspects of my thought and behaviour which I myself most readily recognize as *my own* achieves exactly the opposite result from that intended by its advocates. As I attempt to examine and acknowledge my own motives, I excuse myself for all that my self-estimation judges to be 'unlike myself'. The self which is really *me* is ignored or disowned.

To what extent self-knowledge, in this deeper sense, is requisite is one of the most difficult questions about psychological wellbeing, and it is one to which the attention of professionally qualified students needs to be given even further. The layman is very apt to imagine that a Freudian or Jungian account of the phenomena summarized under the hypothesis of the unconscious are the only possible interpretations. MacMurray's explanation of the findings of psychoanalysis in terms of habit, and the theories of writers such as Melanie Klein, W. R. D. Fairbairn and others concerning the influence of 'internal object-relations' (that is, the

[1] op. cit., pp. 283, 279.

ACCEPTANCE OF THE FACT OF IGNORANCE

adult's inner world of relations to people who influenced him in his infancy), are but examples of other interpretations.[2] It has by no means been scientifically established that all that is buried 'in the depths of the mind' can or should be brought into the light of consciousness, yet there is much evidence to suggest that the techniques of psychoanalysis, perhaps in modified forms, will continue to play a part in the work of healing.

I think, however, that those who have the professional knowledge and skill might clarify for us, to a greater extent than has yet been done, the significance of what the analyst terms *transference*. It may be that the psychotherapist and the Christian pastor alike must see in the familiar fact of *transference* a clearly-recognizable symptom of the need of human beings for God. It is possible that the very proper desire to help men and women to become self-reliant may over-reach itself and become a hindrance to the way of living for which they were created. I imagine that the psychiatrist must often discover, as the Christian pastor certainly does, that both idol-worship and the attempt to be 'without God in the world' appear as deep-seated troubles, sometimes in the same person.

Comments such as these are no more than suggestions for expert examination, but two statements may be made with greater confidence. Firstly, there is need for acceptance of the truth about ourselves if we are to enter into the joy of sins forgiven. Secondly, there is need for recognition of the *limits* of such self-knowledge, and for full confidence in the power of God to refashion our inner life.

(*a*) If there is some doubt about the extent to which our 'unconscious' life needs to be brought into consciousness, there is no doubt whatsoever that any *fact* about myself that is, by any method, brought to my notice must be accepted by my consciousness. The refusal to do this not only lies at the root of much psychological abnormality but is also a supreme hindrance to Christian life. (This is but one reason for the urgent necessity for cooperation between psychiatrists and ministers of religion.)

One of the major considerations which lead me to think the Tennant-type of definition of sin injurious, as well as inadequate,

---

[2] cf. an illuminating summary by Nigel Walker, *The Listener*, 6th October 1955. For a discussion of the 'internal objects' theory by a Christian psychologist, cf. H. Guntrip, *Psychology for Ministers and Social Workers*, pp. 256ff.

is that it directs attention to the self that I 'know', and this is never the *true self*.

> *The self that can say, 'I want this—or want that'—*
> *The self that wills—he is a false creature;*
> *He has to come to terms in the end*
> *With the obstinate, the tougher self, who does not speak,*
> *Who never talks, who cannot argue.*[3]

It is, therefore, imperative that 'sin-sick' souls should not be further hurt by any action that would prevent them from 'coming to terms' with the truth about themselves.

This 'tougher self, who does not speak', is by no means inactive. Nobody who has listened to his fellow men in their hours of self-pity and self-fear, or who has known such hours himself, can fail to be aware of the misery suffered by those who 'feel' within them this other 'self'. It is not only those who suffer from serious mental afflictions, and not merely those who have been influenced by repressive and morbid types of religious teaching, who know much about the working of the 'obstinate' self; many, today, share the emotions of William Cowper, although they would be incapable of expressing them in similar language:

> *This heart, a fountain of vile thoughts,*
> *How does it overflow,*
> *While self upon the surface floats,*
> *Still bubbling from below.*[4]

It is not surprising, therefore, if those who have no understanding of either sin or the way of God's salvation take their problems to doctors and psychiatrists who clearly recognize the existence of 'the hidden depths', rather than to those who, in the name of Christ, offer only moralistic counsel and ethical judgement, and who insist upon the 'voluntary' nature of all their faults and troubles.

Yet it is not pity that we need, but healing, and for that healing it is necessary that we should accept, not grudgingly, the truth about ourselves. When I discover even part of the truth about myself, I recognize that I have by no means been wholly responsible for being what I have been and for becoming what I am. 'Responsible' in that context describes one who has deliberately

[3] T. S. Eliot, *The Cocktail Party*, I.2.   [4] *Olney Hymns*, No. 45.

and wittingly made himself what he is. But, in another sense of the term 'responsible', it is precisely my own responsibility that I recognize. That man who did that action, this man who is so utterly unlike what I thought myself to be, is myself. This gives me no cause for either excuse or blame.

Those who fear that the kind of self-knowledge which I am attempting to describe will lead to mere self-excuse must, I believe, be thinking about other people rather than about themselves. When I pay attention to myself, rather than to other people, I find that the more I know about myself the more fully do I recognize conscious, wholly deliberate, and fully understood thoughts and actions of mine which have been contrary to what I myself have believed to be right and good; nor have I ever met any human being who, in the moment of self-acceptance, did not share that recognition. The fear that, if we refuse to make a rigid distinction between sin and moral disease,[5] we shall prevent any acknowledgement of blame-worthiness is a theoretical fear.

On the contrary, acceptance of my real self is destructive of all pride. No longer can I boast of my wrong-doing. I have been mastered by myself—sin is greater than I. Moreover, what I have done and been, what I do and am, is inextricably bound up with the whole life of mankind. I come to see that I cannot say, 'my sin' without saying 'our sin'. The type of spiritual direction which encourages men and women to assess their own worth, so that they may see in themselves characteristics that merit praise and features that earn blame, is to be deplored. The more detached attitude of the physician is one that the Christian pastor may profitably emulate. Indeed, no man who has begun to recognize himself as a sinner—in the true sense of that term—can any longer thus measure his own character. He knows that this type of self-evaluation is itself a symptom of his egocentric refusal to recognize that he exists under the judgement of God alone.

(*b*) If it is needful that we should accept the truth about ourselves, so far as we can know it, it is no less imperative that we should recognize the limitations to that self-knowledge, and that we should have confidence in the power of God to remake the 'unknown' self. No more need be said here about the limits to self-knowledge, save to urge that we must not estimate these less lightly in relation to consciousness of sin than we do in reference

[5] By the method described in Chapter 6, *supra*.

to ordinary introspection; it must, on the contrary, be recognized that our knowledge of our own sinfulness is even more greatly limited than any other self-knowledge.

The term 'knowledge of sin', like 'ignorance of sin', has been employed very freely in previous pages and it contains an ambiguity of which previous warning was given. (See p. 14, *supra*.) I hope that it has now become plain that we cannot have 'knowledge of' sin—in the sense of acquaintance with our own sinfulness—unless we have 'knowledge about' sin—knowledge of what is meant by the word *sin*. In the former sense, we can never have *complete* 'knowledge of' sin, whether our own or our neighbour's.

If sin relates to character, to the total personality, it becomes plain that I can never wholly know myself. That is especially, but not exclusively, true when we consider the *enduring ego*—the man who is more than 'the man of the moment'. What do 'was' and 'am' and 'shall be' signify when I think about myself?

What kind of hieroglyphics are these, which we accept daily with so much certainty, as though they were not riddles and secrets, and by means of which we believe that we know all about what we are and what we experience? 'For we are but of yesterday, and know nothing', it is written in the Book of Job. These words have a much deeper meaning than we are always willing to admit. God alone knows what time really is, and thus He knows all about our 'then' and 'now' and 'I' both past and present.[6]

Again, if we take seriously the *solidarity* of sin, we cannot hope to comprehend our own sin without far greater understanding of other people then we possess. More important is the fact that, just as only the pure in heart can see God, so only the pure in heart can wholly recognize sin, including their own past sin.

Miss Dorothy Sayers, commenting on Canto xxxi of *Il Purgatorio*, has noted that Dante, although he had 'seen himself as he was' at Peter's Gate and repented, did not come to an overwhelming conviction of sin, and to an abject and passionate confession, until '*after* his (symbolical) purgation by the ascent of the Mountain'. Miss Sayers adds:

What is meant, I think, is that not until the state of innocence has been recovered can sin be apprehended in its full horror. So long as any taint of sinfulness remains, there is always something in the soul

[6] H. Gollwitzer, *Unwilling Journey* (1953), p. 310.

ACCEPTANCE OF THE FACT OF IGNORANCE

that still assents to sin; only when the last, lingering vestige of unconscious assent has been purged away can one see one's own sin as it appears to God. . . .[7]

Only Christ knew to the full what sin means; not even the repentant sinner can fathom the Cry of Dereliction. We may, and should, pray with Charles Wesley,

> *Show me as* my soul can bear
> *The depth of inbred sin—*

but there is a morbid type of craving for self-knowledge and a boastful way of pretending to 'sin-consciousness', which are inverted forms of the self-justification which is the supreme barrier to our salvation. It is not by knowledge of my sin that I am saved, but by the divine forgiveness and restoration of me—the sinner.

We must, therefore, as Christian believers, have no hesitation about the power of God to deal with the whole of our personality, including all that is hidden from our own observation and understanding. There appears to be considerable reluctance, on the part of some who fully accept the facts that are described under the term 'the unconscious', to stress this aspect of the work of God. When speaking of *justifying* grace, few Christians would limit the Divine work by man's ability to recognize what God is doing, and the concept of *prevenient* grace implies belief in the work of God that anticipates all conscious awareness on man's part. Why should there be hesitation in this respect about *sanctifying* grace? There are not different 'kinds' of grace; there are diverse operations of the same gracious activity of God.

Dr R. N. Flew and Dr W. E. Sangster have made searching and valuable criticisms of Welsey's definition of sin, to which I have previously referred. Flew briefly drew our attention to the significance of the faulty distinction between conscious and unconscious sin for Wesley's doctrine of perfection.[8] Sangster devoted considerable space to this matter in two books, but he shows, it seems to me, undue hesitation in following to its conclusion his own insight into this weakness in Wesley's idea of perfection. He evidences fear of stressing too greatly the power of God to work unbeknown by man. He is willing to reduce the conscious element

---

[7] *Il Purgatorio*, Trans. D. L. Sayers (Penguin Books), p. 319.
[8] *The Idea of Perfection*, pp. 134f; cf. p. 27, *supra*.

to 'a thousandth part'; he adds other qualifications; but he finds it impossible to refrain from stressing that 'our hand must lift the latch that lets God in'.[9] Elsewhere he writes:

No man can say to what depths of his being this holy influence may not extend but it only becomes a subject of full moral cognizance as it is willingly received into a mind which is aware and responsible.[10]

What—it is needful to ask—has 'full moral cognizance' to do with the *fact* of sanctification? I suspect that Sangster has in mind the Augustinian doctrine of irresistible grace, and wishes to avoid that error. But the error in that doctrine is the denial of man's power to resist God (although this power itself is God-given). We can say 'No' to God; any rejection of that truth makes nonsense of the Cross of Christ. This need not, and should not, lead to the assertion that we can, or should, always know what God is doing for us and in us.

We must, I believe, follow Sangster's own criticism of Wesley farther than he himself does. John Wesley's tendency (in his formal theology as distinct from many of his brother's hymns which he approved) to identify sin with *conscious* sin led him to identify perfection with the *absence* of conscious sins.[11] Thus he set before us an ideal of perfection which is both partial and dangerously apt to encourage a pharisaic type of self-appraisal. The desire to find some concept of perfection that permits of various types of non-sinful imperfection is still to be found in the writings of some Methodists;[12] the temptation to want to estimate the extent of God's work within us is still a temptation for all who seek the 'path to perfection'.

Most serious of all is the danger of equating conscious moral rectitude with that wholeness of character, and that completeness of dependence upon God, which are equally important meanings of sanctification. The hymn which reminds us, 'Thy kind but searching glance can *scan* The very wounds that shame would

---

[9] *The Pure in Heart*, p. 235. [10] *The Path to Perfection*, pp. 118ff.

[11] Wesley, as is well known, was not wholly consistent in this matter. In a letter (26th December 1761) he refers to the effect of *bodily* influences upon character, in a way that causes us to speculate about what his attitude would have been to modern psychiatric findings. But the remainder of the letter is both psychologically and theologically obscure (Standard Edition, IV.167).

[12] cf. J. H. J. Barker, *This is the Will of God* (1954), Chap. 9, 'Perfect but not Perfected'. For a more restrained discussion, see J. B. Atkinson, *The Beauty of Holiness* (1953), pp. 61ff.

ACCEPTANCE OF THE FACT OF IGNORANCE 169

hide', tells us but part of the truth. The re-creating grace of God can *heal* those wounds, although a man be unaware of the healing operation. So all-embracing is His work that it must be described by vivid metaphors of re-birth and re-creation; the totality of our sinfulness is met by the completeness of God's salvation. As the worst consequence of my self-estrangement from God is that I am self-estranged, so the perfection to which I am called is that of loving God with all my heart and mind and soul and strength. The removal of particular 'sins'—overwhelming as such a prospect appears to the sinner—is but a prelude to that one-ness with Him which is the meaning of my existence, the meaning that I have denied.

II. IGNORANCE ABOUT OTHER PEOPLE

All that has been said about ignorance concerning myself must be remembered when I think about other people; I must not, for example, demand from others a type of self-knowledge which I know to be impossible for myself. There are, however, additional consequences of the 'fact of ignorance' for the attitude of Christians to the sin of their neighbours.

Little further reflection is needed to recognize the limitations to our *moral* judgement upon other people. Even the moral evaluation of particular actions is a precarious task, but when judgement concerns character, the fallibility of man's moral assessment of his fellows becomes obvious to all but those who are either self-righteous or superficial in their thinking. It is not sufficient, however, to recognize this fact. Tennant, as I have repeatedly noted, clearly taught that only God can distinguish 'sin' from other 'moral imperfection', and H. D. Lewis, in *Morals and the New Theology*, freely admitted the difficulty of determining which actions are exclusively the fruit of wrong choices knowingly made. Lewis, however, like Tennant and all who agree with him, asserts that only such choices are sinful in God's sight. I have argued that this distinction, even when qualified by recognition of our inability to use it as a practical guide, is a hindrance rather than an aid to the Christian understanding of sin. If that is so, the Christian must recognize this truth whenever he regards other men and women as sinners.

The implications of our ignorance about other people, and of our recognition of the elements of both ignorance and impotence in their sinning, are varied. (*a*) In the first place we shall never be tempted to forget that judgement of sinners belongs to God alone. 'Judge not that ye be not judged' is one of the few explicit commandments of the Lord Jesus, and one of the most forgotten. I should not wish to minimize the right and duty of the Church to excommunicate, but I have been thankful, on the happily rare occasions when such an action has been taken by my own denomination, to join in prayer that God will over-rule the decision of the Church, if it has been wrongly made. Moreover, the corporate judgement of the Church is a very different matter from the kind of individual moral judgement which Christians sometimes claim the right to make.

(*b*) Secondly, we must not fall into the error of *minimizing*, when we regard the sin of others, the element of deliberate, fully aware choice of what is believed to be evil. Whether those who argue that no man can ever choose evil *as* evil are right I do not know; could I trust to introspection I should fear that they are wrong, and it appears to me that Tennant's statement that men can only choose evil '*in spite of* its being evil'[13] under-estimates the truth that men 'love the darkness rather than the light' (John 3^{19}). However that may be, the fear that if we recognize the existence of unconscious and unavoidable elements in all human thought and behaviour we shall remove any possibility that men will confess their guilt before God is, as I have previously argued, a fear that is dispelled by Christian experience.

All of us make excuses for ourselves; some of these excuses are based upon actualities, some are unjustifiable. When we are bidden to concentrate our attention upon the voluntariness of our actions ('voluntary' being interpreted in the libertarian way) we inevitably take comfort in our legitimate excuses and ignore our empty, fictitious excuses. This is the fact which makes the denunciatory aspect of the prophetic task of the Church both difficult and dangerous. That there is a place for such denunciation cannot be denied, although Christians, with monotonous consistency, are prone to denounce the type of offenders, and the kind of offence, which our Lord treated with gentleness, and to deal lightly with those that incurred His wrath. It must never be forgotten, however, that if denunciation could have sufficed there would have been no occasion for the death of Christ. The man who called

[13] *Concept*, p. 246; cf. p. 247.

ACCEPTANCE OF THE FACT OF IGNORANCE

himself 'a Pharisee, a son of Pharisees' was not saved by denunciation, but by the presence and power of the Lord whom he had, knowingly and unknowingly, persecuted.

(c) Perhaps we are nearest to the example of our Lord Himself when our denunciation is of offences that injure other people, and when our severity is toward those who are 'blinded' and 'hardened' by their own self-righteousness. For—and this is a further implication of our acceptance of such blindness—we must never allow ourselves to be content that men and women should 'sleep in their sins'. Tennant argues that an echo of Paul's reference to 'the times of ignorance' (Acts 17^{30}) is provided by Browning's words in *Ferishtah's Fancies*:

> Ask thy lone soul what laws are plain to thee,—
> Thee and no other,—stand or fall by them!
> That is the part for thee: regard all else
> For what it may be—*Time's* illusion. This
> Be sure of—ignorance that sins, is safe.[14]

Tennant emphasizes that there is a *guilty* ignorance which is 'without excuse', the result of 'indolence, indifference, or aversion to consequences'. But this assertion that 'ignorance that sins is safe' is the inevitable outcome of Tennant's whole position.

When sin is known to be man's self-alienation from God, when particular offences are seen to be manifestations of the self-love that has taken the place of love of God and love of our neighbour, when, therefore, man is recognized to be most truly sinful when he seeks to be 'as God' by claiming mastery over his own and his neighbour's destiny, then no sin is *safe*. That fact must be ever present in the minds of those whose duty it is to intercede for sinners and to speak to other men about their sin.

When sin is interpreted in purely moralistic terms, it is easy for us to lose sight of the fact that to tell men about their sinfulness is to bring them good news. That would not, of course, be true were it not for the proclamation of God's forgiveness and His victory over sin; nevertheless, we need to regain the conviction that it is *good* for men to learn the truth about their predicament, so that they may no longer walk in darkness. This was the conviction that dominated the mind of Paul, as of his fellow Christians. The opening chapters of Romans raise some of the questions about

[14] Quoted in *Concept*, p. 105.

personal responsibility and opportunity to know God which have been mentioned in these pages, but (as we saw in Chapter 8) Paul's dominant concern was not with these questions but with the urgent necessity to call men to repentance, to *metanoia*. For Paul, the announcement that men everywhere 'do not see fit to acknowledge God' (Romans 1^{28}) was but the prelude to the promise that they could 'have peace with God through our Lord Jesus Christ' (Romans 5^1). To Paul, as to John, it was the best of news that at last 'the light shines in the darkness, and the darkness has not overcome it' (John 1^5). The only dread possibility which remained was that men should love the darkness rather than the light.

I imagine that our Methodist forefathers, had they known that many of their twentieth-century successors would deem their attitude to sin morbid, would have been astonished. Did they not sing,

> *The people that in darkness lay,*
> *In sin and error's deadly shade,*
> *Have seen a glorious gospel day,*
> *In Jesu's lovely face displayed.* (MHB 379)

There is no uncertainty in the Wesley *hymns* about the ignorance of sin—

> *By Thy Spirit, Lord, reprove,*
> *All my inmost sins reveal.* (MHB 348)

We have no right to speak to men about their sins unless we know that we bring them good news; indeed, we cannot otherwise do so, for to know what sin means is to have unmasked man's true enemy.

(*d*) When considering the sin of others, as when repenting of his own, the Christian must also have in mind the *corporate* character of sin. In view of what has already been said, I need only comment that to take an exclusively individualistic attitude toward the sin of another man, even though it be motivated by the good intention of helping him toward conviction of sin, is to encourage in his mind an individualistic conception of salvation, which is a denial of the Gospel and which leads to many perversions of true Christianity. In a generation in which the pressure of world-events is toward a totalitarian type of society, a recognition of the corporate, yet truly *personal*, nature of both sin and salvation is specially important.

(*e*) For the attitude of the Christian to other people, the most significant consequence of 'the fact of ignorance' is that moral concern must become an expression of compassion rather than of censoriousness or contempt. We may see in once-familiar descriptions of the Christian ministry such as 'the cure of souls' and 'the office of a pastor', a conception of that ministry which has, perhaps, tended to be forgotten. Even the old evangelical phrase, 'a passion for souls', may serve as a rebuke to those of us who have allowed our ministry to be fully occupied with exhortation, organizing enthusiasm and amateurish psychiatric counsel. We have tended to forget that we minister to sin-*sick* men and women. The hardest word that I have ever heard spoken about the Church in our own country was spoken (in private) by a Christian leader who is honoured by us all. He said: 'The Church in this country is better known for its faith than for its love.' Can it be denied that we constantly reprove when we should comfort, tolerate when we should both disturb and entreat, denounce sin when we should love sinners?

Whether the extent to which mental and physical disorder affects human thought and behaviour becomes more fully understood depends upon progress in the sciences that deal with such matters. If, in an earlier chapter, I rejected one particular method of distinguishing moral disease from sin, that rejection led to the recognition of the element of disease in *all* sin, rather than to the denial of 'moral disease'. In a fully Christian community, all who were engaged in the ministry of healing would know themselves to be the servants of Christ, and suffering men and women would no longer be subject to rival and antagonistic ministrations. That day has not yet come, but its advent will not be hastened if Christians fail to recognize the element of sickness in all sinning; neither will the fullness of healing be found if it is forgotten that man's greatest need is to know his sins forgiven. 'Whether is easier, to say, Thy sins are forgiven, or to say, Arise . . . walk?'

III. IGNORANCE ABOUT GOD

The Christian believer, especially when he is regarding the sin of other people, must also accept without reservation the facts about ignorance of God. Such acceptance involves more than the acknowledgement of diverse opportunities to know about God as

He is revealed in His 'mighty acts' recorded in Holy Scripture; it is equally necessary to appreciate that many people have been quite unaware that they have sinned against *God*, and that all of us, as sinners, have been ignorant about the extent of our unbelief.

The description of sin as *unbelief* leads to much misunderstanding which arises in two ways, and about each of these something must now be said, although full discussion would carry us far beyond the scope of this book. (1) There is possibility of confusion concerning the *intellectual* aspect of belief, and (2) there is need to appreciate that unbelief, lack of faith in God, is not a merely *negative* description of sin.

(1) Gustaf Aulén (to whom I am especially indebted in this section) remarks that 'the meaning of sin as unbelief is . . . the chief problem', and he suggests that this problem is insoluble 'if "faith" consists primarily in an intellectual acceptance of certain statements about God'.[15] With that comment I am in agreement, provided that it is fully recognized that 'the acceptance of certain statements about God' is *part* of the meaning of faith. The ambiguity in the terms 'knowledge of' and 'ignorance of', to which reference has previously been made, is again brought to our notice by the frequently made distinction between *knowledge about* God and *knowledge of* God. I presume that the same distinction is implied when *belief in* is contrasted with *experience of*, and also when *belief* is itself contrasted with *faith*. It is a sound rule to assume that frequently-made linguistic distinctions are made with a purpose and therefore have some claim to be considered necessary, but it is never wise to accept them uncritically. This particular differentiation calls for careful criticism.

Apart from the fact that the verbal contrast between belief and faith is out of harmony with general New Testament usage,[16] there is implied in the various pairs of contrasted terms that I have mentioned a false isolation of conceptual thought from other mental processes. This is yet another example of the type of

[15] *The Faith of the Christian Church*, p. 262f.

[16] cf. *TWB*, Article, 'Faith'. There are, of course, a number of suggestive facts about New Testament usage, such as the uses of *pisteuein* followed by a dative and by a preposition, and the fact that the two concepts of *credence* and *confidence* 'are more closely related' in the Fourth Gospel than elsewhere in the New Testament (W. F. Howard, *Christianity according to St John*', pp. 156f). But the simple fact that *pistis* is translated by 'faith' and *pisteuein* by 'to believe' is often forgotten, especially in popular exposition of the New Testament.

ACCEPTANCE OF THE FACT OF IGNORANCE

faculty psychology which we have previously encountered. Thinking, feeling and willing (to use the familiar words) are distinguishable, and from the point of view of conscious-awareness, one or other of these may be very faintly recognized, but the notion that there is any kind of belief or faith which does not involve an element of *thinking about* must be rejected. Similarly there is no *belief about* which does not involve some degree of feeling and willing. It is not necessary for us to inquire whether there are any exceptions to these general rules (I do not think that there are), for we are discussing belief (faith) in *God*. Faith in God cannot be wholly compared with any other act of faith. That is not, as is often mistakenly assumed, because some peculiar psychic faculty is operative in religious faith; it is because God Himself is unique that faith in Him is distinguishable from any other act of faith.

Faith (belief) in God means treating Him *as God*, that is to say, as Creator, Ruler, Judge and Saviour. It is possible for the believer to adopt an attitude of antagonism toward the God in whom he believes—that is why certain types of atheism, as contrasted with agnosticism, have the appearance of what may be described as *perverted faith*. Nobody believes in God more firmly than does the man who says 'Thou shalt not be *my* God'. James 2[19], 'Even the demons believe—and shudder', is often cited as proof of the difference between belief and faith, whereas it is a terrible description of the rejection of a God who is recognized as God. James was illustrating the contrast between true, living faith and dead, pseudo-faith, but it may be permissible to comment that, when we recall the activities of the 'demons', this picture of their shuddering faith may be taken as the equivalent in the realm of discarnate beings to the human sin against the Holy Ghost, the only sin in which there is no degree of ignorance.

There is, therefore, a valid distinction between actual faith, which treats God as God, and pseudo-faith, which is another name for lip-service. But in all faith there is a necessary element of *belief about;* theological concepts, however rudimentary, are involved in any faith. On the other hand, no kind of actual belief or faith in God is possible without the adoption by the believer of some attitude toward God, even if that attitude be one of enmity.

It is important to refrain from contrasting intellectual belief and faith for two reasons: Firstly, by so doing we run the risk of forgetting that many people whose beliefs about God are nebulous or even false, when compared with Christian beliefs, are nearer to the faith that God requires than are some who have learnt much more about Him. Secondly, the alleged contrast between thought and faith is liable to encourage a search for some type of mystical experience as the normal and essential type of Christian faith.

The notoriously vague term *mysticism* is best reserved for religious experience which does not involve conceptual thought. Only a mystic can assure us that such is possible; the rest of us can neither deny nor affirm that it is. It must be noted, however, that as soon as the mystic seeks to report his experience, he makes use of intellectual concepts, that is, of the theological ideas with which he and his hearers are familiar. More important is the fact that Christian faith—the faith needful for salvation—is not to be identified with mysticism. If Paul in 2 Corinthians 12^{3ff} was referring to a mystical experience, it is noteworthy that he said that it was impossible for him to describe it; he did not suggest that such experience was essential to, or normative of, Christian life.

In the previous paragraphs I have been seeking to make one point, and I do not wish to minimize the reality, and (for those who are thus favoured by God) the significance of the 'glimpses of His presence' which God sometimes grants to some of His children. I remember hearing William Temple say that such moments, although of sublime worth to the experiencer, have not been granted very often even to the greatest of the saints, nor have those who experienced them proffered them as evidences for the validity of Christian faith. St Paul himself, unlike many of his readers in modern times, did not invite men and women to share his 'Damascus-road experience'; he pointed to that event as proof of his own peculiar place in the apostleship, but he invited all men to believe in the same Lord Jesus and to trust in His work for and within them. I suspect that some who draw a sharp contrast between 'experience of' and 'belief about' God are wishful for the vision of God which awaits us in heaven, rather than for the 'communion' with Him which is promised to us here on earth.[17] If many hours spent in trying to help people who have been seeking an experience of God which does not require thought about Him has led me to exaggerate this point, the reader will correct the exaggeration, but the urgency of the Church's mission will

[17] See A. R. George, *Communion with God, passim.*

never weigh upon us as it should if we forget that men must learn about Him in who they are to believe.

How are men to call upon him in whom they have not believed? And how are they to believe in him of whom they have never heard? And how are they to hear without a preacher? (Romans 10^{14}).

(2) The second risk of misunderstanding concerning the nature of sin as unbelief lies in the ease with which unbelief is taken to be a merely *negative* fact, so that sin becomes a negation rather than a positive act. This error is due to forgetfulness of the total character of faith itself.

In the previous section we noticed that there is no belief (or faith) in God which does not involve 'taking up an attitude toward Him'. That was a somewhat simplified method of describing faith as a total response by man to God. Faith is, as Dr H. F. Lovell Cocks has said, not a prelude to the Christian life; it *is* the Christian life. 'Faith *is* adoration ... prayer ... obedience ... communion with God ... Faith is an act.'[18] That is a description of 'saving faith', of the faith which God requires from us and which He makes possible for us. It is only God who can make this faith possible; if we say *sola fide* without implying *sola gratia*, we turn the truth into a lie.[19]

The opposite of faith is, therefore, not a mere negation; unbelief is but a negative description of a positive way of living. Man, created to love God and his neighbour, lives *incurvatus in se*—turned in on himself; subject to the sovereignty of God, he pretends to self-dominion; destined to be an obedient and loving child of the Father, he behaves as though he were a neglected orphan.

This unbelief manifests itself in many diverse ways, but not by some causal process, as though something called *sin* caused actions called x, y, z—we have seen the need to rid ourselves of this vague causal concept. Loving himself, man is lustful in a thousand ways; seeking to determine his own destiny, he offends against the reality of his own nature, his neighbour's nature and the nature of the rest of the created universe. The workings of his pride and sensuality are multitudinous, but his sin is seen most clearly in his ethical arrogance and in his idolatry. The injunction, 'Little

---

[18] *By Faith Alone* (1943), Chap. 8.
[19] cf. Philip S. Watson, *Let God be God*, p. 61 *et passim*, for a refutation of the opinion that Luther's doctrine of faith issued in salvation by works.

children, keep yourselves from idols' (1 John 5[21]) is among the last words of Scripture. Many a humble agnostic, worshipping an unknown God, is nearer to the Kingdom of God than is a theologian confident in *his* theology.

'Whatever does not proceed from faith is sin' (Romans 14[23]). That truth is only known *to* faith, and that is why we need to be brought to know our sins by being restored to God. Knowingly and unknowingly, we do not 'see fit to acknowledge God'; we only begin to comprehend this fact when 'we have peace with God through our Lord Jesus Christ'.

Intruding repeatedly in the mind of the writer of the preceding pages, as, perhaps, in the mind of the reader, was the familiar question about *guilt*. How can men be blamed for this unbelief? I shall not return upon my tracks and repeat what I have previously said, for it must be now quite evident why I have felt it needful to give repeated reminders of the obvious truth that we cannot measure the sinfulness of our neighbours. If sin has to do with man's relationship with God, it is abundantly plain that only God can estimate that relationship. New Testament teaching about the judgement of God upon those who have had most opportunity to recognize Him in Jesus Christ must never be forgotten, but further speculation concerning His judgement of our fellow-men would be of little profit. To the non-believer, questions about how God judges him can be of little interest, and how we may judge his sin ought not to concern him. From the point of view of the believer, anxiety about God's judgement is but evidence of lack of trust in God's wisdom and justice, and serves but to lessen obedience to the command to preach the Gospel to all creatures, whilst yet there is time.

CHAPTER TWELVE

SOME FURTHER CONCLUSIONS AND QUESTIONS

THERE are several further conclusions which, I believe, follow upon what has been said about sin in this book. It may be that some of these conclusions are falsely drawn; it will be apparent that many of them take the form of question rather than assertion. One of the purposes of any inquiry, in any field of study, is the search for further questions, because firstly, we are prone to ask trivial, inadequate or even false questions and need to discover the important ones, and secondly, the answers that we reach very greatly depend upon the questions that we ask. When we brought our contemporary questions to the Old and New Testaments we discovered that some appeared trivial whilst others required to be modified; we also found it necessary to ask additional questions. We found, for example, that we cannot ask questions that are appropriate to the study of sin unless we ask questions about God and about man's relationship to Him. Yet, important as it is to ask appropriate questions, it is no less necessary to recollect that there are other questions to which other answers will be found.

Theologians, pastors and all thoughtful Christians must constantly be aware of the many points of view from which questions need to be asked, and they should not expect that answers to one set of questions will be identical with those that belong to a different set. Much confusion will be avoided, for example, if the Christian pastor, when contemplating or exercising his specific function, fully recognizes that he is asking different questions from those properly asked by the psychiatrist, and that, at least in the present stage of knowledge, the questions and answers that belong to varied types of psychological research will differ from each other. Nor is it sufficient for students in one area of inquiry to respect the points of view taken by their colleagues in other spheres of study; the fact that all questions over-lap is equally important. The confidence that reality is a *whole* is shared by theists and non-theists, and if for the believer in God this confidence is part of his faith in God, that faith should both prevent fearfulness when alleged facts appear to be contradictory and give humility and zest to his search for knowledge. Both the wholeness of truth and the varied character of man's ways of seeking it must ever be born in mind. The Christian believes that Everyman is a sinner, but this does not imply that sin is the whole truth about him, nor that the questions which yield answers about sin are the only questions requiring an answer.

But, whilst it must be denied that man's sinfulness is the whole truth about him, it must be affirmed—if the Christian understanding of sin is accepted—that his sinfulness is a fact about the *whole man* and about *mankind as a whole*. It is for this reason that Christian assertions about sin must always appear, to one who misunderstands or rejects them, to provide a glaring example of the specialist failing to keep to his proper sphere. It is exactly that impression which is made upon the 'humanistic' moralist or psychologist, as well as upon many others. Many would grant that sin belongs to the vocabulary of religion but would argue that religion, along with its vocabulary, must keep to its proper place. The Christian, however, rejects the concept of a religion that can be departmentalized. It is well, therefore, to inquire how it is that the truth about sin has to do with all human thought and behaviour, although it is not the whole truth.

I have rejected any reply to this query that involves the assumption that sin is nothing but deliberate disobedience to the known will of God, and the mere assertion that men everywhere do wrong actions provides only a superficial answer. But if it be true that men both think and behave in opposition to the *actuality of their own nature*, then both their conduct and their understanding of the reality which they seek to interpret are perverted. This is the belief that is somewhat concealed in the term *total depravity*. If that belief is false, the antagonism with which many receive it is well deserved; if it is true, its significance cannot be overestimated.

The Christian believes that *what man is* has been made known to us through the revealing acts of God which are recorded in the Bible; he further believes that the power to *become what he is* has been made available to man through the work of Jesus Christ and the gift of the Holy Spirit. This belief is exemplified by the way in which the New Testament writers speak of God as our Father yet teach that we must *become* His children. This New Testament insight is often obscured in contemporary evangelism, but it is unmistakable in the Bible itself. Men need to become what they are; the children of the Father must be adopted, born again; they must receive *exousia* to become children of God (John 1¹²). It is because God is creator, upholder and redeemer of all life that questions about sin provide answers that are relevant to every aspect of human experience. This statement, however, is distorted if a false understanding of sin is operative. A purely moralistic, legalistic, or (using the term in the sense that I have described and rejected) 'voluntary' concept of sin is too small to embrace all human activity.

If Christian thought is to remain faithful to the biblical doctrine of the *total* character of sin, without falling into the error of making a partial truth carry universal significance, full weight must be attached to several of the characteristics of sin which have been discussed in previous chapters. It is to these, and to the conclusions and further questions which they suggest, that I now turn, and, for the reasons that I have given, we shall not be surprised if many of these questions direct our attention far beyond the study of sin.

I. GOD AND SIN

F. D. Maurice's criticism of early Methodism has often been quoted, but has never, to my knowledge, been subjected to careful historical examination. Maurice said of eighteenth-century Methodism: 'It made the sinful man and not the God of all Grace the Foundation of Christian Theology.'[1] To what degree that judgement is true some student of historical theology might fruitfully inquire. I only wish to emphasize how deplorable would be any such reversal of priority in Christian theological statement and—by implication—in Christian living. Maurice's comment must be interpreted in the light of his own expressed purpose:

My desire is to ground all theology upon the name of God the Father, the Son, and the Holy Ghost; not to begin from ourselves and our sins; not to measure the straight line by the crooked one. This is

---

[1] *Theological Essays* (1871), p. xvi. Contrast the comment of G. C. Cell: 'The picture of that revolution [wrought in Wesley's teaching] was the radical shift of the centre of gravity in preaching from a humanistic doctrine of faith to the meaning of God in Christian experience.' (*The Rediscovery of John Wesley*, p. 272.)

the method which I have learnt from the Bible. There everything proceeds from God. . . .[2]

If sin is 'egocentric unbelief', the futility of grounding theology in sin becomes unmistakably clear. The importance of recognizing that the word *sin* belongs exclusively to the vocabulary of religion, lies in the fact that knowledge *about* sin, as well as the acknowledgement of my own sin, is the result of, rather than the way to, faith in God.

I do not suggest that the term *sin* can be moved into the background of Christian propaganda, but I do suggest that our use of it should be much more cautious, less promiscuous and more fully explained than is now common. Several facts to which attention has previously been drawn point to this need for care. The absence from both the Old Testament and the recorded teaching of Jesus of any one, dominant term for sin, the fluidity of terminology even in St Paul's writings, and the diverse uses of the term by Christian teachers of later generations (only some of which we have noted) should prepare us to recognize that, so far from being one of the simpler words that Christians employ, *sin* has become a very vague word. A careful factual inquiry about the meanings which the word possesses for various groups of our contemporaries would, I suspect, provide information of considerable interest.

Problems about language cannot be too seriously estimated by those who believe that men need to hear or read a Gospel, but even more important is the nature of that Gospel itself. Recent study of the primitive *kerygma* has reinforced Christian conviction that this Gospel does not consist in moral exhortations, although it does include the proclamation of a new way of life (see pp. 135ff, *supra*). All too often, we reverse the method of the primitive Church and offer ethical reproof and advice to the unbeliever whilst we confine the instruction of the faithful to a reiteration of the *kerygma*. Our rightful reason for claiming the attention of the non-Christian is that we are able to tell him about God.

This we must do, whether he hears or whether he refuses to hear (Ezekiel 2 and 3), but we have not even begun to fulfil our mission when we have told him that he and his neighbours are doing evil deeds, a fact of which he is probably well

[2] *The Doctrine of Sacrifice*, p. xii. See discussion by A. R. Vidler, *The Theology of F. D. Maurice* (1940), p. 40.

aware. Whatever may have been the faults of the first Methodists, none of their successors (nor, I venture to suspect, their fellow Christians) can escape the need to ask whether they are not today more ready to diagnose (more or less successfully) moral evil (especially that of 'the world') than to make known, with humble confidence and compassionate concern, the Name of the unknown God. To repeat a previous question, have we not tended to forget that we bring good news about sin because we announce both what it means to be a sinner and that sinners have been redeemed?

If this essential evangelistic task of the Church is to be pursued, we must not ignore another conclusion about the nature of sin which I have repeatedly mentioned. We must never, as evangelists, attempt to estimate the sinfulness of other people. How far they are in fact rejecting what they have apprehended of the Divine nature, or to what extent they have already responded to God, we can never know. Many an 'atheist' is rejecting false conceptions of God which he assumes to be Christian beliefs about Him; many an agnostic has a reverence for the unknown God which puts to shame the pride of a superficial dogmatist. A remark made by Karl Barth in the heat of controversy should, perhaps, not be taken as a generalization, but I think that the immediate disagreement with which many of us read it is modified by reflection:

In my experience the best way of dealing with 'unbelievers' and modern youth is not to try to bring out their 'capacity for revelation', but to treat them quietly, simply (remembering that Christ has died and risen also for them), as if their rejection of 'Christianity' was not to be taken seriously. It is only then that they can understand you, since they really see you where you maintain that you are standing as an evangelical theologian: on the ground of justification by faith alone.[3]

Of two facts the Christian is, by faith, certain whenever he regards his fellow: there is no man who has not in some measure rejected God, and there is no man for whom the news about God as He is manifested in Jesus Christ is not a matter of supreme importance. These two certainties provide the sole and sufficient justification for an evangelism which must, to the unbeliever, always appear to be presumptuous.

Because Christians believe that man can only become what God

[3] *Natural Theology*, Trans. P. Fraenkel (1946), p. 127.

intends him to be when he is reconciled to God, they must deem it much more important that this should happen than that a man should learn the truth about himself. The 'sense of sin' is not the goal of repentance, neither is it the cause of repentance. We are truly sorry for our sins because we are made-at-one with God; we know what we *are* only when we are reconciled to God. This is why, as many very experienced Christians have noted, a deep awareness of sin is by no means always a prelude to conversion. Is there not some danger that the pre-conversion experiences of, for example, Luther and Augustine may be assumed to be a necessary stage in salvation?

The classical records of the religious experience of Luther and Augustine, as of Wesley and Paul, are the stories of men who, prior to the liberation that came to them through the knowledge that man is saved by grace alone, had been intensely religious men, devout believers in God and strenuous seekers after freedom from sin. It is, I believe, erroneous to assume that the processes of thought, and the types of emotions, which men such as these experienced should be shared by all men. Nor do the records of the lives of Christians in all periods of history support such an assumption. Ever since William James wrote his famous study of conversion, interest in the psychological processes involved in religious, as in any other, conversion has attracted too great attention. If John Wesley in his *Journal* seems sometimes to have anticipated that excessive interest in his preaching and teaching, he preferred, as he himself wrote, to use more scriptural words than the term conversion.[4] Moreover, neither Wesley nor Luther nor even St Paul preached to a generation that was conditioned by godlessness as is our generation over a large part of the world.

It is by faith in God's redeeming mercy, not by recognition of their own evil ways, that men and women are saved, and the task of Christian evangelism is that of making God known. I suggest that we have not completely adjusted our evangelical methods to the situation in which we exist. Is there not need, for example, for much preparatory work, if the minds of modern men, nurtured from birth, as multitudes are, to assume that God does not exist, are to be helped to believe in Him? This task must be pursued in many ways and on many levels, but I suggest that it will include

[4] See my discussion of the use of the term 'conversion', *London Quarterly and Holborn Review* (January 1942), pp. 45ff.

SOME FURTHER CONCLUSIONS AND QUESTIONS 185

the work of specialists able both to join in and to learn from the contemporary discussion about theological language. The Christian is unable to pretend that when he speaks about God he is speaking nonsense, but he may have much to learn from those who want to understand what he is talking about. At a different level, is there not room for a revised form of the teleological argument offered, not as a 'proof' of God's existence, but as evidence that the *denial* of His existence is not an essential characteristic of intellectual honesty?[5] Other methods of preparation for the Gospel must be adapted to the needs of those who have less capacity for conceptual thought, but all that can be done to break through the presuppositions of the unbeliever must be attempted.

Yet all this is but a preface to the proclamation to which the Church is commissioned, and that proclamation is about Jesus Christ. There are theological tendencies today which are liable, I believe, to substitute dogmatic generalizations about 'God' for that showing forth of God-in-Christ which is the theme of the New Testament and the supreme responsibility of all Christians. The word *God* is as obscure as is the word *sin*, and the false meanings that are evoked by *sin* are matched by those called up in men's minds by *God*. The impotence of much Christian propaganda is due to the fact that whilst much is said little is made plain. It is very easy for us to prevent men from being confronted by God because we are focusing their eyes upon their own offences; it is even easier for us to conceal God behind our statements about Him. There are few more humbling and rewarding Bible-studies that a Christian advocate can make than is provided by a study of the New Testament references to the *Name* of Jesus.

Before we conclude this brief discussion of evangelism, we may recall the distinction between the Pharisees and 'the sinners', to which reference was made earlier (pp. 106ff, *supra*). Whilst our Lord treated both alike in their need for salvation, and thereby destroyed the concept of sin as a generic classification, He did not speak and behave toward Pharisees and 'sinners' in the same way. I think that much may be learnt from this fact. Wesley, Luther,

[5] F. R. Tennant's large-scale presentation of this 'wider teleological argument' (*Philosophical Theology*, Vol. 11, chap. 4 *et passim*) was offered not as a proof but as grounds for reasonable 'certitude'. Even if our purpose be the slighter one of removing apparent obstacles to belief in God, there is much in Tennant's argument which deserves more attention than it has received.

N*

and Augustine, prior to the decisive period in each of their lives, had much in common with Paul the Pharisee. Luther and Wesley clearly recognized this affinity; Augustine, I conjecture, had been more of a Pharisee and less of 'a sinner' than he realized. It is no accident of history that we can trace the influence of Romans and Galatians through Augustine and Luther to Wesley. It is always the Pharisee type for whom the recognition of both God's grace and the true meaning of sin is most difficult and most painful. Is it unseemly to suggest that it is because very many of us preachers belong to the same type that we most often preach to those who are like ourselves? How few of us have ever fully understood why our Lord was called the friend of sinners!

II. SIN AND MORALITY

The comments that I have made in the previous section may be criticized as showing a dangerous toleration of moral evil and a forgetfulness of the duty of the Christian to condemn sin, however greatly he loves the sinner. This criticism must be treated with respect, for one of the tests of the validity of any interpretation of the Christian doctrine of sin is the seriousness with which it treats moral evil. If the interpretation that I have set forth is not to merit this type of criticism we must do full justice to both the distinction and the relationship between sin and moral evil; in particular, we must recall the difference between remorse and repentance, and the association of *didache* with *kerygma*. Several conclusions, and a number of questions that require further consideration, follow upon what has been previously said about each of these matters.

When repentance is identified with remorse, true repentance becomes impossible; the hopeless 'sinner', whose crimes have become an intolerable burden of guilt, stands alongside the 'Pharisee', who is confident that he has won forgiveness for all his sins; but the door of repentance, which leads to the knowledge of sin as well as salvation, is fastened shut against the Pharisee. Once again I ask a question which I am not competent to answer: Are there not many ways in which present-day Christian witness, both individual and corporate, should reflect these truths more clearly? When we think of ourselves as sinners, rather than as Christian witnesses, the manifold ways in which a 'sense of sin'

SOME FURTHER CONCLUSIONS AND QUESTIONS 187

can be a barrier to repentance and faith become plain. The only actual hindrance to our salvation—that is, the only hindrance which God permits to be a real rather than an imaginary one—is our refusal to accept the salvation which has already been won for us and all mankind. Such refusal may be due to a belief that we cannot be forgiven, or to a confidence that we no longer need to be forgiven because we have in some way 'atoned' for our sins.

Sin is not seen to be what it is until the divine forgiveness is, at least, in sight. Some words of Kierkegaard are apposite, although I have somewhat torn them from their context:

> Is there not a secret relationship between sin and forgiveness? When a sin is not forgiven it demands punishment; it cries to men or to God for punishment; but when a sin cries for punishment, then it looks different, far greater than when the same sin is forgiven.

Kierkegaard was well aware that those last words would sound false; surely, it would be asked, we only know how great our sin is when we have been forgiven? He explained his remark thus:

> Is this only an optical illusion? No it is actually so. It is, to use a rather imperfect figure, not an optical illusion that a sore which has looked dreadful, after the doctor has drained and treated it looks far less dreadful, although it is, nevertheless, the same sore. What does the one who refuses forgiveness do? He increases the sin, he makes it greater.[6]

Much that was said in Chapter 10 about guilt is relevant at this point. A false 'sense of guilt' is equally inimical to the knowledge of sin whether it takes the form of despair about our lot, or of pride that we need no longer judge ourselves guilty. The implications of this fact, both for our personal lives and for our Christian preaching and service, provoke questions upon which I must not enlarge, save to say that they recall us to the truth that it is only the Holy Spirit who convicts of sin, of righteousness and of judgement (John 16[8ff]).

It is equally important, if our concept of sin is not to involve minimizing moral evil, that we hold fast to the relationship between *kerygma* and *didache* (see pp. 137ff). Christian history offers us many warnings of three types of error into which we may fall. There is the danger of *antinomianism*, the denial of the moral

---

[6] *Works of Love*, quoted from *A Kierkegaard Anthology* (Edited Robert Bretall [1947]), p. 320.

law by those who claim to accept the gospel; there is *ethical indifference*, the lack of interest in moral problems and duties shown by some professing Christians; there is a type of '*perfectionism*' which holds that the 'saved man'—or one who has received a 'second blessing'—has been delivered from moral problems, moral faults, and strenuous moral endeavour.

Against all these errors the fact that the Christian gospel includes the announcement of a new and authoritative moral teaching is a salutary warning. A declaration that man is offered divine pardon and restoration to one-ness with God would be less than true to the gospel itself if it did not include the summons to a new way of life. If *didache* without *kerygma* is impotent, *kerygma* without *didache* is false; Christian life is both a new birth and a new way. Once again, considerations such as these suggest many questions which I can merely indicate. Let us, therefore, look briefly at each of the errors that I have mentioned.

In opposition to *antinomianism* we require sustained Christian thinking about the doctrine of justification, but there is also especial need for deeper comprehension of the Christian doctrine of justice and law. We may hope much from the ecumenical discussion of the latter subject which is now taking place.[7] The 'Protestant' has often been too readily content with protest against 'Catholic' beliefs about 'natural law'.

Ethical indifference is a shameful fault in a follower of Jesus, and what most needs to be said on this matter was said by our Lord Himself in much of His teaching. It is only about this indifference as it is associated with thought about sin that I have any comment to make. About this, as about many other matters, it is seemly for me to refer only to the part of Christ's Church in which I live; one of the bitter fruits of disunity is that we can neither rightly criticize nor truly learn from Christians with whom we do not live in common worship; we can but invite others to ask themselves questions which we ask ourselves. In the denomination in which I have been privileged to receive the grace of God, have not careful moral teaching, detailed and honest corporate examination of complex moral problems, and—above all—painstaking pursuit of the good life, made in true fellowship which includes discipline, become less familiar aspects of our Church-life? Have we not, in recent years,

---

[7] cf. *The Biblical Doctrine of Justice and Law* (1955; the Report of a Group set up by the World Council of Churches), Eng. Trans. by W. A. Whitehouse.

preached Romans 1-11 more often than Romans 12-16? And have we not, in so doing, obscured much of the meaning of the Gospel itself as well as forgotten much of the 'Teaching'? John Wesley was never a more faithful servant of Christ than when he sought to fashion the structure of the Methodist societies so that it might truly be said of their members:

They were built up in our most holy faith. They rejoiced in the Lord more abundantly. They were strengthened in love, and more effectually provoked to abound in every good work.[8]

The third error that I have mentioned is less easy to describe. A doctrine, or unformulated assumption, that 'the saved' man both knows what he ought to do and necessarily does it is not the prerogative of perfectionist sects. It is a falsity against which the 'evangelical' Christian must ever be on guard, but—to employ once more the unhappy mis-use of the word 'evangelical'—it is not only the 'evangelical' who must be wary.

The Christian understanding of *conscience* calls, I believe, for very much closer examination than it often receives, and Mr C. A. Pierce has recently provided us with a basis for such discussion.[9] His book consists of detailed linguistic study, and is therefore one which can only be accurately estimated by those who share the author's scholarship. But, however necessary it may be to await critical judgement upon some of his detailed exposition, he seems to me to have established a fact of considerable importance. The New Testament use of *suneidesis* provides no warrant for those who would make conscience the sole determiner of action, whether in all men or in 'the saved'. 'Conscience in the New Testament', writes Mr Pierce,

is the painful reaction of man's nature, as morally responsible, against infringements of its created limits—past, present by virtue of initiation in the past, habitual or characteristic by virtue of frequent past infringements. It can be secondarily depicted as his capacity so to react, and this capacity in turn can be represented in terms of a near-personal metaphor.[10]

He proceeds to discuss the ways in which conscience may mislead, and he comments: 'St Paul would have granted that, for all its

---

[8] J. Wesley, *A Plain Account of the People called Methodists*.
[9] *Conscience in the New Testament* (1955). [10] ibid., pp. 108f.

liability to error, conscience must be obeyed; but he would never have added "for man has no other guide". He is definite that conscience only comes into play after at least the initiation of a wrong act.' I can find in scripture no warrant for the belief that conscience is an infallible guide to future moral actions, nor any suggestion that divine redemption diminishes the need for ethical inquiry. Salvation from sin confers neither moral perfection nor a power of moral insight which renders needless a careful consideration of all the aspects of moral behaviour.

The further questions thus presented to us are many, and they concern both the specific duties of Christians and the relationship between Christians and non-Christians at various levels of ethical study and moral decision. The term 'moralistic', which I have found it necessary to use in reference to a particular concept of sin, must not be employed to deprive morality of its dignity and importance. The revival of interest in New Testament ethics is greatly to be welcomed, but is there not also need for *comparative* ethics, that is, for a careful examination of varied moral standards? Very often the Christian needs to discover that 'he that is not against us is for us '(Luke 9^{50}), and to learn from those who lack faith in God what it means to do justly. Is there not also need, in the activity of the Churches themselves, for more moral teaching, and for the corporate thought and activity in which such teaching can never become sterile? None of these tasks is a substitute for the giving and receiving of the Gospel, but all of them belong to the new life to which the Gospel calls.

I need not remind my readers that *didache*, in the early Church, included much besides ethical instruction; it included instruction about the Faith and about the means of grace. I have laid stress upon the ethical content of Christian *didache* because without it the announcement of salvation from sin is fraught with danger. Yet it is not with thought about moral teaching and moral endeavour that our study can close; we must recall again those 'abysmal depths' of human nature where sin abounds and where grace may yet more abound.

III. GOD AND THE UNCONSCIOUS

One of the premises to my argument has been the conviction that, however unclear may be the word *unconscious*, and however far we

SOME FURTHER CONCLUSIONS AND QUESTIONS

are from explanation of the varied phenomena to which that term points, some word is needed to describe the aspects of human personality which are not known by self-consciousness. Perhaps more than one word is needed to describe these phenomena, but certainly not less than one. I have attempted to indicate some of the ways in which recognition of the 'unconscious' must affect our thought about sin and salvation. We have also seen that it is not through knowledge about our sin, nor even through knowledge about the nature of our salvation that we are saved; we are saved by God; and it is the whole man who is saved.

This *wholeness* in divine salvation has (as we have noted) a twofold significance. It means that man, who never sins as an isolated individual but always as a member of the human family, is a member of a redeemed race, is rescued from the illusion that he is a solitary being, and is made a member of the redeemed family of God. This very important part of the Christian doctrine of sin and salvation is one of several aspects of that doctrine which has received but scant notice in this book. The *wholeness* of God's saving work also means that it is the whole individual, not merely the self-consciousness of each man, that is saved by grace. To that matter my concluding words are directed.

There are exceptions to the common neglect of the unconscious by Christian theologians. Professor Tillich, a few years ago, gave a warning against a tendency which he believed to be present in contemporary Protestant theology, the tendency 'to overburden the personal centre, and to make the relation to God dependent on continuous, conscious decisions and experiences'.[11] More recently, Dr H. H. Farmer, quoting these words of Tillich's, has enlarged upon this danger.[12] I believe that what Farmer has written on this subject is of great importance for Christian thought and practice. He approaches this theme from two converging points of view: consideration of human need, and remembrance of the work of the indwelling Holy Spirit. These two points of view are brought together when he writes:

> ... the problem is to give the unconscious deeps their proper place as an indispensable factor in the religious life, and this Christianity does, at least in part, by insisting in its worship, first, that God as spirit is at work in those deeps, so that the worshipper can trustfully commit himself to His recreating, cleansing, illumining, empowering, vitalizing,

[11] *The Protestant Era* (1948), p. xxiii.   [12] *Revelation and Religion* (1952), pp. 67ff.

integrating presence there; and, second, that nevertheless the worshipper must all the time, in full self-consciousness, direct his mind to a responsible and personal 'I-thou' relation to God through the historic figure of Christ.[13]

The perils implicit in any attempt to surrender to our own unconscious processes is fully recognized by Dr Farmer, and he endorses K. E. Kirk's suggestion that we must distinguish 'between the relation of the soul to God through "communion" and the relation of the soul to God through "possession" '.[14] It is, however, Farmer's insistence that 'the need for unification has its source not in the daylight area of man's rational self-consciousness but in the mysterious unfathomable depths'[15] that I especially wish to stress, and, as I can add nothing to what he has said, I must be content to refer to his theological discussion of the work of God within human personalities.

Important as such theological statements are, they are not the primary concern of any Christian; our primary duty and our supreme need is, as my first quotation from Dr Farmer implies, to *worship* God. True theological thought or speech will always end in a *Te Deum*. If we need to learn about our sin, and if we must acknowledge our sin, these are but a preparation for the worship of Heaven to which, by God's mercy, we trust to be brought. Here, we belong to the Church of pardoned sinners and, in that Church, confession must ever be mingled with our praise, but, as the evangelical task is the declaration of the good news about God, so the Christian life is worship of God and not meditation upon sin. The egocentric unbelief of man must—to use Abbé Bremond's expression—be disinfected from egotism by worship.

Does not much of our *corporate*, public worship often leave too little room for the work of God which is not recognizable by our own self-consciousness? This is liable to happen if we lay all emphasis upon conceptual thought, and if we ignore all the senses except hearing, so that we are deprived of those associations which are mediated by the other senses and which can most powerfully influence us. Even the revival of doctrinal preaching may lead us to over-estimate the degree to which we are dominated by our intellectual life. I do not mean that we can command God's indwelling Spirit; the Spirit bloweth where He listeth, and

---

[13] *Revelation and Religion* (1952), p. 71.   [14] ibid., p. 73.
[15] ibid., p. 209. Farmer is asserting his agreement with Jung on this point.

SOME FURTHER CONCLUSIONS AND QUESTIONS 193

not even our man-centred religion can prevent Him from working as He wills; but we may hinder, as well as grieve, Him.

Is there not, in this and in other ways, need for further study of the significance of *symbolic actions*, as well as of symbolic words?[16] There is a growing consensus of opinion that symbolism (of various kinds) plays a major part in the whole life of mankind. Thoughtful Christians, in all denominations, are gaining fresh interest in liturgy and ritual, and 'Protestants' are now more ready to acknowledge that an action such as the solemn rising of a congregation for the offertory is as much a ritual act as is any 'Catholic' practice. More important than any such study of the words we use and the actions we perform in worship is an awareness of why we speak and act. We may hope that the time is drawing near when every Christian worshipper will think of 'acts of worship' in terms of God's activity and man's response, rather than of the immediate impact upon our conscious thoughts and feelings, and when all the rich experience of a divided Church will be shared, so that we may all more fully submit ourselves to God in corporate worship. The lamentable truth about many of our Church services is that they leave us thinking about ourselves, or, at best, pondering our own and the preacher's ideas about God. From the place of prayer we then return to our self-centredness, and the cleansing and renewing tides of God's mercy may not have flooded the buried depths of our hearts.

Acts of worship are but momentary interludes in our daily life unless all our life is lived in the worship of God. We are to live by faith, and faith *is* worship. The sinner seeks to be as God, and the terrible truth is that in a measure he succeeds; the tenant claims to be lord,[17] and the Lord allows him to ruin the estate. We are all sinners, and we live in a ruined world; but we are all redeemed, and we live in a redeemed world. To men who have snatched at what is not theirs the word is spoken: 'All things are yours . . . and you are Christ's; and Christ is God's' (1 Corinthians $3^{21\text{ff}}$). The totality of our sinfulness is met by the boundless generosity of God, and He has shown us the meaning of our sin only in order that we need no longer be sinners.

[16] See F. W. Dillistone, *Christianity and Symbolism* (1955), for a discussion of this topic which opens up many promising fields of inquiry.
[17] cf. Matthew $21^{33\text{ff}}$; Cf. E. Brunner, *Revelation and Reason*, p. 7.

INDEX OF SCRIPTURE PASSAGES

OLD TESTAMENT

Genesis
3...132

Leviticus
4^{13}ff...94
19^{11}ff...83

Job
6^{24}...93

Psalms
8^4...81
19...18
19^{12}...93

Isaiah
1^{2f}...91
1^3...115
1^{12}ff...83
1^{20}...91
$6^{5, 10}$...95
13^{14}...93
28^7...93
29^9...95
40^{23}...143
53^6...93

51...89, 148
51^4...16, 81

Jeremiah
17^{9f}...89
31^{31}ff...89

Ezekiel
34^6...93
36^{25}...89

Amos
3^2...115

Hosea
2^{20}...115

58^1...97

NEW TESTAMENT

Matthew
5^{21}ff...108
6^{12}...102n
9^{13}...105
11^{23}...118, 145
12^{35f}...110
12^{41}...118
18^{24}...102n
23...106
23^{23}...107
26^{28}...104n

Mark
7^{14}ff...103, 109
7^{18}...108
7^{21}...102, 108f
10^{45}...104n
11^{25f}...102
14^{24}...104n

Luke
4^{18f}...121
12^{47f}...145
13^4...102n
13^5...103
15^{11}ff...112, 132
15^{18}...149
18^{9}ff...111
18^{11}ff...105
23^{34}...159

John
1^5...119, 172
1^{12}...181
3^{15f}...104
3^{19}...170
9^{39}...106

9^{41}...106
12^{31}...152
12^{47}...152
15^{22}ff...116, 118
16^{8}ff...187

Acts
2^{21}...104
17^{30f}...116, 120, 171

1 Corinthians
2^8...159
3^{21}ff...193
13^{12}...115
$15^3, ^{17}$...122n

2 Corinthians
11^7...122n
12^{3}ff...176

Romans
1^{16}...117
1^{18}ff...118
1^{28}...172
2^{10}...117
2^{12}...117
3^{23}...123
4^{7f}...122n
4^{15}...64
5^1...172
5^{11}...129
5^{13}...64, 101, 116f
5^{14}...120, 132
5^{21}...122
6^{12}...122
6^{17}...122
6^{20}...122

7^5...122n
7^7ff...101, 115
7^8...64, 116
7^{13}ff...108, 110, 129
7^{17}...151
7^{20}...109n
8^3...115
11^{27}...122n
14^{23}...122n, 178

Galatians
1^4...122n
3^{24}...115
4^9...115

Colossians
1^{14}...122n

1 Thessalonians
2^{16}...122n

Hebrews
5^1...123
9^9...123
10^{2}ff...123
10^{26}...147
10^{81}...123

James
2^{19}...175

1 Peter
3^{28}...120

1 John
5^{16}ff...147
5^{21}...178

INDEX OF PROPER NAMES

ACH, N., 24
Atkinson, J. B., 168n
Augustine, 18, 22, 28, Chap. 3 *passim*, 184ff
Aquinas, 18, 34ff, 147
Aulén, G. x, 31n, 39, 81, 126, 130, 133f, 149n, 150n, 174ff

BARKER, J. H. J., 168
Barrett, C. K., 107, 118
Barth, K., 109n, 183
Barth, M., 118f
Bevan, E., 22
Bertran, G., 97
Black, M., 102n
Bonhoeffer, D., 111, 151
Browning, R., 171
Brunner, E., 8, 13, 32, 126, 128f
Bultmann, R., 135f
Burnaby, J., 32n, 115

CALVIN, J., 18, 117
Cell, G. C., 139
Cocks, H. F. L., 177
Cowper, W., 164
Cranfield, C. E. B., 120n

DAVIES, H., 68
Dillistone, F. W., 193n
Dodd, C. H., 132, 136, 138, 147

EHRENWALD, J., 72
Eliot, T. S., 7, 164

FARMER, H. H., 191f
Flew, R. N., 27, 52f, 58, 167
Forsyth, P. T., 11
Freud, S., 21ff, 74f, 110
Fromm, E., 23, 73, 155

GEORGE, A. R., 159n, 176
Gollwitzer, H., 166
Grayston, K., 102n, 122n
Grensted, L. W., 29

HADFIELD, J. A., 69f
Howard, W. F., 174n

JAMES, W., 21, 184
Jeremias, J., 104n
Jocz, J., 98
Jung, C. G., 29, 74f

KANT, 32, 55
Kierkegaard, S., 155, 187

Koestler, A., 155

LEE, R. S., 50
Lewis, H. D., 53, 125, 169
Lindström, H., 139
Luther, M., 18, 19n, 39, 126, 130, 152, 184ff

MACKINTOSH, H. R., 47f, 159
Manson, T. W., 104n
Maurice, F. D., 181f
Mortimer, R. C., 35, 146
Moxon, R. S., 49

NIEBUHR, R., 39, 47, 75, 133, 143
Nygren, A., 109n, 122n
Northridge, W. L., 69f, 144
Nott, K., 6, 17n
Nowell-Smith, P. H., 162

PAUL, 16, 64, 100, 115ff, 122ff, 171f, 176, 184ff
Pederson, J., 86ff, 91
Phillips, G., 137n
Pierce, C. A., 189
Plato, 19, 22, 45
Price, H. H., 29

QUELL, G., 83, 92ff, 97
Quick, O. C., 96, 148

RITSCHL, A., 47f
Robinson, H. W., 38, 84ff
Robinson, N. H. G., 61f, 126, 130ff, 150
Rupp, E. G., 18, 19n
Russell, B., 4ff, 10f, 19, 20, 44, 159

SANGSTER, W. E., 109, 167f
Sayers, D. L., 7, 166
Scott, C. A., 102
Smith, C. R., 25, 87, 89, 92ff, 102, 107, 109, 116f
Snaith, N. H., 53, 90, 95f
Stauffer, E., 121

TAYLOR, V., 104, 112ff
Temple, W., 157, 176
Tennant, F. R., ix, 8, 15, 20, 32f, Chap. 5 *passim*, 66, 100, 106f, 113, 159, 169ff, 185n
Tillich, P., 155f, 191
Tyrrell, G. N. M., 21, 74

WATSON, P. S., 133n, 177
Weatherhead, L. D., 67, 69, 73, 144, 154

Welch, A. C., 94n
Wesley, C., 158, 167f, 172
Wesley, J., 52f, 113, 139f, 168, 184ff, 189
Whale, J. S., 146
White, E., 50f, 68f

White, V., 24, 34, 67f
Whyte, L. L., 21f
Williams, N. P., 50, 98
Wright, G. E., 122

INDEX OF SUBJECTS

The main references to SIN *and* IGNORANCE *are not cited*

'ACTUAL' SIN, 31ff, 75, 127ff
Angst, 155
Anxiety, 154ff
Atheism, 19f, 183
'*Awon*, 95

BELIEF, 175ff
Blindness, 106f, 118

CAUSE, 91, 128f
Chata', 90
Classical tradition, 46ff
Conscience, 155, 189f
Conversion, 140, 183ff
Covenant, 82, 115

DEATH, 120, 145, 147
Demons, 121
Didache, 138, 187ff

ESCHATOLOGY, 115ff, 152ff
Ethics, 6, 8, 11, 23, 44f, 64, 111, Chap. 9 *passim*, 188ff
Evangelism, 9, 182ff
Evil thoughts, 109f

FAITH, 106, 115, 129, 174ff
Fate, 46, 160
Flesh, 17f, 49, 84, 105
Forgiveness, 10, 112ff, 126, 187
Formal sin, 127f, 146f
Frailty, sin of, 37ff
Freewill, *see* Will

GOD, KNOWLEDGE OF, 16ff, 115, 174ff, 182ff, 191
Gnosis, 45
Gospel, *see Kerygma* and Salvation
Guilt, 9, 34, 37, 64, 94f, 126, Chap. 10 *passim*

HABIT, 35
Hamartia, 16, 67, 102f, 122
Heart, 84, 86, 89, 98
Holiness, 95, and *see* Sanctification
Hubris, 48

IMPULSE, 25, 59f, 98
Indeterminism, 33, 38, 151, 162
Instincts, 59ff, 162
Intention, 109f, *and see* Motives

JUDGMENT, MORAL, 54, 75ff, 117, 169ff
Justification, 35, 111, 115, 129, 136, 140, 152, 188

KERYGMA, 137ff, 187ff

LAW, 110, 117f, 135ff
Lebh, *see* Heart

MANICHAEANISM, 18
Material sin, 127f, 146f
Mental health, 73f, 76f
Metanoia, *see* Repentance
Moral Disease, Chap. 6 *passim*, 165
Moral Theology, 35ff
Mortal sin, 147
Motives, 24, 71f, 87f, 109f
Mysticism, 176

NEPHESH, 84
Neurosis, 26, 67ff, 72ff, 155

ORIGINAL SIN, 7, 17n, 33f, 39, 75, 127ff, 144, 162

PARABASIS, 16
Paraptoma, 16
Perfection, 52, 167f, 188
Pesha', 90, 92
Pharisees, 104ff, 114, 156f, 185f
Pride, 18, 133, 165, 177
Priests, 95ff, 123
Prophets, 92ff
Psychiatry, 25ff, 50, Chap. 6 *passim*, 156, 163ff, 173, 179
Psychology, Hebrew, 84ff
Psycho-somatic, 26, 85
Punishment, 144f

REASON, 60
Reatus, 127ff, 147f
Rebellion, 18f, 90ff, 132f
Repentance, 113f, 172, 186
Repression, 25, 145
Responsibility, 20, 28, 33, 37ff, 70f, 108ff, 150ff
Revelation, 45, 48
Righteous, the, 104ff
Righteousness, 138ff

SACRIFICES, 94ff, 123

Salvation, 98f, 104ff, 118ff, 171ff
Sanctification, 136, 139ff, 167ff
Sarx, *see* Flesh
Science, 43f
Self-determination, 37ff, 62f, 151, 160ff
Semantics, 6, *see* Vocabulary
Sense of guilt, 144, 149ff, 153ff, 158, 187
Sense of sin, 4, 7, 10, 149, 166ff
Sensuality, 17f, 133, 177
Shagah, 93
Sinners, the, 103ff, 185f
Solidarity of race, 28, 62, 82, 121f, 149
Subconscious, *see* Unconscious
Symbolism, 193

TELEOLOGY, 184f
Telepathy, 25, 28f

Total Depravity, 8, 133f, 180
Transference, 163
Trespass, 102

UNBELIEF, 133, 174, 177ff
Unconscious, 21ff, 28f, 49ff, 53, 63, 67ff, 74ff, 98, 110, 162ff, 190ff

VENIAL SIN, 147
Virtues, 129ff
Vitium, 127ff, 148
Vocabulary, 1ff, 12f, 57ff, 90ff, 102ff, 181f

WILL, 32ff, 38ff, 52ff, 68ff, 84, 87, 109, 151, 160ff
Worship, 193

www.ingramcontent.com/pod-product-compliance
Lightning Source LLC
Chambersburg PA
CBHW051737230426

43670CB00012B/2059